The scramble for art in Central Africa

Western attitudes to Africa have been influenced to an extraordinary
degree by the arts and artifacts that were brought back by the early collectors, exhibited in museums, and celebrated by scholars and artists in the
metropolitan centres. The contributors to this volume trace the life history
of artifacts that were brought to Europe and America from Congo towards
the end of the nineteenth century, and became the subjects of museum displays. They also present fascinating case studies of the pioneering collectors, including such major figures as Frobenius and Torday. They discuss
the complex and sensitive issues involved in the business of collecting and
show how the collections and exhibitions influenced academic debates
about the categories of art and artifact, and the notion of authenticity, and
challenged conventional aesthetic values, as modern Western artists began
to draw on African models.

The scramble for art in Central Africa

Edited by

ENID SCHILDKROUT

Department of Anthropology,
American Museum of Natural History, New York

and

CURTIS A. KEIM

Department of History,
Moravian College, Pennsylvania

CAMBRIDGE
UNIVERSITY PRESS

PUBLISHED BY THE PRESS SYNDICATE OF THE UNIVERSITY OF CAMBRIDGE
The Pitt Building, Trumpington Street, Cambridge CB2 1RP, United Kingdom

CAMBRIDGE UNIVERSITY PRESS
The Edinburgh Building, Cambridge CB2 2RU, United Kingdom
40 West 20th Street, New York, NY 10011–4211, USA
10 Stamford Road, Oakleigh, Melbourne 3166, Australia

First published 1998

Printed in the United Kingdom at the University Press, Cambridge

Typeset in Minion 10½ on 14pt, in QuarkXPress™ [SE]

A catalogue record for this book is available from the British Library

Library of Congress cataloguing in publication data
The scramble for art in Central Africa / edited by Enid Schildkrout
and Curtis A. Keim.
p.   cm.
Includes bibliographical references.
ISBN 0 521 58349 7 (hbk). – ISBN 0 521 58678 X (pbk.)
1. Art, Congolese – Collectors and collecting.   2. Art – Collectors
and collecting.   I. Schildkrout, Enid.   II. Keim, Curtis A.
N7399.C6S39   1998
709′.6751′075–dc21   97–3061   CIP

ISBN 0 521 58349 7 hardback
ISBN 0 521 58678 X paperback

CONTENTS

❻

v

FIGURES

❦

Chapter 2

Chapter 5

Chapter 6

Chapter 8

CONTRIBUTORS

&

MARY JO ARNOLDI is Associate Research Curator in the Department of Anthropology, National Museum of Natural History, Smithsonian Institution. She has done research on visual and performance art in Mali and has published widely on African art and material culture. She is currently working on a major re-installation of the National Museum of Natural History's African collection.

DAVID A. BINKLEY is a Curator at the Nelson-Atkins Museum of Art and Associate Research Professor at the University of Missouri-Kansas City. He has published a number of articles on Kuba and Northern Kete arts associated with funeral and initiation rites. His current research interests include colonial and post colonial discourse on Central African artistic traditions and their interpretation in Western scientific and popular thought.

PATRICIA J. DARISH is Assistant Professor in the Kress Foundation Department of Art History and the Department of African–American Studies at the University of Kansas. She has conducted extensive research in Congo on Kuba textile traditions, focusing on the work of individual artists and the role of textiles in social relationships and ceremonial contexts.

CHRISTRAUD M. GEARY is the Curator of the Eliot Elisofon Photographic Archives at the National Museum of African Art. Smithsonian Institution, Washington, D.C. An anthropologist by training, she has published extensively on the art and history of Cameroon and photography in Africa.

JOHANNES FABIAN is Professor of Cultural Anthropology at the University of Amsterdam. His recent publications include *Time and the Work of*

Anthropology (1991) and *Remembering the Present: Painting and Popular History in Zaire* (1996). *Moments of Freedom*, a summary of his work and thought on popular culture in Africa is forthcoming in 1997. He is now working on a study of non-rational aspects of the exploration of Central Africa, to be titled *Out of Our Minds.*

CURTIS A. KEIM teaches African history and politics at Moravian College, Bethlehem, Pennsylvania. His field research and writing focuses on the pre-colonial history of the Mangbetu. With Enid Schildkrout, he is the co-author of *African Reflections: Art from Northeastern Zaire* (1990).

WYATT MACGAFFEY is the John R. Coleman Professor of Social Sciences at Haverford College. He has written extensively about the politics, religion, social structure and history of Kongo, Congo and Zaire, and has recently turned his attention to African art. His most recent book, accompanying an exhibition of the same name, was *Astonishment and Power: Kongo Minkisi and the Art of Renee Stout* (with Michael D. Harris) (1993).

JOHN MACK is Keeper of Ethnography in the British Museum. In addition to conducting fieldwork in Africa, he has written extensively on the British Museum's holdings from Central Africa. He is also currently a Visiting Professor in the Anthropological Department of University College, London.

ENID SCHILDKROUT is Curator of Anthropology at the American Museum of Natural History in New York and adjunct professor at Columbia University and at the Graduate Center of the City University of New York. She has published on African ethnicity (*People of the Zongo, Transformations of Ethnic Identities in Ghana* (1978), on women and children in northern Nigeria, and on the arts of Africa. She was exhibit curator and co-author of *African Reflections: Art from Northeastern Zaire* (1990).

(b)

The papers in this book were selected from among fourteen contributions to a symposium held at the American Museum of Natural History in New York in October 1990 in conjunction with the exhibition "African Reflections: Art from Northeastern Zaire." The symposium consisted of a wide ranging discussion of Western collecting and changing modes of representation of the arts of Zaire now called Democratic Republic of Congo. The title of the symposium: "Tradition, innovation, and interpretation: Issues in the collection and display of the arts of Zaire in historical perspective" hints at the broad scope of those discussions. In preparing this volume we have selected papers with a narrower focus, concentrating on those that deal specifically with late nineteenth- and early twentieth-century collecting. The one exception is MacGaffey's paper which frames the discussion in a novel way, provoking a certain reconsideration of basic terms and definitions. Johannes Fabian and John Mack were invited but unable to attend the conference and both submitted their papers with the theme of this volume in mind.

We are very grateful to the presenters and discussants whose papers and comments could not be included in this volume. A certain number of these papers have appeared elsewhere and are referred to in this book; all of the presenters benefited immensely from the provocative comments of these individuals. We wish to thank Didier Demolin, Gordon Gibson, Lema Gwete, Bogumil Jewsiewicki, Mary McMaster, Valentin Y. Mudimbe, Mary Nooter Roberts, Pierre Salmon, all of whom presented papers at the conference. We are also very grateful to the discussants who read and commented on the papers: Thomas O. Beidelman, Jack R. Goody, Simon Ottenberg, Roy Seiber, and Susan Vogel.

The symposium was supported by the National Endowment for the Humanities, as one part of the interpretive component of the exhibition, "African Reflections: Art from Northeastern Zaire." Additional support was provided by the Wenner-Gren Foundation for Anthropological Research and the American Museum of Natural History.

We would also like to thank the staff of the library at Moravian College who helped with the references and bibliography. Karen Keim, Alisa La Gamma, Thomas R. Miller, John A. Van Couvering, and Ann Wright Parsons helped in various ways, from constructive criticism to gentle prodding, to bring this project to fruition.

ONE

Objects and agendas: re-collecting the Congo

ENID SCHILDKROUT AND

CURTIS A. KEIM

ᘯ

When the papers in this volume were presented at the American Museum of Natural History late in 1990, a discussant commented that "one of the nice things about studying African art is that we are all so ill at ease doing it."[1] People who study Florentine art, or French Impressionism, he said, seem to have such enormous certainty about what they are doing and what it all means, whereas among the Africanists, "there is so much angst in the air with people who are studying something that appears alien to them. This helps get at more fundamental questions."

The papers in this volume are about some of the issues that cause this angst, in particular with respect to one body of African material culture: art from the Congo collected around the turn of the century, most of which has found its way into Western museums and private collections. We start with the premise that although African objects belong to, and derive meaning from, their use in Africa, once collected they enter into the repertoire of Western material culture. In the last decade such trans-formations in the meaning of things have been discussed from many points of view, most often in terms of processes of appropriation, commoditization, and recontextualization. Many of these discussions have summarized and outlined general processes in which artifacts become art; objects of use become objects of desire; cultures have been constructed and imagined through objects; and objects have been used to "speak for" or stifle the voices of various classes of culture bearers.[2] These issues frame much of the discussion that follows as well as the papers in this book, even though many critical essays on these subjects have been written since these papers were first presented. All the authors in this book have revised their papers, but some with only minimal changes, mainly because the case studies presented here exemplify and provide texture for many of the more general discussions that have taken place. In this introduction, we attempt to relate the subject matter of these Congo case studies to the theoretical concerns mentioned above, as well as to sketch out the relevant history of what is now the Democratic Republic of Congo (hereafter Congo) and what was, at the time these collecting expeditions took place, the Congo Free State or the Belgian Congo.

On the simplest level, the angst is the result of attempts by Westerners to understand the art of Africa. This is not a straightforward project, since Western ideas about the nature of art have changed over the past century with the advent of photography and the move from naturalism and realism to expressionism, abstract expressionism, modernism, post-modernism and so on. Even at the turn of the century when the scramble for curios, scientific specimens, and much of what we now declare to be art took place, there was no consensus about the status of these objects. Material things, as the papers in this volume will show, have been crucial to Western understanding of Africa, but there has been a century of debate about how African objects fit into Western descriptive categories. Fabian, in his contribution here, speaks of "commodities of distinction" – a phrase that has many apt connotations, but most importantly suggests that these collectibles helped people think about other people. They were essential to the project of describing, defining, and apprehending Africa.

Defining the nature of art has always been important in relation to cat-egorizing the status of collected objects (and their creators) since it brings us directly into the debate about which peoples do and do not have art. This argument, of course, is really about everyone's relative status in some sort of global inventory of societies and cultures, arranged more or less hierarchically depending on when and where the discussion is taking place. At the time the collections discussed in this book were made, it was assumed that art was a product of civilization. Realism, naturalism, and the ability to make symmetrical objects were still dominant ideas at that time. Asian societies were grudgingly recognized in the West as having antiquity and art but the door remained closed to the rest of the world. Nor had these concepts of art yet been moved aside by the nascent avant garde in Europe itself.

Thus the ideas brought to the Congo by late nineteenth- and early

2

twentieth-century collectors in Africa reflected not only assumptions about the nature of art but also theories about the relationship between certain forms of art and civilization and theories of racial and cultural hierarchy. Most travelers could not conceive of Africans producing art nor, indeed, of having history. Naturalism, when it was found in Africa, was assumed to have exogenous origins, while symmetry was thought possibly to come from Egypt or even Atlantis. Nevertheless, from the earliest encounters with certain kinds of objects – the Kuba king figures, for example, or Mangbetu ivories – some collectors, whether traders, scientists, missionaries or explorers, began to question their own descriptive categories.

While African objects had been displayed as curios in the homes of the wealthy for centuries, they first began to go on public display in Western museum settings at the end of the nineteenth century, not coincidentally just when the collections discussed in this book were made. While conventions of display have changed a great deal during the past century, and recent exhibitions like the Royal Academy of Art's traveling exhibition, "Africa: Art of a Continent" suggest that African art has been incorporated into the West's expanding catalogue of world cultural heritage, there is still reason to think that many people remain ill at ease with the display of non-Western objects.[3] After almost a century of exhibitions, ranging from curio cabinets to ethnology displays to fine art exhibits, and considerable scholarly research in the field of African art, collectors, scholars, the press, and the public are still pondering on how to deal with context – how much, what kind, and in whose voice it should be stated. Context includes questions about the historical and ethical circumstances of collecting, the social and cultural world in which objects were first created and used, and the transformations in meaning as objects travel about on the global stage and are finally "digested by" (Vogel 1991) the West and incorporated into changing aesthetic categories and exhibition formats.

Collecting is fascinating, not only because of the way in which it speaks to an inner, psychological drive in so many people (see Elsner and Cardinal 1994), but also because its study provides some insight into the interactions and transactions that shaped history and defined the relationship between the West and Africa, not only the colonial relationship, but also the proto-colonial relationship with all its intellectual baggage of

3

imperialism and racism, and the post-colonial situation. Many recent discussions about collecting offer important insights into the way collecting created and defined Africa as well as contributed to various epistemological paradigms, for instance anthropology as an academic discipline (Coombes 1994), African studies in general (Mudimbe 1988) or the genre of travel writing (Pratt 1992). This growing literature shows how objects have been used economically, politically, and cognitively in the encounter between the West and colonized peoples. However, the history of collecting, like that of representation, is complicated and cannot easily be summed up using words like "pillage" or "appropriation" or even "commodification". As valid as these descriptors may be in certain situations, the transactions were often complicated and multifaceted. This book offers a set of case studies which fill in parts of the picture outlined in these discussions and, in some instances, raise questions about the general paradigms.

From a late twentieth-century perspective, the collectors discussed in this book were engaged in a hasty and somewhat indiscriminate scramble for Central African objects. With the exception of Herbert Ward (see chapter 8) most of them were not particularly interested in art, and even Ward did not think of his African objects as art. These collectors' agendas had to do with saving souls, opening up markets, gathering commodities to sell, and gathering scientific specimens to fill in evidentiary blanks in various theories that were meant to explain Africa and carve out an intellectual space for it vis-à-vis the West. For example, in the case of William H. Sheppard, Emil Torday, and to a more limited extent even Herbert Lang, there was the expectation that the display of their collections might cast a more positive light on the peoples of Africa.

Several of the essays in this book focus on individuals who converged in the same area during roughly the same period, in some cases literally bumping into each other. For reasons that will become clear in the brief outline of the history of the Congo presented below, Leo Frobenius, Emil Torday, William H. Sheppard, Samuel P. Verner, and Frederick Starr all met or followed each other in rapid succession in the Kasai region of the Congo Free State, home to the Kuba, Luba, Lele and related peoples. With the exception of Verner and Starr, their collecting itineraries and activities were mostly planned independently of each other. Nevertheless, through gossip, as well as through actual encounters, knowledge of each others' activities intensified competition and influenced what was collected.

This convergence of collectors is especially important when one considers the issue of African agency, since the suppliers were finite in number and many of the African artists and sellers encountered and dealt with a number of the collectors. Some Africans certainly understood the desires and tastes of the collectors, and some became quite adept at manipulating the market. Patterns of trade and manufacture that have been described for the recent period (Steiner 1994) were also typical of this early period, although many people today erroneously assume that before the cash economy had enveloped Africa, the situation was more pristine and authenticity could more easily be defined. On the contrary, in this period at the dawn of the colonial era, exchange values were being established and objects that had not previously been commodities were being defined as such for the first time. Artifacts and the texts that came with them were an important part of this process of economic redefinition – new scales of value developed as different sorts of wealth, both material and immaterial, entered into the economy.

The exchange of objects between Africans and Europeans also created an arena in which material objects could be used to define African ethnicity and culture. Labels and explanations were needed to connect objects, cultural practices, and people. Fabian notes (chapter 4) how each collected object provided an answer to a question not yet asked: knowledge was created as things were collected, defined, and redefined in a Western epistemological system. The people who made the objects were associated with them through a labeling process that acquired great importance in the subsequent administration of the Congo Free State and the Belgian Congo. As MacGaffey and Fabian suggest (see chapters 4 and 9), these texts are an integral part of the creation of art, but they go further and are a way of classifying people, communities, and social systems. It is in the search for labels for artifacts that much of the contemporary map of Central Africa was created.

Generalizations about the nature of early colonial collecting often make Africans appear more passive than they were. Although African participants in the collecting process often remain anonymous, in some instances they have left their "signatures" on the collections – signing works, making replicas or fakes, or making choices about parting with certain pieces and not others. Africans made conscious choices about what to give, sell, or make for the collectors, based on their perception of the outsiders' interests and desires. Force and bribery were used to secure objects, both in warfare and as part of the daily imposition of colonial power, but when one looks closely at what actually happened, to the limited extent possible using the available sources, African agency becomes as important as the fantasies and intellectual schemes of the scientists, ethnographers, missionaries and entrepreneurs who take the spotlight in the written history of African collections in the West. To take just one example, Frederick Starr notes with frustration how Frobenius' recent purchases in the Pende area had affected both the quantity and quality of what was available; and on another occasion, how his request for objects showing signs of age led to the appearance of quantities of suspiciously aged objects (see chapter 7).

Central Africa, specifically the Belgian Congo, was both typical of collecting in other parts of Africa and other parts of the colonial world, and at the same time unique. The search for exotic artifacts has been described in terms of the early development of museums, colonization, and the emergence of various bodies of knowledge that placed colonized places and peoples in the West's orbit. World's fairs and commercial expositions, both pre-dating museums and contemporaneous with them, competed for the attention and pocketbooks of the public (Coombes 1994; Rydell 1984). In Africa, by the end of the nineteenth century, specifically after the Berlin conference, all of the colonial powers began sponsoring systematic collecting expeditions that brought back trophies and artifacts for display in expositions and museums. Personal collecting and public and private sales also continued, reaching into different pockets of society at different times. In some respects, however, King Leopold's Congo was unique, for here was a territory both claimed as a personal possession – by a foreign king who never set foot there – and supposedly opened through his largesse to the world for exploration and exploitation. As we shall show, the financial and public relations problems that developed in the Congo, as well as the very organization of the Congo Free State, led to certain kinds of international outreach among investors, the press, museums, and scientists associated with the latter, hence the international nature of the collectors mentioned in this book.

The Congo Free State's employees and officers were likewise an international mix, as were the destinations of the artifacts.

Within the Congo, there was a concentration of collecting activity in those places where other forms of economic intervention were taking place. Villages along the major rivers – particularly those tributaries that supported steamers – became trading stations, and many collectors made short collecting sojourns as the river boats stopped for supplies of wood for fuel, food, and trade goods, especially ivory and rubber. Both the nature of the artifacts produced and the way they were valued were affected by this convergence of collectors in particular areas. In the Kasai, beginning with Sheppard's visit in 1890, a rapid succession of visitors sought artifacts among the Kuba and collected massively over the next two decades. Five of the papers in this volume (Arnoldi, Binkley and Darish, Fabian, Mack, Schildkrout) discuss collectors in this region. Three of the papers (Geary, Keim, Schildkrout) deal with collectors in the northeastern part of the Congo, including Lang and Chapin and their predecessors, Schweinfurth, Junker, and Casati. Even though these collectors followed one another in succession over a forty-year period, they clearly influenced each other. As Geary (chapter 6) shows in her discussion of book illustrations of the Mangbetu and Azande, tropes were created about Africa and specifically about these groups, and provided models for subsequent collectors. Moreover there was time for Africans to adjust to the expectations and demands of the collectors, and this had a marked impact on the art of the region (see Schildkrout and Keim 1990a).

A BRIEF HISTORY OF THE CONGO

An overview of the history of the Belgian Congo will be useful at this point, to set the stage on which artifact collecting took place. While the collectors described in this book were minor players in the history of the region, they brought back tangible objects that were used to construct the Africa of popular imagination. Themes in this story include the slave and ivory trades, the scandals of the Congo Free State, and the subsequent regularization of Belgian rule. The scene begins on a river – the Congo (also called the Zaire River), the world's second largest in volume and length. Its basin, stretching over 2,000 kilometers both north and south and east and west, covers most of Central Africa and comprises many ecological zones ranging from dry grasslands, to rain forest, to marsh, to riverine. This was the jungle of Tarzan, the river of Conrad's *Heart of Darkness*, and the backdrop of museum dioramas and live expositions.

For at least two millennia, Bantu-speaking peoples have been colonizing the Central African environments, settling new lands, improving technologies, increasing population densities, and linking communities through long-distance trade and conquest. By the time the Portuguese arrived on the West Coast in 1483, Central African political organizations included thousands of village chiefdoms and several centralized societies such as Kongo, Luba, and Lunda, as well as a web of long-distance trade routes for commodities such as copper, salt, and iron and shorter distance routes for articles such as crops, game, medicines, and crafts (e.g., Connah 1987; Phillipson 1985; Vansina 1990).

The Central African slave trade has been justifiably characterized as a massive wave that spread destruction across the continent (Miller 1988). Nevertheless, from the fifteenth century the slave trade had the paradoxical effect of both destruction and development. Notorious for its negative impact on African people, it nonetheless did not end the long-term intensification of human activity in Central Africa and provided some Africans who were left behind with new political and economic opportunities. By the time the Belgians began their conquest in the late nineteenth century, nearly the whole of the Congo River basin was inhabited. The grasslands north and south of the rain forest were home to many African kingdoms and empires, and the forest regions were moving toward larger-scale social organization. Extensive trade networks reached everywhere (Harms 1981; Miller 1983; Reefe 1983; Vansina 1966, 1990).

Among the first to feel the effects of the slave trade were the Bakongo, a people who live on the West Coast just south of the mouth of the Congo River. The Bakongo kingdom welcomed the Portuguese arrival and soon profited from its middleman position between the supply of slaves and other products coming from the interior and the Portuguese buyers on the coast. However, conflicts and trade between Portuguese, Euro-Africans, the Mani Kongo (the king), and provincial nobles, led to frequent warfare. Moreover, interior peoples such as the Imbangala regularly invaded the Kongo while other Europeans established competitive trading posts to the north and south. By the late seventeenth century

Kongo had broken into fragments and many of its citizens became slaves themselves (Hilton 1985; Martin 1972; Thornton 1983).

This sequence of prosperity followed by destruction repeated itself many times as the slaving wave advanced eastward into the continent. In the seventeenth century, slaving states such as Kasanje and Matamba flourished about 300 kilometers inland. In the eighteenth century the violence was concentrated about 500 or 600 kilometers from the coast, and in the first half of the nineteenth century the Lunda empire, centered on the upper Lulua River, benefited from the raids and trade. Violence subsided behind the wave, but the slave trade continued to define much of the chaotic life of the region. The poor and powerless suffered from warlords who taxed, kidnapped, and conscripted labor. The powerful remained so only as long as they had access to firearms and trade goods from the coast.

In the east and north of the Congo basin, Arab traders developed similar patterns. An Arab trade in African slaves that had existed for nearly a thousand years reached Central Africa in the middle of the nineteenth century. From Zanzibar on the far east coast, the Swahili–Arabs crossed Lake Tanganyika in 1840 and thereafter developed Maniema, an ivory and slave empire ruled loosely by Tippu Tip in the 1870s and 1880s. To the south, other Swahili–Arab and African traders established states (e.g. Reefe 1983: 198–202). On the Nile River to the north, slavers and ivory traders founded Khartoum in 1822 and by the 1860s had reached the Azande and Mangbetu, located on the northeastern edge of the rain forest (Keim 1983). Generally the Arab trade from the east was as destructive as the European trade from the west, but unlike the Europeans, the Arabs themselves entered the interior of the continent and organized large areas of what is now eastern Congo under their own leadership. Thus at least some aspects of Swahili–Arab and Sudanic–Arab culture including new crops, language, and clothing styles spread rapidly into eastern and northeastern Congo.

THE EUROPEAN SCRAMBLE FOR AFRICA

Until the nineteenth century most European interest in Africa was satisfied by staying on the coasts. In terms of art, collecting focused on objects made of rare and valuable materials, particularly ivory. Artists were commissioned to make specific objects such as salt cellars, spoons, and horns that often depicted the earliest encounters between Europeans and Africans. The criteria for collecting reflected the tastes of wealthy Renaissance merchants and their interest in exotic curiosities. These were very different criteria from those that developed in the nineteenth century with the emergence of ethnology, anthropology, and the reification of the "primitive." It is these later collecting agendas that are explored in this book, although it is important to note that even during the Renaissance some forms of African art were adapting to global markets (Bassani 1977; Bassani and Fagg 1988).

In the nineteenth century important changes in European society such as industrialization and the rise of the middle class led to a growing interest in Africa and eventually to colonization of the entire continent. In Africa, the first evidence of change came at the very end of the eighteenth century with efforts to stop the slave trade and tentative explorations of the interior. Throughout the nineteenth century a growing European involvement in Africa led to an extensive campaign to end the trade in humans, ever more frequent explorations, the founding of numerous Christian missions, increasing trade in non-slave commodities (e.g., vegetable oils, ivory, rubber) and the establishment of a few coastal colonies. Meanwhile, technological advances in firearms, transportation, communication, and medicine made life in Africa much less costly to Europeans.

Given the voracious colonial appetite of modern Europe and the knowledge and interest that had accumulated, except in South Africa there had been surprisingly few efforts to take African territory by the 1880s. This failure to colonize meant that Europeans still perceived the costs of large-scale colonization in tropical Africa as greater than the potential benefits. By the 1890s, however, they were in the midst of a rapid and violent "scramble" to take all territory possible. What changed from the 1880s to the 1890s seems to have been an intensification of European nationalism. The growing European identification of personal well-being with national well-being led to incident after incident in which the states of Europe clashed abroad while masses of citizens at home demanded that there be no slight to their nation. The great powers – Britain, France, and the newly-formed Germany – found that every spark could ignite a fire and indeed, in 1914 a spark lit the conflagration of

World War I. In this atmosphere Africa could not long remain uncolonized. No matter how hypothetical its riches, European fear that "the enemy" might gain a monopoly over some potentially valuable African resource drove countries to believe preemptive colonization was essential for national prestige and even for national survival. By the 1880s only an incident was needed to spark a rush for African territory.

It is somewhat ironic that the fire was lit by Leopold II, King of the Belgians, for Belgium had stayed out of most of Europe's late nineteenth-century national conflicts. Itself divided between Flemish and French, Belgium found its niche in farming, commerce, and industrialization rather than in projecting its national self on the wider world. However, King Leopold, its constitutional monarch, wanted vastly more than his country could provide. Most of all he wanted colonies and global commercial enterprises that could fund an aggrandizement of himself and Belgium. He made a fortune speculating in Suez Canal stocks, but his biggest effort took shape in Central Africa.

In 1871 Henry Stanley, an American newspaper reporter, had gone to East Africa to locate the famous British missionary, David Livingstone. Captivated by Livingstone's humanitarian and religious vision of opening Africa to Europeans through exploration, Stanley returned in 1875 and crossed the continent in 999 days by descending the Congo River, an incredible feat for the era (Stanley 1878). Back in England in late 1877, Stanley tried unsuccessfully to convince the British government to undertake colonization on the Congo. Rebuffed by a government already overloaded with colonial possessions, he responded to a call from Leopold who said he wanted to undertake philanthropic and humanitarian work in the Congo. Thus Stanley was soon back on the Congo building a road around the rapids near the mouth and organizing a 1,500-kilometer line of trading posts from Stanley Pool (Malebo Pool) to Stanley Falls (Boyoma Falls). Leopold also directed Stanley to organize local chiefs into a Confederation of Free Negro Republics with Leopold as their king. Meanwhile Leopold had other agents push into Central Africa from Zanzibar and from farther south on the West Coast (Stanley 1885).

By the middle of the 1880s France was also eyeing the Congo Basin and there was the possibility that Leopold would be denied his colonial dreams because, as a private individual, he had no legal "right" to colonize. Britain, intending to thwart French claims without investing in another colony, offered to recognize Portugal's ancient claim to the river. Germany objected, fearing that either Britain (through Portugal) or France would limit trade access to the Congo. Leopold now showed his mastery of European politics. In return for European recognition of his personal right to colonize the Congo, he made promises he never intended to keep. To France he offered trading rights on the Congo and the colony itself should his effort fail. To both Britain and Germany he offered most favored nation trading rights on the river, and to all he proffered that his only aim was philanthropic. At a conference in Berlin in 1884–85, the deal was completed, Leopold was to administer the Congo which remained a Free Trade Zone (Anstey 1962).

The Berlin Conference also sparked the more general scramble for Africa by stipulating that a European country could only claim a territory in Africa after having occupied it. Britain, France, Germany, Portugal, and Spain each saw that they would need to send armies to prevent others from taking too much, and the race for territory was on. Over the next fifteen years the entire African continent was occupied by Europeans, and although it took many more decades to establish effective administration in most parts of the continent, the division of modern Africa was basically accomplished.

THE CONGO FREE STATE

Leopold's ambition was extraordinary.[4] He intended to occupy and control not only the Congo basin, but also Lakes Victoria and Tanganyika and the entire upper Nile and upper Zambezi basins. To do so he needed his newly formed army, the Force Publique, to defeat the well-established Nile–Arabs and Swahili–Arabs as well as many powerful independent African peoples. Thus Leopold needed vast amounts of money, but unlike the other conquerors of Africa, colonization was Leopold's personal affair and he could not count on national resources. By the late 1880s his private fortune was severely depleted, so he turned to Belgium for loans secured by promises in 1888 and 1895 and by the Congo itself in 1890. In 1891–92 he also began to apply his earlier ordinance that declared that the vast uninhabited lands used by Africans for hunting and gathering were "vacant" and belonged to his private "domaine." This effectively allowed him to claim every wild product of the Congo and since wild products were practically the only products worth trading, he thus circumvented the Berlin Conference and excluded private traders from most areas. On the Lower Congo and in the Kasai Basin private traders were strong enough to insist that they be allowed to trade freely, but they were taxed. Elsewhere, state agents were authorized to collect taxes from Africans in goods and labor, which meant Leopold no longer intended to trade for ivory, rubber, food, or labor. Each local agent would simply require Africans to supply whatever he desired, with little over-sight from the State. Agents received commissions (or year-end bonuses after 1896) from the State for the ivory and rubber collected.

To solve his money crisis, Leopold further began to allocate "conces-sions" of territory to companies willing to pay for rights to exploit the land and its peoples. He retained a substantial interest in many of the companies. Two concession companies, Anversoise and Anglo-Belgian India Rubber Company (ABIR), received huge tracts of land in the rubber producing areas and adopted the methods of the state. The Congo Railway Company, which built the essential rail link around the rapids near the mouth of the Congo River (Matadi to Stanley Pool) at terrible cost in African and European lives, received land grants during the 1890s as incentives to speed up work. Other grants included land concessions and 99-year leases of mining rights in Katanga in 1891, given mostly to secure Leopold's claim to Katanga (today's Shaba) from the British. The first mines in Katanga opened in the early 1900s and the operation led to the formation of the hugely profitable Union Minière du Haut Katanga. In 1906 Leopold gave Forminière a 99-year lease on all Congo minerals outside Katanga (excluding the new state-run gold mines at Kilo-Moto in the northeast), a benefit that eventually led to the company's diamond riches (Anstey 1966; Vellut 1983).[5]

These moves had long-term potential, but did not resolve Leopold's immediate financial problems. By the middle of the 1890s Leopold was still desperate for funds and on the verge of bankruptcy. Only the discov-ery of vast resources in wild rubber saved the Congo for Leopold (Stengers and Vansina 1985: 319). Naturally, he claimed all rubber for himself, and began to pressure Africans for production. The method, begun with ivory, was to require Africans to pay arbitrary taxes in rubber and to give agents bonuses based on production.

Revenues mounted and by the late 1890s a budget surplus allowed

Leopold to obtain private loans and investments. However, rather than reinvest surpluses in the Congo, Leopold began the lavish expenditure on himself and on Belgian public projects that he had always desired. He purchased luxurious private estates in Europe, enjoyed his mistresses, and eventually undertook massive building projects in Brussels, Ostend, and Laeken. Leopold also sponsored a Brussels–Tervuren Exposition on Congo in 1897 to publicize his work. The objects collected for the Exposition were eventually housed in the magnificent Royal Museum of the Congo (later called the Musée Royal de l'Afrique Centrale and now called the Musée Africain) which Leopold constructed at Tervuren.

Rubber profits also allowed Leopold to finish the push to the Nile and begin the transition to civilian administration in the Congo. The Force Publique finally defeated the Nile–Arabs in 1898 at great loss of life to both Belgians and Arabs, but Leopold lost the upper Nile valley because Britain considered the Nile River vital to the security of Egypt, the Suez Canal, and India (Collins 1968). The administration of the Free State slowly began to change from a military occupation to a civilian administration in the late 1890s, although most civilian agents had to be regularly backed up by the Force Publique well into the first decade of the 1900s. Only after about 1910 is it possible to think of the Congo as having a civilian government.

The Berlin Conference had stipulated that Christian missionaries from all countries should have access to the Congo. In practice, this meant that Leopold encouraged Belgian Catholic congregations to go to the Congo and grudgingly admitted British and American Protestants. Among the Protestants, the Baptist Missionary Society began work near the coast in 1878 and other Baptists moved up the Congo River in the 1880s. The American Presbyterians founded their station on the upper Kasai at Luebo in 1891 (see chapter 2). The Plymouth Brethren were in Garenganze by 1886. By 1908 there were nearly 400 priests, monks, and nuns and just over 200 Protestant missionaries. Most Africans had not yet seen missionaries (Slade 1959; Stengers and Vansina 1985: 346).

The prosperity produced by rubber did not end Leopold's extreme exploitation of Africans. Indeed, the exploitation increased because collecting wild rubber involved destroying the rubber vines so that by about 1900 the rubber was running out and Leopold's agents had to put increasing pressure on Africans in order to maintain revenues. Enforcement of production was sometimes through taking hostages, cutting off hands, and other barbaric methods that were eventually detailed in the reports of Casement, Morel, and others in the Congo Reform Movement. Moreover, the growing number of European enterprises required more food, porters, soldiers, buildings, and services and these meant more violence. The state administration refused to introduce a monetary system because it would have enabled Africans to avoid the State by earning money through trade to pay taxes.

The impact of the invasion on African life was enormous. Whenever possible Leopold was interested in tapping the power of the strongest African rulers, as well as the trade routes, and farm labor. Rulers who resisted were crushed while those who cooperated were asked to fight other Africans. Long-distance trade routes along the extensive river system of the Congo basin were expropriated and by about 1890 had ceased to serve Africans. Farmers were forced to become porters, canoeists, soldiers, food suppliers, and rubber collectors. The diversion of food and labor from Africans to the invaders caused widespread hardship and frequently resulted in dislocation and famine.

Different African peoples deployed different strategies for addressing the invasion. Some rulers cooperated because they expected to gain an advantage such as power over neighbors. In the northeast, for example, the Mangbetu-Matchaga king Yangala and his successor Okondo found it useful to cooperate with the Belgians after 1891. They supplied soldiers, porters, food, and land for a major post at Niangara in return for Belgian protection from neighbors. The Belgians relied on the Matchaga even though Yangala was once discovered to have plotted to attack them and one of his sons murdered a Belgian head of post. Many other groups resisted the Belgians with force, either upon their arrival or after taxation grew too heavy. In the northeast there were at least four larger rebellions – Bakoyo in 1898, Ababua in 1900–06, Djabir in 1904, and Enguettra in 1895–1904 as well as many smaller incidents. Guy Burrows, an Englishman who served as Belgian commander on the Upper Uele wrote in 1903 that the Azande were "so powerful that the State cannot afford to quarrel with its chiefs, and the result is that the Zande are quite exempt from military service. They are really a state within the State" (Burrows, 1903: 18). The most spectacular revolt of the era took place in 1897 among the troops of the Force Publique who were setting out from

Stanleyville (Kisangani) to dislodge the Arabs on the upper Nile. As they crossed the deep rain forest they were badly mistreated and consequently mutinied, killing their white officers.

Two main ways to escape the foreign invaders were flight into the forest or across the State border. While both involved enormous cost to Africans, the State exactions were so great in some areas that missionaries reported depopulation of whole regions. Mission stations, both Protestant and Catholic, also served as refuges for Africans who were fleeing oppression. And those Africans who stayed to deal with the State – both rulers and villagers – often became masters at dissimulation, obfuscation, procrastination, and other survival tactics including various forms of trickery.

By the early part of this century there was little danger for civilians travelling in much of the Congo. The collectors described in this volume met little or no African violence during this era. But one should not mistake African hospitality toward civilians for evidence of general cooperation with the State. In the well-defended European centers a growing number of Africans succeeded through interaction with whites (including providing them with artifacts), but in the vast rural areas violence against State agents still occurred regularly, if less and less frequently, and Africans could still overturn practically any local government post even though the price they would pay was increasingly high.

It was in this context that many of the collections described in this book were made. While some of them reflect the insertion of Europeans into a purely African patronage system where art was used as tribute among local rulers (Schildkrout and Keim 1990a: 217–28), some art from this period also became the embodiment of resistance. Torday, Lang, and others, including many missionaries, gave Africans European books and magazines and encouraged depictions of European people and artifacts. Since the fifteenth century, when the Portuguese along the coast commissioned ivory carvings of the European/African encounter, African artists had been meeting European demand for objects that incorporated images of the West. In the time of Leopold, some of this art can be seen as an expression of resistance, for many images mocked the Europeans and the Africans who worked for them (Jewsiewicki 1991a). Moreover, in contrast to the methods used to extract ivory, rubber and labor, the growing demand for handicrafts must have seemed to most Africans to be relatively benign. Unlike rubber and ivory, the Europeans did not have production quotas for artifacts and Africans had much more control over the quantity and quality of the merchandise.

Most Europeans felt that the Congolese were paying a necessary, if sometimes unfortunate price for the benefits of civilization. In a racist, nationalist, and colonial era, even the non-Belgians in the Congo – mostly traders and Protestant missionaries – did not always see the harsh actions of the Free State as problematic. In fact, one might say that given European views of Africa and its peoples, complaints about the system were bound to be mixed and to surface slowly. For example, Joseph Conrad's famous *Heart of Darkness*, published in book form in 1902, was set on the Congo River and is today considered by some to be an early indictment of Leopold. However, Conrad's racist subtext was that all Africa was primitive and – like the primitive human mind – best left alone. This esoteric message was not aimed solely at Leopold, and though he believed Leopold should be removed from Congo, Conrad did not become an anti-Leopold activist.

Missionaries in the Congo also complained about the State, but the complaints were often weak. As Protestants, mostly British and American, began to speak out in the 1890s, state administrators put various kinds of pressure on them. Moreover, the missionaries themselves were products of a civilization that felt imposed discipline and work was "civilizing" for Africans. Thus although Protestant missionaries were the prime source of reports on atrocities, these reports were often mixed, containing either praise for the State and blame for individual administrators, or vice versa. Catholic missionaries tended to be Belgian and to support Leopold. In fact, this support during the anti-Leopold campaign led to a formal policy of large land grants for Catholic missions.

A few Belgians – including a former Congo Governor-General, a respected legal scholar, and opposition members of parliament – protested in the 1890s, and the British Aborigines Protection Society spoke out in 1896. But complaints did not gather sufficient momentum to make a difference until after 1900 when merchant John Holt, activist E. D.

Morel, British Consul to the Congo Roger Casement, and others began to be heard by the British government. Especially effective was Morel, a private British citizen, who publicized widely his discovery that guns and ammunition, not trade goods, were Leopold's major exports to the Congo. Morel was a main founder and organizer of the Congo Reform Movement which publicized atrocities in Congo (Morel 1968).

British accusations aroused Belgian nationalism and fostered a great deal of anti-British feeling. Belgians generally admired their fiercely patriotic king and the country was already feeling the benefits of the enormous Congo revenues. Moreover, during the recent South African War (1899–1901), the Belgians had sympathized with the Boers who seemed to be standing up to gold-greedy Britain. Now Britain looked as if it might be planning to take the Congo and Belgians were easily per- suaded that the Belgian nation – not just Leopold – was under attack (Stengers and Vansina 1985: 324–25). Leopold and the Free State mounted a large-scale public relations campaign to convince the world that the Congo was indeed civilizing Africans. This counterattack included bribery of journalists in Britain and the United States and efforts to discredit missionary reports. Leopold, who seems to have truly believed that things were not as bad as they were, also sought to tie his Congo enterprise to scientific advances that would be appreciated by Western elites.

In 1903 the British government asked Consul Roger Casement to undertake an investigative tour of the Congo. He visited the middle Congo River and interviewed Protestant missionaries, white agents of the state and concession companies, and Africans. His report, detailing the extreme violence and depopulation carried out by European agents and by Africans working for them, forced Leopold to appoint his own international investigative commission. When it released its findings in late 1905, they confirmed in muted tones Casement's report, and made it inevitable that the Congo would be transferred to Belgium. The Belgian Parliament began to work on reform in 1906. Late that year the United States and France joined Britain in pushing for rapid change. It took until 1908 to transfer Congo to Belgium because Leopold tried to preserve the revenue of his *Fondation de la Couronne*, the institution that had done so much to adorn Leopold and Belgium with Congo profits. Both Britain and the United States finally had to pressure

Belgium into abolishing Leopold's private domain and ending revenues to the foundation.

After 1908, many reforms improved the situation for Africans. These included the introduction of a colony-wide monetary system, ending forced rubber collection and regulation of taxes, establishment of legitimate chiefs and full civilian administration, reorganization of the Force Publique, and freer movement of traders, missionaries, and scientists. In fact, they satisfied E. D. Morel sufficiently that by 1913 he closed his Congo Reform Association. From a historical perspective, however, it has been much harder to close the books on Leopold's Congo. It is easy to find examples of Westerners in post-Leopold Congo who felt the king had been right and who continued to treat Africans in deeply exploitative ways. Frederick Starr, for example, a collector discussed in this volume (chapter 4), wrote numerous newspaper articles defending the regime (later published as Starr 1907), for which he won a Medal of Honour from the Belgian government. Even Herbert Lang, leader of the American Museum of Natural History expedition to Congo (see chapters 5 and 7) and a man who was not openly exploitative of Africans, wrote in 1915 that the Congo reform campaign had been "impetuous" and "unfortunate" while the government was "wise" and "responsible" toward Africans (Lang 1915: 382). Indeed, modern scholars Louis Gann and Peter Duignan urge us not to exaggerate the evils committed in the Congo. While they accept that the Congo Free State was coercive, they add that much of Leopold's bad press was not based on fact in that not only did some anti-Leopold campaigners tell outright lies, but also that violence was localized and observers in the Congo often misunderstood what was going on (Gann and Duignan 1979: 134–37).

Such continuing ambiguity concerning Leopold should lead us to conclude that the 1908 transfer of power marks neither the abrupt end of foreign exploitation nor the abrupt beginning of peaceful interaction between Westerners and Africans. Rather, the year symbolizes the longer transition from a wild and violent scramble for territory to other milder but still exploitative scrambles for African resources. By 1908 the other scramblers – missionaries, traders, entrepreneurs, prospectors, sportsmen, bureaucrats, scientists, anthropologists, collectors, and the like – had already begun their harvests of everything from ivory to souls to art. The 1908 change in government accelerated the process by making it easier for civilians to operate throughout the Congo.

The 1910s saw the spread of civilians and civilian rule to all corners of the colony. To take the far northeast as an example, the Dominicans began mission work in the Uele in 1908 and the Protestant Heart of Africa Mission and the African Inland Mission both entered in 1913 (Braekman 1961: 245–63, 349–60). By 1916 there were thirty-one Portuguese and twenty-three Greek traders in the Uele (Belgian Congo 1916: 11). In 1915 the Belgians introduced cash crops and a 1917 decree allowed adminis-trators to require cash crop cultivation of all Africans (Anstey 1962: 52). In 1912 the automobile arrived, and by the early 1920s a decent road and adequate supplies of fuel and parts made road transport more or less reli-able. Costs were high, however, and porters continued to be employed into the late 1920s (Chalux 1925: 630–37).

The influx of whites into the northeast continued in the 1920s and 1930s as mission work, cash crops (cotton and coffee), gold mining (at Kilo-Moto), and commerce intensified. Relations between Africans and Europeans were rarely good. Lower level state administrators, those most in contact with Africans, were frequently young, poorly educated, racist, and opportunistic (e.g. Anstey 1962: 54). Non-state Europeans were generally abusive. Thus Africans mostly cooperated only to avoid punish-ment and from time to time revolts broke out, usually over excessive demands for cash crop cultivation, food for mines and government posts, and labor for road building, mines, porterage, and European enterprises. Significant revolts occurred in this region in 1915, 1929, 1930, 1933, and 1934, and there were regular occupations of chiefdoms by the Force Publique. The colonial effort was shaped by this unrest. For example, one of the reasons given in the late 1920s for not building a railroad through the deep forest to the mines was frequent unrest among forest peoples, and a more northerly route was chosen (Choprix 1961: 22). A 1931 report by an investigative commission noted that conscriptions of males aver-aged 20 per cent and rose to 50 per cent in some parts of the Uele. It rec-ommended that recruitment for work away from villages be limited to 10 per cent, a rate that would have left the colonists with insufficient labor (Belgian Congo 1931: 246–59). Elsewhere in the Congo the situation was similar, few Africans escaped the grasp of these latter-day opportunists.[6]

THE SCRAMBLE FOR ART

African material culture had been coming out of the Congo basin since the Portuguese arrived in the fifteenth century. For the first three quarters of the nineteenth century Europeans saw most African objects as curios or as souvenirs of travel to a strange and backward continent. In the last quarter of the century, however, this vision of Africa began to change as theories about the arts and crafts of Africa developed. Georg Schweinfurth, who visited the northeast in 1871, constructed a hierarchy of African material culture by elevating Mangbetu material culture over that of their neighbors. The high quality of Mangbetu objects was correlated with their more centralized political structure and, taken together, these were seen as evidence of their greater biological evolution compared to that of their African neighbors (see chapter 5). The accounts of Schweinfurth and other nineteenth-century visitors were widely disseminated in books and images published in many languages. Christraud Geary (chapter 6) shows how these representations of Africa altered, yet remained consistent in their iconic message, from one edition and one author to another.

Before the Berlin Conference of 1885, traders and explorers made haphazard collections of souvenirs and curios wherever they went. This was the first stage of Western collecting beyond the coast, for one cannot ignore the important commissions of ivory objects made along African coasts centuries earlier. The period dominated by curio collecting, in which objects serve as souvenirs of contact, was followed by a period of trophy collecting in which large collections of artifacts (often mostly weapons), along with animal skins, horns, and tusks from hunting expeditions, were a tangible means of showing penetration, conquest and domination. The many objects looted by soldiers in the campaigns against Asante and Benin were examples of this kind of collecting. As spoils of war, many of these objects made their way into national museums, where they were first displayed as propaganda for continuing the campaigns.

Scientific discovery was also a motive for many nineteenth-century explorer/collectors. Accurate descriptions of the landscape and people were seen as prerequisites to an array of colonial programs including the extraction of resources, the spread of civilization and political control, and the salvation of souls. Schweinfurth, a botanist, Junker, a physician and Casati, a cartographer, for example, all traveled up the Nile and contributed to the map-making project of the Uele River region. In the same period, Stanley descended the Congo River and opened up the vista of Central Africa from the west. (Stanley actually depicted African material culture in terms of its threat to his more or less violent passage, thus presaging a massive effort by the soldiers of the 1880s and 1890s to take home trophies of their conquests [Stanley 1878].) These explorations, from the 1870s on, laid the groundwork for much subsequent collecting.

This was precisely the period in which ethnography was emerging as the science concerned with exotic cultures. The desire for ethnographic information was especially strong in the United States where, despite the lack of colonies *per se*, a century of dealing with native Americans had led to the creation of the Bureau of Ethnology as well as the formation of anthropology departments in natural history museums. For Leopold, these established museums provided a golden opportunity for publicity through supporting scientific collecting and research. Leopold's financial adviser and friend, John Pierpont Morgan, was a Trustee of the American Museum of Natural History, and plans were soon made to have Congo Free State agents collect more than 3,500 artifacts. These became the basis for a new African Hall that opened in 1910 (Schildkrout and Keim 1990a: 48–50). Meanwhile, a group of American Museum Trustees, some of whom had been given mining and rubber concessions in the Congo Free State, followed up Sir Harry Johnston's 1902 discovery of the okapi in the Ituri forest with plans for what became the 1909–1915 Lang-Chapin Congo Expedition.

Scientific expeditions in the Congo Free State were not dissimilar to expeditions in other parts of Africa. The French had begun systematic studies of Islam and traditional law in French West Africa by 1909; the British government had commissioned a series of ethnographic surveys and employed anthropologists in most of their territories by the 1920s. The Germans sponsored more than ten major expeditions to various parts of tropical Africa, including the Congo, in the decade after 1905. However, because of the Congo Free State's policy of open access, in the early years the Congo expeditions were decidedly international: Belgians, British, Swedes, French, Germans, Poles, and Americans were encouraged to sponsor scientific research and collecting expeditions. After Leopold, the Belgian government continued to sponsor scientific expeditions as when, for example, King Albert, Leopold's successor, sent Hutereau to northeastern Zaire in 1911 to study the fractious Azande. Belgian sociologists began systematically to organize the disparate reports of travelers, soldiers, missionaries, and bureaucrats on various Congolese peoples into a series of compendia on various ethnic groups (see for example, Van Overbergh and de Jonghe 1909).

The cumulative result of this activity was a massive "scramble" for objects during the first fifteen years of the twentieth century, in the period surrounding the transfer of power from Leopold to Belgium. It is difficult to calculate the number of artifacts removed in this period, but many museum collections (in Belgium, Britain, Germany, and the United States) came in lots of 3,000 to 4,000 or more objects. In the case of Hutereau the museum in Tervuren acquired 12,000 objects. There are several dozen systematic collections including one made by agents of Leopold for the American Museum of Natural History, and the collections of Frobenius (much of which was lost in transit), Lang, Sheppard, Starr, Torday, Verner, and Ward, all discussed in this book. When added to many smaller collections and isolated objects, and considering the fact that a certain number of lots were lost in transit, between 70,000 and perhaps as many as 100,000 objects may have been removed before World War I.

In 1884, even before the foundation of the Congo Free State, Leopold's company had proposed the foundation of a museum to publicize the Congo. In 1885 the new State displayed some objects in Belgium and began to store objects at the Musée d'histoire naturelle. In 1891 Leopold ordered all his agents to allow the State to keep all confiscated "arts and crafts" which were judged "significant." This decree points to the fact that there was already a market developing in Congo material culture, because other confiscated objects were normally sold for the benefit of the ailing treasury. It also shows that the market was still small, since Leopold did not order agents to collect arts and crafts for sale in Europe but felt rather that he could make more of the material culture by displaying it. In 1894 and 1895 the State displayed ethnographic objects at small Belgian expositions. More important, two expeditions were sent to the Congo in 1895 to bring back objects and natural products for a much grander exposition in 1897. That exposition was held in Brussels and in the new palace of the new Musée Royal du Congo in Tervuren.

The purpose of the 1897 Brussels–Tervuren Exposition was to justify and publicize Leopold's activities in the Congo. The official guide noted that a good government protects its citizens' art. While Africans were characterized as children, some of their sculpture had "real worth," especially that representing the human face. Along the coast, where Europeans assumed undeserved credit for influencing African forms in the direction of realism, such anthropomorphic art was said to be superior. As one penetrated the continent and left the zone of long-term European contact, the art forms supposedly became more expressive and less valued as art. The authors complained that the African artists from the former Arab zone in the far east who carved or decorated ivory tusks were degrading the ivory, presumably an attack on Arab influence which was thought at the time to be destroying the Congo (Salmon 1992). This exposition guide contains one of the first explicit distinctions between African anthropomorphic and non-anthropomorphic art, associating anthropomorphic art with Western art. More important, however, is that such art was taken to be an illustration or justification of why Belgians should be colonizing in the Congo. Art – here used as a metaphor for African society – was thought to improve in direct proportion to contact with Europeans.

In the period from 1900 to 1915 collectors began to focus on objects more closely identified with art in the West. Weapons, tools, jewelry, and other objects continued to flow out of Africa, but there was a growing effort to collect figurative objects, those representing humans and animals. Many missionaries collected these "fetishes" as part of their effort to turn converts away from idol worship. Yet there were also significant nods to aesthetic qualities, even among missionaries. The African American William Sheppard, an American Presbyterian missionary who arrived in the Kasai in 1891, collected Kuba material culture and displayed it when lecturing and preaching in the United States (see chapter 2). Sheppard recognized the aesthetic qualities of this art and set up an exhibition at the Hampton Institute to display it. In the decades following, a Western aesthetic that grew to include African objects was certainly germane to people like Emil Torday (see chapters 2 and 3) and Herbert Lang (see chapter 7) both of whom, like Sheppard, recognized the art as indigenous.

Although it is easy to overstate the case for the transformative power of African art, collecting could and did sometimes pose challenges to Western assumptions about cultural evolution, race, and colonialism. Kuba king figures, considered art from their first appearance, led to the conclusion that the Kuba, like the Mangbetu, had a well-developed political system that could be described in historical terms. When Torday saw these figures and was unable to find an exogenous origin for them, the Kuba were deemed to have had a history in a way that was never acknowledged in Benin, where degeneration from a more glorious but also not indigenous past was posited (see chapter 3 and Coombes 1994). Similarly Herbert Lang, among the Mangbetu, was convinced, no doubt naively, that the display of the newly discovered Mangbetu ivory carvings would contribute to a changing perception of race in the United States since, in his view, the public would be confronted with evidence of African skill and artistic talent. But as all of the papers in this book discussing these collections make clear, even though indigenous origins were acknowledged for objects that were valued as art, in every case the production of art was tied to the idea of kingship, repeating many of the tropes of nineteenth-century European cultural evolutionary thinking.

THE EFFECTS OF CONTACT ON THE PRODUCTION OF AFRICAN ART

From the earliest contacts, Westerners deliberately or inadvertently influenced certain spheres of African craft and artifact production. Missionaries' attitudes towards African material culture were by no means monolithic, but many of them nevertheless had some effect on African production processes, at least among people living close to mission stations. Protestants usually discouraged all art as idolatry, though this did not always stop them from collecting, while Catholics accepted the idea of iconic representation but asked for a shift to representations of Christian themes and images (Goody 1991). Whatever their views, many missionaries introduced new woodworking techniques such as carpentry and joinery, and new needlework techniques using sewing machines (to increase the demand for imported cloth). Particularly among Protestants, an emphasis on the written scripture and on two-dimensional graphics sometimes also shifted aesthetic interest away from sculpture. Certain types of artifact were affected more than others: in some places furniture and utilitarian objects were obviously affected more than medicines and ritual artifacts; in other places sculpture began to be dissociated from, or inserted into, particular ritual contexts.

The way in which objects were exchanged between Africans and Europeans itself affected the production of art. The early traders used Western trade goods as currency – items like cloth, beads, or wire. But Europeans also bought up African currencies such as cloth and iron bars and used these in their transactions for artifacts, at least until Congo currency was introduced in 1910. African objects soon incorporated imported materials, including currency (glass beads, for example), deliberately-introduced substances (like bakelite, introduced in 1908 and later sold as fake amber), scrap (such as tin from cans), other metals, and some forms of cloth. In many cases, these new materials did not change the meaning or use of the objects for Africans even though it sometimes enhanced their value. However, as Western notions of authenticity developed, collectors often required the rejection of imported materials. This led to the paradoxical situation in which objects made for local use in Africa often incorporated acrylic paint, plastic, and imported cloth, while a lively market emerged in faked authentic objects using only "natural" materials – mostly wood, raffia, hide, copper, and feathers – that met Western consumer expectations.

All the essays in this book touch upon the economics of collecting, suggesting that African objects were part of an international market economy from the earliest days of contact and that this market affected the production of objects at a very early date. There is no reason to assume that African artifacts were immune from market forces before collectors entered the region. The goods that Europeans coveted at different stages, including slaves, ivory, rubber, minerals, and artifacts, all circulated in one or several spheres of exchange long before Europeans entered the system. Metal objects, raffia, livestock, and people circulated in marriage systems; ivory, feathers, animal skins, weapons, sculpture, and even people circulated in relationships of tribute; "fetishes," divination objects, and medicinal objects circulated over vast distances among specialists and between healers and patients; and prestige objects circulated among rulers and between artists, patrons, and clients. The idea of a market, including the idea of commoditizing artifacts, was not introduced into Africa by Western collectors, but the existing system was expanded and sometimes transformed. New ways of standardizing and calibrating value were adopted and new kinds of goods and materials, in addition to colonial currency, entered the exchange system. Moreover, vast differences in the symbolic system into which the African objects entered, once they were traded to Europeans, radically transformed their meaning (see Guyer 1993 and Thomas 1991, for a comparable case in the Pacific).

From the point of view of the collectors, emerging ideas of authenticity prevented the market from being flooded with objects that were created expressly to meet the new demand. In the Kasai, for example, Frobenius, Torday, Verner, and Starr were all busily collecting "fetish" figures and masks around 1905. Several papers in this book (Fabian, Mack, Gibson, Binkley and Darish, and Schildkrout) show how these men were exchanging information about sources and values in their competition for the best objects and the best prices. Not surprisingly, this led to the production of objects specifically to meet the needs of this burgeoning market. While emerging definitions of authenticity seemed to provide a way for the Europeans to distinguish old from new and good from bad, Africans quickly understood Western notions of value, aesthetics, and authenticity and began to shape the supply accordingly. Thus the very criteria that precluded collecting objects made for foreigners assured that this process would take place.

LOGIC OF ETHNOGRAPHY AND ETHNOGRAPHIC DISPLAYS

Collecting is part of the inherent logic of ethnography, and objects were part of the empirical foundation of the discipline of anthropology. This point has been raised frequently in recent years by Clifford (1988), Coombes (1994), Stocking (1985) and others, as well as by Fabian (1983) and Mack (1990) who again touch on this issue in their essays in this volume. Coombes suggests that because objects were presented in public exhibitions with agendas of entertainment and promoting imperialism, anthropology had trouble dissociating itself from the most racist and sensationalist theories. Schildkrout's discussion of Starr (chapter 7) is a case in point, although in the end it was Starr, the arch imperialist, who was rejected by the discipline even while he was accepted by the public as the discipline's representative. The essays in this book consist of descriptive case studies that show how the logic of ethnography developed on the ground, and how this logic structured the texts and formats of visual representations of Africa in exhibitions and illustrations. The artifacts, or "commodities of distinction" that came from Africa in this period made it possible for Westerners to make sense, or think they were making sense, of the confusing mixture of cultures and peoples they encountered. MacGaffey's essay (chapter 9) focuses on the importance of the texts that were constructed to explain the artifacts, comparing the relationship between objects and texts in the context of art and magic respectively.

One theme running through this book is the relationship between the intentions and agendas of the collectors and the narratives and texts that were constructed to display the objects to the non-traveling Western public. We are interested in the changing, intersecting space between collection and representation. In the decades since these collections were made, the explanatory labels attached to many of the objects, in museums, galleries, and books, have changed. Fetishes have become power objects; curios and specimens have become art. Once the social and political context in which exhibitions exist changes, the exhibitions, like the artifacts themselves, take on new meanings. Today, the animal trophies displayed amongst symmetrical arrays of weapons in Herbert Ward's studio (later reconstructed in the National Museum of Natural History, Smithsonian), or in the 1910 African Hall at the American Museum of Natural History, resonate as testimony to the ego and audacity of the colonial collectors, whether King Leopold, the artist Herbert Ward, or the hunter Teddy Roosevelt. Today we can see such displays as expressions of European arrogance and greed, blatant reflections of the age of colonial expansion. They can easily be construed as expressions of voicelessness and disempowerment, since they suggest that Africans stood by as their means of defense became benign wall decorations. The co-presence of African artifacts, weapons and animals can now be seen as part of a process of naturalizing African people and denying them civilized status (Bal 1992; Haraway 1985). However if we are able to see these artifacts and exhibitions in a different light today it is only because we have distanced ourselves from the colonial project. These exhibitions then become historical artifacts of history and grist for the mill of cultural criticism. The subtexts about imperialism, conquest, cultural hege-

28

mony, and hierarchical comparisons of culture are more obvious today precisely because they have lost some of their affective power.

THE PERSONAL AND THE PARTICULAR IN THE MAKING OF HISTORY

While much recent discussion about museum collecting and museum representations has been framed in terms of the grand encounter between colonizers and colonized, "the West" and "Africa," it is also possible, and in some ways much more productive, to be a bit more specific and embellish the general narrative with case histories. As the papers in this book show, every one of these collectors was part of a historical process, with values and opinions typical of their class, gender, and national culture (which varied significantly even among those described in this book). Yet they were also "characters" with various personal agendas and odd habits. We encounter a range of personalities including some who were audacious and intrepid, and others who were more nervous and diffident; some were avaricious, others generous; some tolerant, others blatantly racist. These individual experiences do not "explain" colonial collecting on a grand scale, but they do inform us about what happened in particular places at particular times. However, we must also consider these collectors retrospectively as historical figures, since they have gained a place in Western history through their collections. Forgotten in Africa as most of them are, in the West they have gained a status similar to that of the artist, the builder of railroads, or the architect; through their collections they have left something tangible and public behind, by which they are remembered. They have become immortalized through the collecting enterprise.

The collectors described here went to and returned from Africa with an assortment of motives and justifications. In some cases artifacts were seen as scientific specimens, in others they were used as "evidence" of African inferiority, and occasionally, as in the case of Sheppard, Torday, and Lang they were intended to demonstrate the African's higher-than-expected abilities. Frobenius' and Starr's domineering and sometimes brutal behavior towards Africans; Starr's lustful even obscene fascination with African sexuality; the disgust or satisfaction that some missionary-collectors experienced when they removed "idols" and made converts;

Schweinfurth's, Sheppard's, Lang's, and Torday's awe at the pomp and ceremony of African rulers, are all relevant as we revisit the history of this period based on the collectors' accounts of their travels. This aspect of collecting is rarely discussed, partly because people interested in the artifacts usually focus on the larger picture and not on the messy details of collectors' personal lives. The evidence abounds, however, and usually in the collectors' own words. As Fabian notes in chapter 4, we can read hypochondria and illness metaphorically in the documents and diaries these men left behind.

Besides grand ideas about science, or the discovery of African art, the day-to-day experiences and emotions, the meal-time gossip, and the interpersonal rivalries between collectors all made a difference in the kinds of objects these men collected. As we have said, Africans understood and manipulated the experiences of the Europeans more than is generally acknowledged, and their perception of the motives and tastes of the collectors made a difference in terms of what they supplied in the way of information and artifacts. These detailed biographical accounts, which show how collections were made in the field, therefore offer valuable clues to the African response to Western interest in Africa. They serve as a corrective, however incomplete, to the problem of the muted African voice in the history of this period.

RE-COLLECTING AND RE-CONTEXTUALIZATION

To return to the issue of disquiet raised at the beginning of this essay, we conclude with some further remarks on the matter of the context of artifacts as they are used in exhibitions of Africa in the West. It is accepted that once removed from their original context, all artifacts are decontextualized and given new meanings which reflect the values and views of museums, curators, collectors, and Western audiences rather than the minds of the Africans who made and used the objects. Thus the changing ways artifacts are used to represent African culture say little or nothing about Africa, but a great deal about the collectors and viewers of artifacts and exhibitions. This is precisely why the kinds of collection histories presented in this book are so important. Even though they focus on Westerners, they still bring us back to Africa and closer to the original scene of decontextualization. Although we seem to focus on Western collectors, we also find Africans standing in the background as witnesses to the collecting enterprise.

The essays in this volume suggest that the manner in which collecting was carried out in Africa in real time had a lot to do with defining the categories used over the years to interpret African artifacts. Although material culture changes continually in Africa as everywhere else, until recently our understanding of it became frozen in a system of anthropological and aesthetic interpretation characteristic of the turn of the century. Notions of authenticity based on ideas then current in popular anthropology and schemes of ethnological categorization were used to catalogue and interpret the vast collections that came to museums, mission stations, and private collections. The notion of "one tribe/one style" which, despite volumes of scholarship to the contrary, continues to hover like a shadow over the field of non-Western art, came directly out of the circumstances of this period: the need to categorize people and manage them in small, geographically distinct, governable, and conceptually accessible entities. (Nor is it a coincidence that emerging nationalisms at home were preoccupying the same European powers that were carving up Africa.)

Until recently, the way objects were collected has rarely been addressed in exhibitions. This information was only available, if at all, in unpublished and often inaccessible archives. Museum display techniques, as they have moved from typological displays to representations of individual cultures to fine art museum displays, have stripped these objects of their historical context. Only recently have exhibition labels even noted the collection dates of objects, except in cases where early dates were ways of proving the provenance of the pieces (usually the dates they were removed from Africa). Given the ethical questions raised by collection histories, it is not surprising that many museum visitors and exhibitors feel more comfortable with decontextualization than they would with clear indications of the life histories of the objects. Even ethnographic displays which attempt to present the African context and allude to the function and meaning of the objects in their original setting usually leave out the often unsettling history of collection. In an exhibition format, as the controversial exhibition at the Royal Ontario Museum demonstrated, this history can force curators and bid the audience, whether Western or African, to take a position in reference to the circumstances of collecting (see Schildkrout 1991a; Cannizzo 1990, 1991).

Besides the where, when and how of collecting, we need to try to understand the ideas that impelled collectors to collect, how they documented (or did not document) their collections, and how they ultimately used those collections once they were removed from Africa. Some collections were quickly sold for profit, some were dispersed among individuals, and others made their way into museums where they were sometimes exhibited and sometimes placed in storage, unexhibited and unstudied for decades. Using these case studies, one can discuss with reasonable certainty changes in Western perceptions of African objects, from ideas about exogenous origins, to the appreciation of craftsmanship, to the recognition of art and the individual artist. There was a gradual shift in perceptions, but it was by no means a straightforward trajectory. Keim's discussion of Schweinfurth, Casati, and Junker shows how African artifacts were praised as "craft" but rarely acknowledged as art. Although an artist himself, Herbert Ward looked at African art through the lens of academic late nineteenth-century Western art; African objects became decorative elements in his own constructions, not art objects in their own right. Emil Torday saw the Kuba *ndop* figures as proof that the Kuba had a sense of history and as examples of portraiture comparable to great works of classical Western art. Lang and many other observers of the Mangbetu saw the naturalism of Mangbetu-style sculpture, and their propensity for making symmetrical compositions, as evidence of the intellectual superiority of these people over their neighbors.

The idea of art requires a certain conception of the artist and his or her relationship to society. It requires a certain skepticism about the relationship between art and religion, typical of the later twentieth century. Acknowledging that Africans made art, whether deliberately or not, is not simply a reflection of the growing commodification and appropriation of ethnographic objects into Western aesthetic categories. It also requires a particular view of Africa. After the turn of the century a few of the collectors discussed in this book, for example Torday and Lang, began to acknowledge African sculpture as art – not art created accidentally, but what we might call, although it is certainly redundant, intentional art. This idea of intentionality requires separating the idea of art from the idea of the "fetish," something which still has not occurred to many people who persist in associating "authenticity" with religious efficacy. Both Torday and Lang recognized that the power of "fetishes" resided in the materials from which they were made, not in their form (Schildkrout and Keim 1990a: 234–36; Mack 1990: 44). Lang's case is instructive, however, because he also noted that much Mangbetu sculpture was not made for religious purposes, but was "art-for-art's-sake." Mangbetu carvings of women, he said, were not "idols" or "fetishes" but were made "for amusement." This observation allowed Lang to think about the objects in a new way, and for him the idea that they were art both for him and for the Mangbetu was indeed revolutionary. He wrote in a letter to the Director of the American Museum of Natural History that this new way of thinking about African objects would revise the way people thought about "the Negro question." In other words the idea of art, for Lang, challenged the hierarchical relationship between races. Torday, as John Mack shows in chapter 3, had a similar revelation with regard to Kuba history.

Acknowledging African figurative sculpture as art marked a monumental shift in Western perceptions of Africa. In one sense, its importance lies in acknowledging the possibility of parity in the sense that African works and Western works could be at least categorized together. As Mack's discussion of the British Vorticists suggests, acknowledging African art as art meant that supposedly universal aesthetic criteria could be applied to both Western and African art. However, this recognition of African objects as art, described by many people today as a simple (and presumably laudable) act of appropriation, was not quite so simple even in the West. "Art" meant different things to different people, depending on their class status, education, and national culture. There was a long period, lasting from around World War I until around the 1970s, and the Museum of Modern Art's exhibition on African textiles and decorative arts, during which the interest in African art grew, but was focused exclusively on figurative art. In France, what the avant-garde artists and surrealists saw in African objects was quite different from what the British Vorticists saw. The basic idea of primitivism was that the African objects expressed some basic early stage of the human psyche that may have continued to persist among contemporary Europeans. Nor have we arrived at a consensus on these issues even today, for while Torday, the British Vorticists, and the Primitivists could take steps towards universalism, there are still people today who have difficulty categorizing African sculpture as art.

The trajectory toward the idea of a universal aesthetic has required that African objects be appropriated into Western aesthetic categories and stripped of their African context. This decontextualization, with all its problems of intellectual imperialism, nevertheless opened up the possibility of seeing and exhibiting African art and Western art together – within the same museums and the same kinds of exhibition spaces. African art could be displayed at the Museum of Modern Art or the Metropolitan Museum of Art in New York or the Royal Academy in London and admitted into these sanctuaries using the same kinds of critical criteria as were used for Western art.[7] The cost of this recognition has most often been the annihilation of an African reality, and the rejection of the anthropological paradigm that, since the end of the last century, attempted to represent that reality.

It is mainly in the past twenty years that our categories have begun to shift and the rigid distinctions between art and craft, and art and anthropology, are being re-evaluated. We have come full circle to a broad interest in all different kinds of material culture as forms of aesthetic expression, in a sense returning to the perspectives and interests of late nineteenth-century travelers. Like Schweinfurth, Junker, and Casati, we look at shields, hats, pots, and other non-figurative objects as beautiful. But having now acknowledged the existence of the artist in Africa, these non-figurative objects also begin to be perceived as works of art as we re-evaluate our classifications of objects, our definitions of art and artifact, and think further about African approaches to these questions.

Art is now seen not just as a way of classifying things, but rather as a kind of behavior, a way of acting in the world.[8] Thus it is now possible to see how the Western idea of art can be understood through an understanding of the African idea of magic (see chapter 9). Once art becomes an aspect of behavior, a social act, for Westerners as well as for Africans, we again have to look at how we behave towards these collected African objects – how we obtain them, how we care for them, and how we think about them. At the same time, we need to pay ever more attention, as in fact a growing number of scholars are doing, to how Africans think about art and creativity and the meaning of objects.[9]

Ultimately we still experience angst in dealing with these African artifacts because they stand as icons of our inability to resolve our relationship with Africa. They remind us of the details of their African life, how they were removed from Africa, and the ways they have been used to (mis)represent Africa. Museums and collectors often attempt to overcome this angst by accepting the objects as equal to Western art. This effort is laudable, but it is not entirely successful because the supposed universal standards by which the art is then judged are Western standards which impose a new kind of intellectual imperialism on the material. What is needed is not a *uni*versal aesthetic by which we can judge the artifacts of all peoples, but a *trans*versal aesthetic that would require viewers to understand alternate worldviews and acsthetics.[10] As for our angst, it is possible and indeed probable that we will not soon be rid of it. To do so would mean coming to terms with our past and resolving the complex aesthetic, ethical, and political issues these objects raise in the present. Meanwhile, it is in our best interest to honor the objects, their creators, and modern Africans by continuing to study their histories and struggle with their meaning.

NOTES

1 Thomas O. Beidelman was the discussant in question.
2 An annotated bibliography of relevant works, many of them appearing after the symposium where these papers were first presented, would encompass the literature on collecting starting with Baudrillard 1968 and including among many other works Appadurai 1986; Baldwin, Bearden *et al.* 1987; Hooper-Greenhill 1992; Pearce 1988, 1992, 1994; Pomian 1990; Steiner 1994; Stewart 1984; Thomas 1991; Vogel 1991; the literature on representations of culture in museum settings including Ames 1991; Clifford 1988; Danto *et al.* 1988; Fabian 1983; Karp, Kraemer and Lavine 1992; Karp and Lavine 1991; Mudimbe 1988; Pratt 1992; works on the history of museums including Hooper-Greenhill 1992; Impey and MacGregor 1985; Pearce 1988; and references to relevant works in the history of anthropology including Coombes 1994; Stocking 1985.
3 See Beidelman's 1997 review of the Royal Academy of Art's catalogue, *Africa: The Art of a Continent* (Phillips 1996) and the Guggenheim exhibition catalogue by the same name (1996). It is interesting that these survey exhibitions of African art tend to reify myths about African art while the written texts in their accompanying catalogues often work hard to deconstruct those myths (see for example, Blier 1996; Kasfir 1984, 1992).
4 The best general sources for the Congo Free State include Gann and Duignan 1979 and Stengers and Vansina 1985. Older but still useful works include Anstey 1962, Ascherson 1964, and Slade 1962. Forbath 1977 tells the story in a readable, if undocumented, form. Birmingham and Martin 1983 include excellent introductory bibliographies at the end of each volume.

5 In neighboring French Equatorial Africa the French used a similar concession scheme with equally violent results (Coquery-Vidrovitch 1972).

6 The Great Depression brought falling demand for African raw materials and the labor situation eased during the 1930s. In the period of expansion beginning with World War II, labor recruitment again became an issue.

7 Duncan and Wallach's essay on the universal museum and discussions of the 1984 "Primitivism" exhibition at the Museum of Modern Art in New York. (Clifford 1988; Duncan and Wallach 1980; Rubin 1984).

8 Following from Baudrillard 1968 and continuing to Bourdieu 1984; Stewart 1984; Wolff 1981 and others.

9 There is an increasing emphasis on field studies in African art focusing on the use of art in daily life and African aesthetics. This approach offers a welcome antidote to catalogues of art that decontextualize the objects: see for example, Arnoldi 1995; Brett-Smith 1994, MacGaffey 1988. See also Vogel 1980.

10 The idea of a transversal aesthetic is derived from the work of Calvin Schrag 1992 and Hwa Yol Jung 1995.

TWO

"Enlightened but in darkness"
Interpretations of Kuba art and culture at the
turn of the twentieth century

DAVID A. BINKLEY AND
PATRICIA J. DARISH

(6)

This paper ascertains the nature of Western discourse about the Kuba of
southern Congo at the turn of the twentieth century. We examine two
dominant Western voices on Kuba art and culture – that of William H.
Sheppard and other Protestant missionaries, and that of Emil Torday, the
principal early Kuba ethnographer. From the outset, both missionary and
ethnographer were searching for the Western ideal of an advanced
culture in the "heart of darkest Africa" waiting to be Christianized or
studied and collected.[1] We will show that during this period missionary
and ethnographic discourse on the Kuba were essentially the same. Often
expounded in the form of received wisdom from older Africa hands and
as narratives in personal letters, missionary articles, ethnographic field
notes and travel accounts, the discourse encapsulated a variety of images
to support the vision that Kuba peoples formed a powerful, centralized
kingdom whose superior physical development, intelligence, and artistic
achievements elevated them above the barbarism of their neighbors. We
will further suggest that the character of this discourse has profoundly
influenced the direction of Kuba studies during the twentieth century.

THE KINGDOM OF THE KUBA – EXPECTATIONS OF GREATNESS

William H. Sheppard and the Kuba

In the late nineteenth century, the Southern Presbyterian Church of the
United States had established missions in Brazil, China, Mexico, and
Japan, but not in Africa. The church's Executive Committee of Foreign

Missions developed a plan to send African–American and Caucasian missionaries to establish a mission in Central Africa. The two missionaries selected to initiate this bold venture were the African–American William Henry Sheppard and his Caucasian companion Samuel Norvell Lapsley, both committed to evangelical Christianity (Shaloff 1970: 13–25).[2]

Without foreign mission experience, Sheppard and Lapsley sought advice from those already familiar with the Congo Free State. Before leaving the United States, Lapsley visited Grattan Guinness, a British missionary then in Boston, with extensive experience at the Congo Bololo Mission (Shaloff 1970: 20). On the voyage to Africa, he also obtained an audience in Brussels with King Leopold II who recommended that the mission be located in the Kasai region (which was just being opened to commercial exploitation) because, as the king warned, "we cannot protect you, if you go so far from our stations" (Lapsley 1893:44). The American Presbyterian Congo Mission's (APCM) activities in Central Africa began in May 1890 when the two missionaries disembarked at the port of Banana near the mouth of the Congo River. After supplies and transport were arranged in Leopoldville (Kinshasa), Sheppard and Lapsley traveled 900 miles southeast to the confluence of the Kasai and Lulua Rivers at Luebo.[3] On their way, Lapsley visited the Baptist Missionary Society (BMS) station at Tunduwa on the Lower Congo River, in order to gain insights into mission organization (Lapsley 1893: 59–65; Shaloff 1970: 21–2). More importantly, Lapsley spent an entire month at Bolobo, the BMS station on the middle Congo River, in order to discuss their plans and seek advice from the well-known missionary and explorer, Reverend George Grenfell.

Given his long residency in the Congo, it was not by happenstance that Grenfell became a major arbiter of firsthand information for missionary and ethnographer alike, especially among the English-speaking community newly arriving in the Congo State.[4] Colonial communities were small before the turn of the century; fewer than five hundred Europeans and Americans scattered themselves across a vast landscape. Among government and concessionary company officials and among various missionary denominations, word of mouth became the principal means by which information spread as the colonial effort took shape.

The character of the Western discourse on the Kuba in 1890 can be examined in George Grenfell's research on Congolese cultures and in the correspondence of Sheppard and Lapsley before they acquired firsthand knowledge of the Kuba. Grenfell's extensive research on Congolese cultures was compiled posthumously by the British explorer Sir Harry Johnston in *George Grenfell and the Congo* (1908).[5] This two-volume work both summarizes and typifies the prevailing European views concerning Congolese cultures during the early colonial period.[6] Following the then-current evolutionary discourse, the narrative divides the populations of the Congo into four racial types (Congo Pygmy, Bushman, Forest Negro, and Nilotic Negro) hierarchically ranked from aboriginal to advanced, based on physical characteristics including facial features, body proportions, and color, type and placement of hair. Certain cultural features, including material culture and propensity to cannibalism, are also included in the assessment (Johnston 1908: 497–557).

The hierarchy places pygmies at the lowest level: "little else than a primitive and also somewhat degenerate development of the true negro" (Johnston 1908: 504). The so-called Nilotic Negroes supposedly represent the highest level of physical and cultural development in Black Africa. They are believed to be a racial hybrid of Caucasian (including Mediterranean and Arab) types and a "pre-existing negro stock of northeast Africa" (Johnston 1908: 511–12). The intermixture of Caucasian blood was supposed to have produced what Johnston describes as a "superior type of humanity: that aristocratic negroid" (1908: 514).[7] Several cultures, including the Mangbetu, Luba, Lunda, and Kuba, are mentioned as notable products of the "aristocratic negro" (Johnston 1908: 702–3).[8] Johnston confidently characterizes the Kuba as:

> form[ing] a very powerful and industrious people, chiefly occupied in the ivory trade ... They smelt and work iron, weave cloths to perfection, embroider them and dye them. They also make large mats on a frame and carve wood with much artistic taste ... They are described now as the most powerful, conservative, least changed, and most tenacious of their own superstitions and customs of all the surrounding tribes. They are also probably the most capable and intelligent. (1908: 515–16)

That Sheppard and Lapsley took to heart the elevated assessments of Kuba culture even before they had visited the Kuba heartland, is clear from a letter written by Lapsley in the June 1891 issue of the *Missionary*: "It seems the unanimous verdict of the missionaries and the state officers who know the Kassai that the *finest race of people* on the river are those who are found between the Sankuru and Lulua Rivers. Their cloth, vessels, and weapons are simply wonderful for beauty of design and finish" (emphasis added). A letter written by Sheppard in September 1891, the period that the Luebo station was being established, also elevates the accomplishments of the Kuba over those of neighboring peoples.

> The tribe with which our missionaries were, the Bakete, extends for a great distance on both sides of the river. Beyond it is another tribe called the Bakuba, reported to be more intelligent and more widely extended and powerful than the Bakete. To this well-populated region our missionaries now ask to send re-inforcements. (Gibbins 1939: 21)

It is apparent that both Sheppard and Lapsley believed the Kuba were an untapped and potentially fruitful population for missionary endeavor; but it was only after Lapsley's sudden death in March 1892 and the realization that Kete peoples living in the vicinity of the Luebo mission were slow in responding to APCM conversion efforts, that Sheppard traveled north into the Kuba heartland and became the first Westerner to visit the capital of the Kuba confederacy.

Sheppard, who spent four months at the Kuba capital, wrote a glowing description of his experiences for the *Southern Workman* (1893). He noted the political power of the paramount ruler, his elaborate ceremonial regalia, the cleanliness of the capital village, and its advanced form of government. He was especially impressed by the fact that except for the king, who had many wives, the Kuba were monogamous. He also favorably discussed Kuba laws against public drunkenness and gambling, and recounted that the Kuba did not possess idols like the Kete and other neighboring peoples.[9] He described in glowing terms their iron weapons, mats and other decorative arts and collected a number of examples (1917: 105–23). On the whole, Sheppard found the Kuba "exceedingly enlightened and advanced when we remember that they belong to a realm that lies in the heart of Darkest Africa" (Women's Foreign Missionary Society 1895: 14).[10]

Emil Torday and the Kuba

By 1906 the Hungarian ethnographer Emil Torday was widely considered an authority on Congolese ethnography (Mack 1990: 12). His importance is clearly seen in the photographs and other documentation he contributed to Sir Harry Johnston's work *George Grenfell and the Congo*. Johnston praises Torday in his acknowledgments to the two volumes and particularly Torday's ethnographic collections and reports on south-western Congo (1908: v).

Torday's interest in Congo ethnography began while he was an administrative officer of the colonial government and, later, an agent for the Compagnie du Kasai, a concessionary company.[11] While in the service of the Compagnie du Kasai Torday began to collect ethnographic information and artifacts and to photograph people in south-central Congo. In 1907, Torday contracted with the British Museum to collect objects and ethnographic information from the Congo. At this time, Torday began to publish articles by himself and with T. A. Joyce of the British Museum (Mack 1990: 11–12).

From the outset, a central goal of Torday's research and collection activities for the British Museum was to visit the aristocratic Kuba (1925: 79–80). Since his arrival in the Congo State in 1900, he had been aware of earlier reports by Silva Porto, a Portuguese ivory trader who had reached the Kuba market of Kabao at the southern frontier of the kingdom in 1890. Dr. Wolf, of the Wissmann expedition, also recorded fragmentary information about the Kuba when he met their paramount ruler at a frontier market in 1884 (Shaloff 1970: 3). Torday planned to follow immediately in the footsteps of, and in direct competition with, the German ethnographer Leo Frobenius, who had just completed an expedition in the south-central Congo State in 1905–06. In 1908, on his second expedition for the British Museum, Torday visited the Kuba region, spending ten weeks at the royal capital (*nsheng*). He also spent a month at the Kuba-related Ngongo capital of Misumba (Mack 1990: 57–58).

THE ARISTOCRATIC KUBA: THEY ALMOST LOOK LIKE US

The American Presbyterian Congo Mission's accounts and Torday's ethnographic accounts are remarkably similar regarding their assessment of the physical and cultural superiority of the Kuba over neighboring peoples. These accounts are often structured or framed in terms of polarities – contrasting the Kuba with non-Kuba neighboring peoples in

terms of their physical appearance, their clothing and their artistic production.[12]

For Sheppard and other APCM missionaries, the ruling Kuba at the
kingdom's center were most often contrasted with the supposedly less
civilized Kete living in the southern part of the kingdom near the APCM
mission at Luebo. Sheppard found the Kuba superior to the Kete "in
physique, manners and dress and dialect" (1917: 81). They were altogether "the finest looking race I had seen in Africa, dignified, graceful,
courageous, honest, with an open, smiling countenance and really
hospitable" (Sheppard 1917: 137).[13] To the missionaries, Kuba racial
superiority was most clearly seen in the ruling families. The APCM missionary Samuel Verner described the Bieeng chief Ndombe as:

> nearly six feet and a half in stature; of a bright copper color; with broad
> square shoulders, Herculean limbs and massive statuesque features. The
> physical build of the man conveyed a distinct impression of great power
> ... The king's face, however, was his chief charm. He had a broad, high
> forehead, a strait and slightly aquiline nose, a pair of magnificent brown
> eyes ... characterized by an artistic fullness and prominence; those eyes
> were restless and searching, and seemed to take in the whole horizon at a
> glance. His cheek bones were high, his mouth clearcut and rather mobile,
> without the usual thickness and sensuality; his chin firm and broad;
> while the whole face beamed with a kindly intelligence, and bespoke a
> character at once resolute and benign. (Verner 1903: 167–68).[14]

On another occasion, Verner praised Ndombe's son in similar terms,
terms that are clearly gauged against a Caucasian standard (see Fig. 2.1)
(Verner 1903: 175).

The characterization of the Kuba as physically and morally superior to
their neighbors is seen throughout the published and private correspondence of the APCM mission. These characterizations entered the public
record when two missionaries (Sheppard and Morrison) were called to
London to testify against the atrocities of the Compagnie du Kasai in
relation to the rubber trade. In a document presented to Parliament in
1909 confirming many APCM accusations, British vice-consul Wilfred
Thesiger described the monogamous Kuba as "the most oppressed race
today in the Kasai," while the polygynous Kete were characterized as
"more disinclined to accept civilized ways than the Bakuba"; "vicious and
degraded"; "quarrelsome, indolent, dirty, and stricken with disease"; and

2.1 Chief Ndombe and his son.

people who, "not [possessed of] the trading instincts of the Bakuba, steal on every occasion" (*Further Correspondence* 1909: 35–36).[15]

While APCM missionaries compared the Kuba with Kete peoples living on the southern fringe of the kingdom, Torday and his expedition companion, Melville Hilton-Simpson, compared the central Kuba with their northern neighbors – Mongo peoples including the Nkucu and Songo Meno. For Torday, the central Kuba (the Bushoong), were "a branch of the great family" and this was evidenced by the physical features of the Kuba paramount ruler Kot aPe who is characterized as having "refined strong features . . . [with] . . . very little of the African about them and were less negroid than those of many Zanzibar 'Arabs' I had known . . . The nose was nearly aquiline, and the lips finely curved" (1925: 112). In similar terms Torday (1925: 82) described the physical appearance of a Bushoong titleholder at Misumba as "shin[ing] like a diamond in the sky; groomed, oiled, combed to perfection, he would walk down the street, slowly, his staff over his shoulders and his hands negligently slung over its ends. When he stopped he spread his legs and looked a perfect statue."[16] Hilton-Simpson draws the most striking contrast. After praising the "tall dignified Bushongo of the plains," he described the Nkucu as:

> small and very dirty in appearance, superstitious, timid, and treacherous, they appear to have been influenced by the oppressive atmosphere and almost ghostly gloom of their native forest. As some plants require the rays of the sun and the fresh air to develop them, so it appears to be with the negro. The Bushongo of the plains are a fine race of men with a dignity and a certain grace of manner which cannot fail to attract the attention of the European who visits them . . . they have developed to a greater degree than most, if not all, the natives of equatorial Africa such civilized arts as weaving, embroidery, and wood carving. The Bankutu, on the other hand, are undersized and ugly, sullen and disagreeable in their manner, and, with the exception of the building of huts, the only art that has been developed to any extent among them is the art of killing their fellow-men by stealth. (1911: 133)[17]

AFRICANS DRESSED AND AFRICANS UNDRESSED

Missionary and ethnographic accounts during the period are also similar as they relate to the characterization of clothing worn by the Kuba and their neighbors. In these accounts, an explicit correlation is made between the amount of clothing worn by various Congolese populations and their relatively elevated position on the continuum to a civilized state. Both missionary and ethnographic accounts suggested that a developed sense of modesty, and even shame of the naked body, was at the basis of civilized life.[18] While Kuba arts, including textiles, were both praised and collected by APCM missionaries, the missionaries felt that wearing Kuba clothing (i.e. a raffia skirt), whether decorated or not, was not only immodest but an outward sign of unconversion. The historian Stanley Shaloff notes in this attitude adopted by the APCM "an overtly censorious approach to Congolese society" (1970: 182). While on the one hand some APCM missionaries admonished their fellow missionaries not to ridicule the customs of the people with whom they were working, many missionaries believed a transformation of both the outward body and the soul had to take place.[19]

Samuel Lapsley was particularly distressed by the style of clothing and the dances he witnessed occasionally at the northern Kete village of Bena Kasenga. On one occasion he described "some fifty women in their best, i.e., a new waist-cloth" at a dance that he characterized as "often frantically obscene" (1893: 187). He concluded that the dance was a "pitiable sight" in part because of the "little baby girls in the crowd, all innocent looking, many bright-eyed and pretty, imitating the immodest gestures of their big sisters and even their mothers" (1893: 187). In a similar manner a photograph published by Sheppard in *Presbyterian Pioneers in Congo* (1917: 88) is placed in the text discussing Kete peoples living in the area of the Luebo mission. The photograph illustrates a group of men and women dancing on a village square. The potency of this image and its intended interpretation is carried as much by the "immodest" dress of the dancers as by the photograph's caption, "Cannibal Dance in the Congo." Even Kuba decorated ceremonial dress was not overlooked in APCM critiques. William Morrison was equally distressed with Kuba apparel worn during funeral dances:

> Some of the men were gotten up in the most outlandish and frightful costumes, consisting of native cloth of various colors, animal skins, feathers, charms, medicines, bells, knives, spears, with cowrie shell and bead work on the ankles and heads and with the face and other bare parts of the body painted red, white and black. These men were rushing about the streets, gesticulating wildly and wielding big cutlasses and looking the personification of satanic savagery. (Vinson 1921: 31)

The wives of missionaries were important contributors to the rhetoric of proper dress for Africans. An article by Mrs. Motte Martin in the *Kassai Herald* entitled "A Visit into the Bakuba Country" describes clothing worn by inhabitants of the Kuba capital village as "rich heathen apparel" (1910: 3). Lucy Sheppard, the wife of William Sheppard, was actively concerned about the moral fate of African girls and young women: "When I saw the first native woman in her strip of cloth, her hair daubed with paint, her body smeared with grease and her mind filled with sin and superstition, I could not help but wonder if she could be changed" (Kellersberger 1965: 24).

To the early ethnographers such as Torday and Johnston, the Kuba style of wearing decorated raffia textiles gathered and draped over a belt created a regal profile and presence and was considered a sure sign of aristocratic ancestry.[20] Sir Harry Johnston noted that "it is only in the western and southwestern regions of the Congo basin that we find elaborate clothing . . . The *Bakuba-Baluba-Lunda* peoples have adopted an extraordinary costume for the *men* when in full dress" (1908: 594). Torday believed that the elaborate textiles worn by the Kuba were an indication of an advanced civilization, in part because of the technology utilized in the creation of such textiles. This included the use of "iron needles of native make" to sew their garments while "splinters of bamboo or of bone" were in use before the introduction of iron. This was additional proof of the Kuba's advanced civilization as compared with that of neighboring peoples (Johnston 1908: 594).[21]

The decorated raffia textiles worn by Kuba were a significant feature of their elevated status. Early published illustrations of Kuba decorated textiles uniformly tie these textiles to leadership regalia and centralized authority. Johnston (1908: 596) and Torday (1925: facing 112) both publish the same photograph of an Ngongo chief to imply that the more advanced populations of Africa clothed themselves (see Fig. 2.2).[22] In part this assessment was made because these were the clothes worn by leaders.[23] This is made clear when Johnston stated that "all the common people in this region content themselves with a mere loin-cloth or a piece of furred skin. The women are much less clothed than the men, even in the higher classes" (Johnston 1908: 595).

2.2 Ngongo titleholder.

MISSIONARY AND ETHNOGRAPHER AS COLLECTORS OF
KUBA ARTIFACTS

Possibly more than any other cultural feature, the rich carving and decorative art traditions of the Kuba convinced both missionary and ethnographer alike to elevate the Kuba to their high status, designating theirs the
most advanced culture in black Africa. The relative naturalism of Kuba
figure sculpture and the eye-dazzling two-dimensional decoration on
many objects made Kuba arts universally admired by all who saw them.
These were comprehensible traditions in the service of centralized leadership which could be admired for their own virtuosity: art of the nobler
classes as opposed to "fetish" art for witch doctors or sorcerers, which
could barely be interpreted through a remote, bizarre and primitive belief
system.

Many APCM missionaries were avid collectors of Kuba artifacts. Even
before arriving in the Kuba region, Lapsley must have seen, and perhaps
even collected, several Kuba artifacts, for he wrote that Kuba "cloth,
vessels, and weapons are simply wonderful for beauty of design and
finish" (Gibbins 1939: 12). On several occasions in his diary he depicts the
competition between himself, Sheppard and others traveling on the
steamboat, for cloth and carved wooden objects. Lapsley described the
decorated textiles as "rare beauties" and the wood carving as "exceedingly
fine" (Lapsley 1893: 157, 161). When disembarking from the steamboat
at Luebo, Lapsley observed: "The rage with the white men newly arrived
at this El Dorado is to get some of the rare knives and battle-axes . . . and
the *mpusu* palm cloth with velvet figures, and that with the soft satin feel
about it, and the mats, and the fancy baskets" (1893: 163).

Other APCM missionaries were equally taken with Kuba decorative
traditions. In a letter home, Lucy Sheppard, the wife of William
Sheppard, mentioned the beauty and utility of Kuba mats as floor covering (October 19, 1895). The missionary Lucious DeYampert also
described how he used "curios" including Kuba mats to decorate the
newly painted rooms of his mission home (Feb. 28, 1904).[24]

The APCM attitude toward Kuba artistic expressions was often
ambivalent. While APCM missionaries collected a range of Kuba artifacts
including carved wooden cups and boxes, mats, and a variety of textiles
and weapons, often missing from this inventory were objects the mis-

sionaries considered to be heathen, including objects they described as "devil masks," or "idols and images."[25] As noted earlier, Sheppard's interpretation of the Kuba capital as relatively more civilized was based in part on his noting no widespread use of wooden "idols" (Sheppard 1917: 113). Both Lapsley and Sheppard were dismayed by the prevalence of these objects among Kete peoples living near Luebo. After a visit to the Kete village of Bena Kasenga, Lapsley wrote:

> Every corner and cranny in the town has its *nkissi* or image, and generally the rudest you could fancy in construction. The features are portrayed by three cuts in a stick. Two strokes make the mouth, as many each eye and the finish is planting it before the house or at the cross-road. But it is enough to keep them from believing the gospel; and we shall have a hard fight of it, no doubt, for even our boys still believe in the power of *nkissi*. (1893: 166–67)

Worthy of special mention among missionary collections is the one amassed by William Sheppard and acquired by the Hampton University Museum in 1911 (Zeidler and Hultgren 1988). Sheppard notes that, on his return to Luebo from visiting the Kuba capital for the first time, his porters were "loaded down with Bakuba curios, cloth, rugs, masks, mats, hats, cups and plenty of food" (1917: 138). Before Sheppard's collection was acquired by Hampton, Sheppard used these objects to illustrate his public lectures in the United States. The short, choppy style of Sheppard's book *Presbyterian Pioneers in Congo* and articles in the *Kassai Herald* and the *Southern Workman* is due to their initial use as texts for public lectures. In these presentations, Kuba artifacts were displayed as "curios" to stimulate questions from the audience.[26] On one occasion, Sheppard spoke of his friendship with Kot aMbweeky, the Kuba paramount ruler whom he met for the first time in 1892. As he displayed a knife given him by the Kuba ruler (see Fig. 2.3), he spoke of the superiority of the Kuba over other groups in central Africa. The knife, he explained, "had been handed down in the red halls of the Lukengas through seven generations" (1893: 185).[27] The knife and other Kuba artifacts used in this manner were invaluable aids to Sheppard's presentations. Artifacts were tangible proof of Sheppard's visit to the mythic capital and his meeting with its ruler.

Like other ACPM missionaries, Torday was selective in his collection efforts for the British Museum. He purchased over 3,000 artifacts during

2.3 Kuba knife collected by William H. Sheppard. Iron, copper, wood, brass.
Length 14½ in.

his expedition, but ignored certain objects he felt were artistically inferior or of recent manufacture. The Kuba collection Torday amassed was intentionally weighted towards objects which he felt demonstrated aristocratic status and antiquity. Interestingly, when Torday compiled a list of Kuba artistic achievements he included weaving, embroidery, wood carving and metal work but not mask-making. For Torday, Kuba masks were not representative of "the greatest artists of black Africa" (Torday 1925: 203). He witnessed masked dancers among the Ngongo at Misumba and described them as grotesque, and the Ngongo initiation society (*babende*) as a "masked horde" who in the past "invaded the village and carried its victim off to be slaughtered" (Torday 1925: 98, 191–92). It seems that Torday believed any artistic tradition that did not support the authority of chiefs was not significant in the corpus of Kuba arts. There was another reason for his lack of interest in masks. Because Torday's primary interest lay in obtaining objects that validated Kuba antiquity (see Mack, this volume), lavishly decorated masks which did not appear to him to represent ancient traditions were left uncollected.[28] In correspondence with T. A. Joyce of the British Museum, Torday described a mask called Mukenga as "beautifully worked, but unfortunately the natives have ornamented them with trade cloth and beads to such an extent that the original mask completely disappears. Not having seen any that was not thus spoiled no specimen has been purchased" (1905–1908: I: 591).

Among other artifacts missing from the collection are Kuba figure sculptures other than the important royal king figures (*ndop*).[29] While Torday made extraordinary efforts to obtain three *ndop* including the example which represents the culture hero Shyaam, he showed little interest in other figure sculpture such as Kuba hunting charms or the charm figures which had been recently acquired by the Kuba ruler, Kot aPe, from the Songye. In this regard, John Mack notes that for Torday "authenticity had been confidently recast as an aspect of antiquity. The oldest object, like the oldest authoritative informant, provided the most faithful representation of the state of a culture" (1990:74).

Torday and Sheppard's discourse on Kuba art is similar in this regard. Torday was as pleased with the acquisition of the royal king figures as Sheppard was with the gift of the royal knife now in the Hampton University Museum collection. Torday considered the *ndop* of Shyaam aMbul aNgoong to be "the most remarkable work of art black Africa ever produced" (see Fig. 2.4) (1925: 147). It portrays the seventeenth-century ruler and culture hero to whom most Kuba cultural innovations are credited. For Torday, the *ndop* represented Kuba culture at its apogee: a culture basking in a never-ending golden glow of past glory. Torday's king figure, like Sheppard's royal knife, was thought to affirm the greatness and antiquity of the Kuba nation – considered the one remaining advanced culture in all of Central Africa which still exhibited vestiges of its past glory. For Torday, the naturalism of the *ndop* figures like the "non-negro features" of the Kuba elite was additional proof of earlier contacts with advanced non-African populations to the northeast.[30] In a letter to T. A. Joyce in 1909, Torday articulates his reasoning: "I have a kind of idée fixe ... If you look at the portrait of the *nyimi* you will find a chin which is not negro. The same chin is in all the statues ... I could give you from memory fifty more names of people with non-negro features" (January 20, 1909, II).

"ENLIGHTENED BUT IN DARKNESS"

Sheppard's and Torday's romantic accounts of the Kuba follow the pattern outlined by Patrick Brantlinger (1986: 195) who asserts that "the great explorers' writings [on Africa] are nonfictional quest romances in which the hero-authors struggle through enchanted or bedeviled lands toward a goal."[31] Tales of a wealthy feudal monarchy in the heart of Central Africa heightened interest in Kuba culture during the late nineteenth century. Reports asserting that foreigners who entered Kuba territory would be killed only added to the mystery and the fascination felt by explorers and missionaries alike.[32] Sheppard and Torday journeyed through what they considered to be a land of darkness and savagery only to find, in the midst of darkness, a golden civilization – one whose peoples and artistic traditions seemed to them, at first encounter at least, to be more European than African.

The idea of a powerful, advanced Central African kingdom tenaciously maintaining its traditions against foreign influences and interests seems to have been a powerful romantic notion in the Western imagination during the late nineteenth century.[33] So overstated were the initial assessments of Kuba culture, that these estimations were revised in the early twentieth century. Sheppard was disappointed when he finally retired

2.4 *Ndop* figure of Shyaam aMbul aNgoong.

from the mission field and left the Kuba region in 1910 – some twenty years after he and Lapsley had established the APCM at Luebo. The years at Luebo and later at Ibaanc had been difficult. He lost not only Samuel Lapsley, his original associate in the enterprise, but also two of his children who died in their infancy. Stanley Shaloff suggests that he also lamented his inability to convert the Kuba (1970: 170). For Sheppard, Kuba culture was truly "enlightened but in darkness." They were distinctly more advanced than their neighbors but still in darkness.

Like Sheppard, Torday modified his unbridled enthusiasm for all things Kuba when he later reflected on the Kuba in his 1925 publication *On the Trail of the Bushongo*. He characterized the central ruling Kuba (Bushongo) as a "great might have been" (1925: 281). For Torday, the aristocratic Kuba never fulfilled the potential of their seventeenth-century ruler and culture hero, Shyaam aMbul aNgoong. The arrival of missionaries and other intrusive Western influences at the end of the nineteenth century marked the final blow to Kuba creative genius.[34] On his departure from the Kuba capital in 1908, he wrote to T. A. Joyce at the British Museum:

> I have had my say on the Bakuba ... when I think what things of scientific and artistic value have disappeared by the white man's arrival and how the few that perhaps are preserved are in possession of those who cannot value them, I am absolutely downhearted and consider my journey, of the point of view of collecting a failure ... I would give ten years of my life with pleasure to have had, fifteen years ago, a month of stay at the Mushenge [Kuba capital]. (December 17, 1908, II)

After leaving the Kuba capital, Torday searched for a culture which remained untouched by Western contact. He believed he found such a culture to the west of the Kuba region among Kongo and Mbala peoples.[35] He wrote: "Isolated from the rest of the world ... [they are] ... a good picture of the Bushongo before the advent of Shamba, we must admit that the natives of this part of the world were in the sixteenth century a very happy people" (1925: 237). So moved was Torday by the prospect of finding a culture still isolated from Western influence that he suggested to the Belgian authorities in 1925 that they make the region into "a human reservation, and the natives be preserved from all contact with Europeans, so that, when the whole continent has been altered, there should still remain a spot where the black man is left in his original simplicity" (1925: 237–38).

In retrospect, the accounts of Kuba culture by William Sheppard and Emil Torday often seem to read as fairy tales. Bruno Bettelheim in *The Uses of Enchantment* describes how a "fairy tale simplifies all situations. Its figures are clearly drawn" (1976: 8). Social evolutionary paradigms were explicitly stated by Sheppard and Torday. Advanced African cultures were clearly recognizable. So-called refinement of physical features, centralized forms of government and naturalism in the arts were among several key traits in this paradigm. As noted above, the Kuba were not alone in being elevated by Europeans to an advanced status. Schildkrout and Keim (1990a: 30) describe how the Azande and the Mangbetu were judged superior to neighboring peoples during the late nineteenth century in part because of their greater political centralization and because of their tendency toward more naturalistic representation in the arts. (See also Keim, this volume.) However, by the early twentieth century, the Kuba represented the last vestiges of a powerful centralized government in Central Africa.

THE LEGACY OF SHEPPARD AND TORDAY'S DISCOURSE ON KUBA CULTURE

Sheppard's and Torday's discourse on Kuba art and culture has dramatically influenced the direction of Kuba studies during the twentieth century. This relates principally to the continued emphasis in the literature on Kuba royal traditions. Although there are more than seventeen distinct ethnic groups under the designation Kuba, with varying degrees of cultural and artistic diversity, only Bushoong culture as manifested at the royal capital of *Nsheng* has held sustained interest for Kuba scholars during most of the twentieth century.

In scanning the art-historical literature on the Kuba in the twentieth century, one finds a virtual imperative to tie all Kuba artistic production to royal traditions at the capital as if they would otherwise lack scholarly interest or historical credibility. While many artistic traditions are practiced throughout the Kuba region, the literature is overshadowed by emphasis on traditions at the capital. For example, decorative textile traditions are, by and large, discussed in relationship to their fabrication and ceremonial display at the capital. Although extensive traditions of masquerade are found throughout the Kuba region, traditions at the capital, which are more limited and take place less frequently, are emphasized in the literature. Even masks which have their origins among the Ngongo are routinely given Bushoong names in the literature and some discussions of Southern Kuba initiation and masking rituals emphasize their relationship with royal patronage. The authors believe this to be a legacy of the initial encounters with Kuba culture in the late nineteenth and early twentieth centuries and the subsequent preoccupation on the part of Western scholars with royal over non-royal traditions.

In this regard, discussion of the royal *ndop* figures has dominated the discourse on Kuba artistic traditions since their acquisition by the British Museum in 1908 (see Fig. 2.4). The *Handbook to the Ethnographical Collections* describes the *ndop* as "portraits" of the early kings and as "the most striking products of indigenous African art" (British Museum 1910: 222). This assessment is confirmed in many influential publications during the twentieth century. In *Les arts plastiques du Congo belge* (1959), Frans Olbrechts focuses his entire discussion of Kuba sculptural traditions on a group of *ndop* figures concluding that the Kuba "produced their great sculptures at the inspiration and under the stimulating influence of the reigning dynasties" (a produit ses grandes sculptures à l'inspiration et sous l'influence stimulante des dynastics régnantes) (1959: 114).[36] To accentuate the correlation between art and centralized leadership, he draws a comparison between the Kuba and "the princes who surrounded themselves with a galaxy of artists as did the Medici and the Dukes of Burgundy in their own time" (des princes qui avaient à coeur de s'entourer d'une pléiade d'artistes – comme le firent en leur temps les Médicis et les Ducs de Bourgogne) (1959: 114).[37]

When casting about for a single object to represent the Kuba for the exhibition and catalogue *Tribes and Forms in African Art*, William Fagg selected the same *ndop* figure Emil Torday had designated as the work of "the greatest artists of black Africa" (1965). Carl Kjersmeier focuses almost his entire discussion of Kuba arts in *Centres de Style de la Sculpture Negre Africaine* on the *ndop* figures, stating that they "rank among the very rare works of African art that we are able to date with some certainty" (se rangent parmi les très rares oeuvres de l'art africain que nous soyons en état de dater avec quelque sûreté) (1967: 18). Kjersmeier echoes

Torday's understanding that only the oldest artistic traditions can be considered relevant to a reconstruction of the Kuba's archaic past. Because of this, Kuba masking traditions are left out of the discussion as they are believed to be borrowed from neighboring peoples such as the Lulua, Pende and Kete, and are therefore not treated as "*un coutume propre à sa race* (Kuba)" (1967: 18–19).

In a similar manner, the dust jacket for *African Art and Leadership* (Fraser and Cole 1972) is illustrated with the famous Eliot Elisofon photograph taken in 1947 of the elaborately bedecked Kuba ruler Mbop Mabiinc MaMbeky. The visual grandeur of this image suggests the pomp and pageantry of the Kuba royal court and further emphasizes the nature of Kuba artistic production as one primarily associated with royal traditions. Jan Vansina's important contributions to Kuba scholarship focus primarily on the central Kuba. His article on *ndop* figures in *African Art and Leadership* (1972) and his book *The Children of Woot* (1978) published with an illustration of an *ndop* figure on the dust jacket further dramatizes the singularity and dominance of the *ndop* figures over other Kuba artistic expressions. Other studies by T. A. Joyce (1910b; 1925), J. Maes (1936), Jean Rosenwald (1974), Belepe Bope Mabintch (1981) and Joseph Cornet (1982) have further emphasized the importance of this singular royal sculptural tradition to Kuba scholarship.

One can only speculate that if Sheppard and Torday had recognized the overriding importance of the funerary context to art making (*ndop* figures, textiles, prestige regalia, mat making and masks) both at the royal capital and throughout the Kuba region, a very different conclusion would have been reached: a conclusion that would logically situate the *ndop* figures within a broader framework of art-making associated with Kuba concepts of the afterlife and veneration of the recently dead (Darish 1989, 1990; Binkley 1987).

In retrospect, both Sheppard and Torday had limited experience in the Kuba region – Sheppard spent one month at the royal capital of Nsheng. Most of his eyewitness accounts seem to come from this visit. Torday spent ten weeks at Nsheng and one month at the Kuba-related Ngongo capital of Misumba.[38] During these brief encounters with Kuba culture, Sheppard and Torday conversed primarily with the paramount ruler and other titled officials and elite thus further substantiating the importance and influence of the central Kuba, principally the Bushoong, over their neighbors. During these interviews Torday was more concerned with gathering information to validate the antiquity of certain Kuba artistic traditions than with studying contemporaneous traditions elsewhere in the Kuba region. The published accounts which developed from these experiences emphasize artistic production at the capital in support of centralized authority and minimize cultural differences among other segments of the population which would have become apparent with a longer residence in the region. Similarly, the collections they formed, including figural sculpture, decorative arts, weapons, and textiles are weighted with examples acquired at the capital.[39]

These fleeting encounters with Kuba culture and the collections which developed from them form the baseline for Kuba studies in the twentieth century and set the tone for subsequent research. When Sheppard and Torday compared the central aristocratic Kuba (Bushoong) to neighboring peoples to the south and to the north, the apparent lack of artistic accomplishments by those neighboring peoples only made Kuba achievements seem grander and the exploits and discoveries of Sheppard and Torday more significant. Sheppard and Torday were invaluable eyewitnesses to Kuba culture during a period of unprecedented change. However, their conclusions about the Kuba must be understood in relation to nineteenth-century notions of cultural evolution and diffusion. This may in part explain the reductive tendencies of both missionary and ethnographer in trying to get a fix on a culture: to freeze Kuba culture in time and place, much like a photograph. In the late nineteenth and early twentieth centuries, the grandeur and the antiquity of the Kuba royal court were more readily comprehensible than the complexities of a multi-ethnic confederacy undergoing massive change.

ACKNOWLEDGMENT

The title of this chapter "Enlightened but in darkness," is borrowed from William Sheppard's book *Presbyterian Pioneers in Congo* (1917: 132).

NOTES

1 The quoted phrase appeared in a published leaflet describing Sheppard's expedition to the Kuba capital (Women's Foreign Missionary Society, February 1895: 14).

2 See Shaloff (1970) for a detailed discussion of the history of the American Presbyterian Congo Mission.

3 The site of Luebo was chosen because, as Lapsley notes, the Société Anonyme Belge planned to open "four new stations on the Kassai" and Luebo was fast becoming the heart of government administration and trade interests in the south-central region (Lapsley 1893: 133; see also Shaloff 1970: 21–24; Benedetto 1990: 55). In this regard, it should be noted that the Kuba were important middlemen in the burgeoning ivory trade of the nineteenth century. Ivory trade occurred to the south of the Kuba heartland at the markets of Ibaanc, Luebo and further south (Binkley 1993: 277–79; Vansina 1962; 1978: 186–96).

4 After a long residency at a mission station in the estuary of the Cameroon River, Grenfell moved to the Lower Congo River in 1879. From that time until his death in 1906, Grenfell was stationed in the Congo at Musoko and later at Bolobo. In Grenfell's obituary notice of 1907 Alphonse J. Wauters, the editor of the *Mouvement Géographique* wrote:

> Stanley revealed the course of the Congo from Nyangwe to Boma, Wissmann discovered the Kasai and Wolf the Sankuru. It is to Grenfell that we owe the earliest reconnoitering of most of the other navigable tributaries of the Congo . . . The Congo Independent State never had a more faithful auxiliary nor a more reliable adviser than George Grenfell, who, under all circumstances gave proof of his keenest sympathy with the efforts of the Belgians on the Congo. (Johnston 1908: 4–5).

5 Grenfell died July 1 1906 at Basoko.

6 Johnston based his work on photographs, detailed maps, diaries and other documents describing the peoples, languages, and the flora and fauna of the Congo. These research materials were compiled by Grenfell and additional materials by Emil Torday and others were included in the text.

7 William Sheppard and other APCM missionaries ascribed the physical and cultural superiority of the Kuba to previous contacts with the northeast (Shaloff 1970: 35; Sheppard 1893: 187. See also Kellersberger 1947; Verner 1903; Wharton 1927). While Torday believed the Kuba had created their culture by means of their own creative impulses, he also believed, like other Africanists of this period, that the Kuba's apparent physical and cultural superiority was proof of ancient Sudanese origins (1925: 162–166; see also Johnston 1908: 701–03).

8 The term Kuba is used by their neighbors and by Western art historians to refer collectively to approximately seventeen different peoples who historically belonged to the Kuba confederacy. In the Kuba region itself, only the Bushoong refer to themselves as Kuba.

9 Sheppard describes seeing numerous "idols and images" in Kete villages near Luebo but saw no such images in Kuba villages and therefore assumed they didn't exist there (1917: 69–70, 113).

10 Missionaries also praised the Kuba language. The Presbyterian
publication the *Kassai Herald* of July 1905 stated that "the Bakuba dialect is
said to be superior to any other in the Kassai . . . as a means to convey
thought." Another APCM missionary called it "the Greek of the Kassai" (Sieg
1905: 29).

11 In the late nineteenth and early twentieth centuries, government officials and
missionaries were often respected explorers and ethnographers. While
George Grenfell's principal duties were as the head of the Baptist Missionary
Society, he was also an acknowledged authority on the geography and
cultures of the Congo Free State. Even the American Presbyterian missionary
William Sheppard, who never thought of himself as an explorer or
ethnographer, became a member of the Royal Geographical Society
principally due to his visits to the Kuba royal capital.

12 On occasion other polarities were invoked, including aristocrat/commoner
and royal/slave.

13 On entering a Kuba village, Lapsley describes the women as having "specially
fine features, small noses, very thin lips, and are very light colored" (1893:
160).

14 Hermann Norden met Ndombe and described him and the Kuba in general
as tall (1925: 202). The Bieeng are a Kuba-affiliated group situated south of
the Lulua River.

15 Sir Harry Johnston struck a similar note when he characterized Kete peoples
living in the vicinity of Kuba as "a dirty, somewhat retrograde people who
have seemingly degenerated from a state of higher civilization, partly owing
to the degree to which they have been enslaved by the Bakuba and Baluba
chieftains" (1908: 162–63). For a discussion of the Thesiger Report see
Shaloff (1970).

16 T. H. Hardy, the artist who accompanied Torday to the Kasai, must have had a
similar impression of this titleholder for he included an illustration of this
individual in a statuesque pose in Hilton-Simpson's book *Lands and Peoples
of the Kasai* (1911, facing page 91).

17 In a similar tone, Sir Harry Johnston characterizes the Mongo and Nkucu as
"of poor physical development and primitive in mode of life" while Lord
Mountmorres described other Mongo peoples as "small of stature and
meagre of build, a backward forest race" (Johnston 1908: 518).

18 Even though advanced in many ways, the Nilotic negroes were identified as
having a propensity for nudity. Sir Harry Johnston noted that the custom
"before they came within the influence of European civilization – was for the
men either to be entirely nude, or if they wore clothing, to do so with no
intention of preserving decency" (Johnston 1908:558, n.1).

19 Vinson quotes Morrison as stating that "the acceptance of Christ means
complete revolution of their whole social and religious fabric" (Vinson
1921:43; see also Kellersberger 1947:78).

20 In searching for origins for this elaborate attire, Johnston suggested that the Kuba might be imitating "the clothing of European women one hundred and fifty or sixty years ago, though the resemblance may be quite accidental" (1908: 595).

21 According to Johnston the ability of Nilotic peoples to forge metal was one of several technological and cultural innovations which allowed them to become the carriers of advanced civilization into the Congo River Basin.

22 The photograph was taken by either Torday or his traveling companion on the trip to the Kuba area, Hilton-Simpson. See discussion of Torday and Hilton-Simpson as photographers in Royal Anthropological Institute (1980) and Mack (1990).

23 Torday notes that Kuba social classes are differentiated by dress (Torday and Joyce 1910; Torday 1925: 111–12, 178–81). See also Vansina (1964) and Cornet (1982). Johnston (1908) publishes numerous comparative photographs throughout his book to emphasize both physical differences and differences in dress between Nilotic peoples such as the Bakuba and other Congolese peoples.

24 Hermann Norden (1925: 237) describes visiting the colonial administrator's home at the Kuba capital and seeing "many bits of carving and other Bakuba craft." Kuba decorated mats and *madiba* (coarsely woven and embroidered textiles) continued to be a common decorative feature of missionary homes in the 1980s. See also Verner (1903:296).

25 Sheppard does not mention seeing masked dancers; however APCM missionary Verner (1903:251) describes masked dancers performing at a funeral as the "most hideous and appalling vestments of animal skins, bones, beads, red paint, wooden images, and figured cloth."

26 Sheppard was not the only missionary to use Kuba "curios" to illustrate a lecture. The April–June 1941 lecture schedule of the APCM missionary Alonzo Edmiston also listed "curios" to illustrate his lectures. See also Kellersberger (1947: 85).

27 Sheppard's article published in the *Southern Workman* describes his style of presentation (1893: 185).

28 Torday believed that the Babende masking society was not of Kuba origin but was a relatively recent import from the west "in consequence of the slave trade" (1925:98).

29 Torday never visited the southern part of the Kuba region and therefore did not collect Kete post figures that were described as prevalent during Sheppard's and Lapsley's stay fifteen years earlier.

30 See note 7. For a contrasting view on the relationship between Emil Torday's view and diffusionist theory see Mack (1990: 81–86).

31 Vansina (1978: 3, 319) notes the adulation of early travelers to the Kuba region who compare the kingdom to Pharaonic Egypt, Augustan Rome and Imperial Japan.

32 Sheppard's account vividly describes his fear and that of his porters on his initial journey into the Kuba heartland.

33 A strain of romanticism pervades accounts of the Kuba as it does most discourse about Africa in the nineteenth and twentieth centuries.

34 Torday regarded the missionaries as a dominant Westernizing influence who had fundamentally altered the pristine, untouched nature of Kuba life. He accused APCM missionaries of meddling in Kuba politics. He also charged them with inciting government officials against the Kuba by spreading untruths about potential revolts or the sacrifice of slaves at the interments of ruling family members.

35 Torday was especially impressed with the Southern Bambala. Like the Kuba, Torday describes the "un-African" features of all Bambala as "not the ordinary negro type, but much more refined; thick lips, for example, are quite exceptional, and only a small proportion have flat noses" (1913a:78).

36 Frans Olbrechts (1959) identifies two Kuba art styles: a "court style" associated almost exclusively with the *ndop* figures and a "folk style" associated primarily with decorative wood carving traditions. Olbrechts also speculates whether "the great prestige of the court, and the veneration the kings received even after their death, resulted not only in the flowering of court art, but also in the almost complete lack of folk sculpture" ("c'est le grand prestige de la cour et la vénération dont les rois étaient l'objet après leur mort, qui ont été cause, à la fois de la prodigieuse efflorescence de l'art de la cour et de l'inexistence presque absolue de la sculpture populaire") (1959:60).

37 Olbrechts also includes the States of Benin, Abomey and the Ancient Kingdom of Kongo in his discussion of African kingdoms (1946: 114).

38 While Torday differentiated between the Ngongo and the Bushoong peoples in relation to the elite titled classes, he and Hilton-Simpson would often refer to them both as Bushongo. See Vansina (1978: 5) for a list of Central Kuba groups.

39 Torday also collected at the Kuba-affiliated Ngongo capital of Misumba.

THREE

Kuba art and the birth of ethnography

JOHN MACK

The received wisdom is unequivocal: the arts of Africa received international recognition very largely as a result of events taking place in the
artists' studios of Paris in the opening decade of the century. The story has
been patinated with approval in accounts of the cultural developments of
the period ever since, with hardly a dissenting voice to warrant even a
passing footnote. Robert Goldwater, referring with approval to earlier
remarks by William Fagg, put the matter succinctly. "The French," he
reiterated, "took over" (Goldwater 1969: 26–27). Any more anthropological engagement with the visual traditions of Africa was pushed firmly to
the fringes with the emergence of "Primitivism" and did not reappear
until very much later.

The wisdom is unambiguous, but is it unassailable? The period, after all,
was one of significant flux and change in the parallel discipline of anthropology. Indeed, the whole idea of the "primitive," a composite image made
up of bits and pieces embedded equally in the intellectual history and the
popular culture of the previous century, was under revision. If we look
outside France, and to Britain in particular, it is clear that the days of nineteenth-century notions of social evolution which gave succor to the
popular image were already numbered. Frazer's *Golden Bough,* with its
evolutionist and developmental framework, continued to be reprinted
well into the present century – having first appeared in 1890 – and
remained an immense publishing success; but Frazer himself was no
longer at the forefront of the serious scientific discipline that was emerging. From one point of view the invention of "Primitivism" can be seen as
an endorsement of a representation of the cultures of the non-Western,

non-Classical world which was already becoming outmoded in scientific circles at the very moment it was being so warmly embraced by parts of the artistic community.

It is hard to believe that some of the rethinking which, at exactly this time, was beginning to give shape to modern anthropology did not rub off somewhere. What, for instance, was happening in British Art at this time? Britain hardly had a Primitivist movement. The "Primitivism" exhibition at the Museum of Modern Art, New York in 1984, together with its associated catalogue (Rubin, 1984), gave space to Henri Gaudier-Brzeska and to Sir Jacob Epstein. Both worked in Britain, but Gaudier-Brzeska was French anyway, and Epstein, by birth American, had studied in Paris before moving to England. Among indigenous British artists there was a certain resistance to Primitivism, but did these opponents also have a view of the "primitive"? Because they did not notably imitate well-known forms of African or other "primitive" art, were they therefore unaware of it, or immune to its qualities? In any case, do we not under-estimate the complexities of cultural interaction if we judge imitation as the only form of approval, interest and influence?

Equally, it does not seem inherently likely that anthropologists with interests in Africa and elsewhere would forego a concern with visual sub-jects merely because artists happened to take them up. For one thing museum collections increasingly benefited from collections formed in the field, collected and documented by the very anthropologists who, in the conventional view, had succumbed to the French artistic intelli-gentsia. The study of art was already well founded in general cultural studies. Tylor had included art in his evolutionist tract *Primitive Culture* (1871), Balfour and Haddon, two of the leading figures in the field in Britain, had published significantly on the visual arts and occupied the two Directorships at the museums associated with the universities of Oxford and Cambridge, the Pitt-Rivers Museum and the Cambridge Museum of Archaeology and Anthropology (Balfour 1893; Haddon 1895). Indeed of the coming generation, one of the most significant, W. H. R. Rivers had already undertaken studies in the related field of visual acuity and perception in the Torres Straits as early as 1898. Overall there were certainly the beginnings of a general shift of emphasis, characterized by a movement away from a more fragmentary typological interest in objects towards more integrated social and cultural studies. But why shed art from the roster of anthropological interests in the process. Indeed was it really marginalized at all?

The focus of this paper is Central African art and ethnography. Some of these wider issues are addressed by looking at the impact of one culture and one collection of ethnographic artifacts from what is now southern Congo. The collection was made principally on behalf of the British Museum towards the end of the opening decade of the century.

In Britain great discoveries have traditionally been communicated to the scientific world through presentations to the learned societies. The "discovery" of the art and culture of the Kuba was considered worthy and was similarly announced. It was admittedly only a part of the story to be told about an expedition undertaken in the years 1907–09 through the southern parts of the then Belgian Congo. The "discoverer" was Emil Torday, the Hungarian ethnographer, the venue was the Royal Geographical Society in London (Torday 1910b), and the audience a gathering including many of the luminaries of the day in the fields of anthropology and African studies – among them Sir Harry Johnston, A. C. Haddon, Henry Balfour and T. A. Joyce. (Thomas Athol Joyce was Torday's amanuensis and adviser on the staff of the British Museum who, though he never went to Africa, drafted many of Torday's ethnographic reports which were subsequently published under their joint names.)

As with other discoveries, we may argue about precedent: Torday was not technically the first Western observer to work among the Kuba, nor was he the first to collect examples of their arts or make notes on their history and society. The German explorer Leo Frobenius had passed through Kuba country several years earlier (Frobenius 1907). However, the honor of being the first foreigner to visit the capital itself, Nsheeng, belonged to William Sheppard the Black American missionary who formed the first collections in 1892. Among visitors to the Kuba capital, Torday was the most professional practitioner of a discipline which, in the Anglophone world as elsewhere, was beginning to become a more rigorous observational science. Torday with his companion M. W. Hilton-Simpson were however, the first outsiders to cross the area between the Loange and the Kasai Rivers, the territory of the two Kuba-related groups, the Lele and the Wongo. (The expedition painter, Norman Hardy, had by then returned to Europe, though he did visit the northern Kuba with Torday and Hilton-Simpson.)

Even if Torday's claims to priority were questionable, the tale which he was to tell, relating as it did to a territory which was at the very center of Conrad's *Heart of Darkness* was still sufficiently fresh and unexpected to have had a significant impact. Apart from the meeting at the Royal Geographical Society in March 1910, and subsequent press reporting of what had been said, for most of the potential public the main and most accessible version of the story was that which could be deduced from the display of Kuba arts in the Ethnographic Galleries of the British Museum, where the bulk of Torday's collections went and where they were already being put on exhibition while Torday was still in Africa. "Prepare room for the Bakuba collection," he had written from the field to forewarn the Museum authorities, "you will want it!" (March 6, 1908).[1] He was right.

The details of the collection Torday formed are these: the collection as a whole runs to some 3,000 objects of which nearly half (over 1,200 pieces) are from the Kuba or Kuba-related groups. Torday and Hilton-Simpson spent most of their time among two Kuba sub-groups, the Ngongo and the Bushoong at the capital itself. In addition, Torday visited the Ngende, and the two men acquired additional material from the Shoowa and the Kete. The collection is completed by a series of objects from the Lele and the Wongo to the west of the kingdom itself, and from the Isambo, a detached Kuba group in the area of Lusambo to the southeast. Representative collections were also made among other surrounding peoples. The objects were all acquired directly in the field (except possibly a number of textiles from the Shoowa) in association with broadly-based ethnographic research. All were collected in the period 1908–09.

No single category of object predominates in the collection. The purpose of the collection was explicitly stated – to establish another kind of document of social and cultural life, equivalent to the written records, photographic images and the phonograph recordings Torday also created (Mack 1991). To that extent it sought to be as comprehensive as possible. The list of objects acquired includes wooden boxes in a wide variety of shapes and designs; wooden cups, drinking horns, oil containers, molded tukula paste, headrests, seats, wooden figures, gourds, pottery, mats, divination objects, masks, iron-bladed knives and swords together with wooden versions, wooden smoking pipes, drums, musical horns and whistles, thumb pianos, rattles, harps, bull roarers, spinning tops, toy guns and cross-bows, toy boats and toy musical instruments, ivories, iron-working equipment, axes, adzes, oil presses, spears and arrows, fly-whisks, hats; personal ornaments of many types: bells, pins, bracelets, combs, looms, a wide variety of textiles, traps, bags, architectural panels; and enema tubes. Associated information with the objects includes details of where the material was acquired, detailed analyses of patterns and pattern names, and often an indication of ownership, especially in the case of courtly regalia and objects associated with royalty.

Torday had written to the Keeper of the relevant British Museum department, Charles Hercules Read, "I have not chosen objects for their beauty but for the interest they may have for the anthropologist, and I hope that in this I have acted for the best" (November 19, 1905). The spirit of the collection is that of a detailed cultural accounting, not a highly selective, focused interest dictated by external aesthetic or other pre-conception. To that extent it coheres with the aims of accurate ethno-graphic reporting which, however problematic they might seem in retrospect, were being actively promoted as an alternative to the conjec-ture of nineteenth-century social philosophy. The new figures in the field were technicians more interested in social and historical process and detailed accurate description, than adepts of philosophical method artic-ulating the sweep of theoretical ideas. It is not unimportant that many had a background in the natural sciences (notably those who went on Haddon's Torres Straits Expedition in 1898) and carried with them into ethnographic research a well-founded scientific method of investigation. Torday's background was somewhat different. His credentials were essen-tially those of bushcraft rather than scholarship and science. However, armed with the statutory ethnographic questionnaire, and instructed from 1904 onwards by the Museum authorities and a variety of members of the Royal Anthropological Institute in Britain, he had imbibed the spirit of the new documentary fieldwork that was emerging. Indeed, he came to regard himself as an especially gifted practitioner being, for instance, highly critical of Frobenius whose methods he had seen firsthand in the Congo in 1905–06 (Mack 1990: 48–51).

Torday's view of the Kuba, however, was far from dispassionate, what-ever the aims of neutral reporting he brought to the study of their society.

He was a complete enthusiast for Kuba art and culture and an unashamed, even uncritical, admirer of the King himself, Kot aPe. Torday confided that he felt the research he had conducted among the Kuba was the best he had done: "you will think me a conceited ass," he wrote to Joyce, "but I am very proud of the result of my researches here" (December 4, 1908). On leaving Nsheeng he went on to tell Joyce: "There is no man alive who knows as much about the Bakuba as we do; so at least says the chief; for 'I have told you all I know and spoken to you as no Bushongo ever spoke to a white man; the old have told you more than they would tell even to me; you are in all the secrets of our people'" (December 17, 1908).

These comments mark a significant shift which had taken place in Torday's experience of ethnography. The enthusiasm for data collection was still there, but the controls on objectivity represented by the questionnaire, the camera and the phonograph he used to make recordings of indigenous music no longer seemed sufficient in themselves. They were props to be wheeled into place when circumstances, whether language difficulties or shortage of time, prevented other forms of relationship from developing. Knowledge, "facts," could not be advanced as objective merely because they were impersonal, acquired in a rigid and controlled way. Indeed, in Torday's work among the Kuba the various artificial aids to objectivity had been overtaken by a style and quality of relationship which was at once personalized and intimate. The care and tact with which Torday had conducted all his dealings with the Kuba signaled these changes. Fieldwork implies the creation of relationships and responsibilities; and the most profound insight, it now seemed, was to be derived from the closest relationships. The questionnaire had its limitations – it was not a rule book, it could not tell you how to create trust. For that, a background in bushcraft rather than science was a more serviceable tool.

It can be argued that the Kuba were also important to Torday, and the work he undertook amongst them important in the development of African studies and ethnographic writing generally, because the emphasis of their culture closely matched the emphasis of his research. Torday, in the wake of the vagaries of evolutionary paradigms, was concerned with documenting actual pre-existing conditions. And the Kuba were temperamentally historians. Like many centralized states, theirs was a society obsessively interested in precedent. More than that, what Torday learnt from the Kuba did not look like mere folklore. They could recount king lists, locate events in time by reference to the kings in whose reign they occurred – they even talked of a solar eclipse and a passage of Halley's comet, thus providing a means of linking the Kuba account of history to a wider chronology. Oral history as relayed by the Kuba was for Torday real history, of the sort that the European historian might investigate. Memory was documentary.

Torday was always disposed to treat the evidence relayed to him by the senior spokesmen of any society as a literal representation of fact. This had even been so in his work a few years previously in the Kwilu. In discussing the king of the Yaka, for instance, Torday reports an oral account of a ruler who hauled himself up from a sitting position by stabbing knives into the backs of slaves. This is not taken as a statement about wealth and the status of slaves but as an actual event and, as a result he calculated how many slaves would die by such means in a single day, and given the local price of slaves what such a practice would cost over a year.

While no one would now be disposed to doubt Torday's acceptance of oral tradition as an authentic document, there are still considerable reservations. It is authentic in an ethnographic sense rather than a strictly historical one. What Torday was recording was not history as experienced but history as interpreted. Yet no more was Freud, for instance, interpreting dreams as they were dreamed by patients; he too was giving credence to what was remembered of the experience of dreams. Torday may not have had the intellectual sophistication to argue with his contemporary about whether what is perceived to be real is real, yet he did treat the Kuba account of their past as reality, which, for that time already represented a considerable advance over an older tradition of treating native accounts of myth and history as illusion.

On completing his study of the Kuba-Ngongo Torday wrote to tell Joyce:

> There are many things those who may come after me may find but they will find all I wrote is strictly correct. Not a word of all written to this day has been obtained otherwise as from the native himself and all has been controlled with other members of the tribe; and I may say: I swear to have told the truth, all the truth, and nothing but truth. (December 17, 1908)

The aim was not to be the ventriloquist, but the ventriloquist's dummy. Among the Kuba, Torday had discovered a voice that was dignified, regal, and above all one that seemed to be historically informed.

KUBA ART AND THE SCHOLARLY COMMUNITY

Similarly Torday and his Museum masters were far from immune to the qualities of Kuba forms of visual expression. To make the point, the way in which the material was exhibited in the Ethnographic Galleries of the British Museum was somewhat unusual. The main method of display in the British Museum, as at the Pitt-Rivers and elsewhere, had been consistently typological: serried ranks of objects arranged and classed by function, often on a continent-wide basis rather than as localized features. Arrows, combs, textiles, pottery – whether from the Congo Basin or not – all tended to get mixed in with equivalent objects from elsewhere in Africa. The Kuba material, however, was all displayed together. Large prints from Torday's field photographs were included, one of Kot aPe and his court, another of a Kuba elder, and a third of a courtier holding a king figure. This display invited attention to Kuba art as a handle on Kuba culture. In this instance, at least, the integrity of an artistic tradition was retained without forfeiting any anthropological or historical perspective that might emerge to the constraints of typological classification.

The leading characteristics of Kuba arts are perhaps sufficiently well-known not to require extensive comment here. The Kuba obsession with rectilinear configurations is clear. The surfaces of all manner of objects from the most elaborate to the most mundane provide an irresistible canvas for the talents of carver and embroiderer alike. Writing in the 1930s, Henry Lavachery described the essential qualities of Kuba art as decorative rather than sculptural, even where representative imagery is produced. "Here the human figure though widely employed, is presented for the most part as merely an important element in the decorative scheme" (Lavachery 1934: 690). (The translation from the French, interestingly, is by Samuel Beckett.) Of representations of the human figure the *ndop*, royal king figures, were, and remain, the most famous. Torday collected four: those associated with Shyaam aMbul aNgoong, MishaaPelyeeng aNce, and Mbop Pelyeeng aNce went into the British Museum collections; the fourth, that of Kot aMbul, went – it is believed – to a territorial administrator, thence to the Musée royal de L'Afrique centrale in Belgium and finally to the Musées Nationaux in Kinshasa. The most notable feature of these figures is their naturalism.

An early impression of the significance that the Kuba collection was to have can be gauged from Joyce's comments on an Ngongo cup, collected by Torday and published before he and Hilton-Simpson returned from the field (Joyce 1910a). Firstly the evidence of wear indicated "that the cup is a genuine 'antique' in the limited sense of antiquity which can be applied to objects from savage Africa." Yet it was a puzzle: "On the whole the shape of the vessel distinctly suggests European influence, just as the ornamented body suggests the art of Benin. But it is impossible to find in this neighborhood even the remotest traces of direct European influence earlier than the comparatively recent date of Wissman's visit." From the vantage point of the Pitt-Rivers Museum in Oxford, Balfour, in reviewing Torday and Joyce's volume *Les Bushongo*, reiterated the point, again taking off from the baseline provided by the arts of Benin: "If the punitive expedition to Benin astonished the ethnological world by the revelation of the marvelous *cire perdu* bronze-work and the ivory carving of that Nigerian district, Mr. Torday's expedition to the Bushongo reveals a yet more wonderful art–culture, the more to be admired since it is strictly indigenous and uninfluenced by contact with Europeans" (1912: 47). Torday himself conceded that as far as the Bushoong are concerned, Shyaam, the king and culture hero of the Kuba, is reputed in tradition to have traveled widely beyond Kuba territory; but he said nothing to dent the unanimity which was emerging: "the most un-African shapes are found amongst tribes related to the Bushongo [he is referring to the Wongo and Lele], who have never been under the influence of the traveler king, and who are the most conservative and most adverse to strangers of all people I have ever met" (1911: 46).

The implications of this view are far-reaching. Firstly, in advance of the diffusionist debates which were to rage in British anthropology after the First World War, this was to set down an important marker. Torday and Joyce do cast a conjectural glance at the broader affinities of Kuba culture and come up with some highly speculative conclusions about the remoter origins of at least some elements in the complex that constitutes Kuba society. They note similarities with the northern parts of the Equatorial Forest in isolated aspects of material culture – for instance, objects of divination, and a throwing knife then already extinct amongst the Kuba. They identify the ultimate homeland of the Kuba with a distant area in the region of Lake Chad. For the most part, however, they limit themselves in their detailed ethnography *Les Bushongo* (1911) and elsewhere to systematizing Kuba chronicles as they had been related to Torday.

This was a long way from anticipating the characteristic arguments of the emerging body of diffusionist literature. In the second and third decades of the century, studies of the geographic distribution of everything from mummification to pearl fish-hooks were advanced as a means of tracing broad lines of human migration and the transmission of culture. The comparisons were often as uncritical as the evolutionist speculations which they were intended to replace. There was, as A. M. Hocart remarked (1954: 10), a "cranky" element to all this. Grafton Elliot Smith, concerned to demonstrate the Egyptian origin of a megalithic culture-complex, selected his evidence from all quarters of the globe. A monument found at the Mayan site of Copan seemed to portray on each of its four corners an Indian elephant complete with turbaned rider (Elliot Smith 1924). This, to the converts to unicentric diffusion, was proof that Egyptian influence had swept through India and then even reached Central America. Sceptics preferred to see in the monument a more likely subject, whether the representation of a tapir, a macaw, or even a tortoise.

For a review of Kuba art in broad diffusionist terms a modern commentary (Meurant 1986) gives a much better idea of the oddities of such a position than anything Torday wrote. Torday was never in favor of the idea of the Egyptian grand tour, not even in a more restricted form – the influence of Egypt on Bantu culture. Regarding the indigenous origins of iron-working in Africa, Torday wrote, "no bronze implements have ever been found in black Africa; had the Africans received iron from the Egyptians, bronze would have preceded this metal and all traces of it would not have disappeared" (1913b: 414). Beyond that, however, he preferred to start from what he regarded as solid fact rather than speculation. F. W. Maitland had written "by and by anthropology will have the choice between being history and being nothing" (1911, III: 259). His aim was to direct attention back to actual processes of development and the more verifiable events of the past – a goal partly realized in Rivers' *The History of Melanesian Society* (1914) but ultimately subverted in the diffusionist version of historical reconstruction.

Torday's main contribution to the question was his essay on "The Influence of the Kingdom of Kongo on Central Africa" (1928). One of his purposes was to try and explain "the rise of a distinctive high civilization (that of the Kuba) in the midst of peoples of much lower culture" (1928: 159). It is not by any means a theoretical tract, but rather a search of the available historical and cultural sources to establish the merits of the Kuba tradition that Shyaam traveled extensively among peoples to the west of the Kasai. The historical kingdom of Kongo, documented in European sources going back to the late fifteenth century, provided a stimulating set of parallels with the Kuba both in terms of social and craft organization, in titles and terminology, and in art and material culture. Torday concludes that there were significant levels of contact between the Kuba and the Kongo in the first part of the seventeenth century. He is careful, however, to leave the question as to how these contacts were achieved and what form they took for further work. He was prepared to regard the story of Shyaam himself journeying westwards as a metaphor rendered in Kuba idiom for contacts that may or may not have engaged the king personally. This was history in the sense Maitland had intended, a question of dates and chronologies, of events with the authority of written or oral testimony. There were question marks remaining: it was conjectural, but it was not for all that "conjectural history" in its Enlightenment sense, let alone its diffusionist form.

This, of course – a number of years on from Torday's first reflections with Joyce on the issue – was to water down the sense of the uniqueness of Kuba culture: in part the Kuba reflected the glories that were the old Kingdom of Kongo. But it is not, for all that, to move to any greater assertion of European influence on Central African art. In fact, the early arrival of European influence is portrayed as one of the factors contributing to the *decline* of the Kongo by comparison with the Kuba, protected for much longer by their relative isolation from extensive and corrupting external contacts.

The second point to emerge from the assertion of the entirely indigenous sources of Kuba art concerns the standing of African culture in European perceptions of what was still the "Dark Continent." The comparison constantly made with Benin is significant. There the arrival of the Portuguese had been seen as a highly significant moment in the development of its arts. Artistic excellence, so it seemed, could be explained by exposure to European influence. Something similar occurred after the discovery of the immense walls and other architectural features at the site of Great Zimbabwe – that too for a long time was never attributed its true African origin.

In analyzing Kuba art, however, Joyce had been able to detect "no more than the merest shadow" of Portuguese influence. The image of so un-African an African society, discussed with unabashed approval in the writings of Torday, Joyce and others, was frankly unexpected. Its "discovery" posed an awkward question. Perhaps the nearest equivalent in European thought is the imagined kingdom of Prester John. Yet that was a Christian African kingdom, a "lost" culture once in touch with a world beyond Africa. There are echoes, perhaps, of a comparison of the Kingdom of Shyaam and that of Prester John in some of Torday's discussion. He was initially inclined to make something of a Bushoong tale that cited a remote white ancestor. The point was taken up by Haddon: "It is, to my mind, very suggestive that the most civilized, cultured, and artistic people in Central Africa should themselves own that hundreds of years ago there was a white ancestor somewhere behind them" (1910: 55). Torday himself was aware that some elements of Bushoong myth might also be suggestive: "I am afraid," he wrote from the field, "that people will say that the mythology of the Bakuba is a hash up of the Bible" (December 17, 1908). But in the end Shyaam was not Prester John. Kuba art and culture might be exceptional, but it had to be faced: it was a purely African achievement. That, in essence, was the distinctive "discovery" Torday had made.

BRITISH ARTISTS AND AFRICAN CULTURE

Torday himself imagined that the existence of a complex African kingdom in so remote a location, and with a highly elaborate and accessible decorative tradition, would excite more than a small circle of scholars. He wrote from the Congo to the authorities of the British Museum inquiring "Have the staff of police at the Museum been doubled to keep out the publishers?" (March 8, 1909). He anticipated an immense public interest in the cultures he had documented. Up to a point his judgment was vindicated. Even if his "discoveries" did not initiate an intellectual earthquake, there was a quiet revolution, the more imperceptible because of the blustery promotional material coming out of Paris.

James Clifford, in commenting on the 1984 "Primitivism" exhibition in New York pointed to one important missing element in the story of the modernist movement and "the primitive" if it is a tale told exclusively through an emphasis on modern Western art. What is lacking, he remarks, is the world of other more popular forms of expression and performance – the world of jazz musicians, of boxers, of Josephine Baker and the Venus d'Ombre (Clifford 1988). Also omitted, however, is the place the "primitive" began to occupy in a world that included a rich array of other cultures commonly, and approvingly, circumscribed initially under the museological umbrella of "Antiquity." Entry into that select company was as carefully scrutinized as that which prevented Groucho Marx from taking up any club membership. In terms of Antiquity, the museological world granted the Kuba, and by extension aspects of African culture, associate membership.

What did British-based artists make of all this? The naturalism of Kuba art was an immediate contrast with the angular faceted African sculpture the Primitivists were seeing. From the Primitivist point of view *ndop* displayed characteristics they might otherwise have regarded as unwelcome. They show their subjects seated cross-legged in a somewhat flabby condition; they are emotionless, and they are generalized with virtually no distinguishing individual features and very few natural references. Gaudier-Brezska remarked "an enormous stomach if you like, without lumps, without holes, without hardness, without angles, without mystery, and without force – a flabby thing made of wool, which goes in if you lean against it, and what's worse makes a fellow hot" (Ede 1987: 53). He was not as it happens talking about the *ndop* – though he might very well have been for he certainly saw them in his long reflective observations in the British Museum in the period immediately before the First World War. He was in fact referring to the Venus de Milo – a "detestable" creation, "no more than a line enjoyed by pigs."

It is perhaps doubtful that Gaudier-Brezska's fiery opinions of the qualities of the Venus de Milo would have been significantly altered had it suddenly been discovered that it had been created by an African; surprised, however, he and everyone else, would have been. African naturalism, where found, had always intrigued and surprised Westerners. One of the virtues of the "African Reflections: Art from Northeastern Zaire" exhibition initially at the American Museum of Natural History, New York and its associated catalogue (Schildkrout and Keim 1990a) is precisely that it makes clear

the circumstances in which the presence of powerful outsiders, their pur-
chasing power and influence, can lead to the creation of an artistic tradition with strong naturalistic tendencies. The idea that naturalism was
otherwise beyond the untrained, unaffected skill of Africans was common.
African naturalism had, or rather had to have, an external source. In fact, of
course, the development of a naturalistic tradition among the Mangbetu
(the primary subject of "African Reflections") is in one way a form of
confirmation. It is a record of a moment, observed with mature insight in
the "African Reflections" exhibition and catalogue, but a moment nonetheless which had already been imagined, with much less reason, to have taken
place in the distant African past at Benin and Great Zimbabwe. The Kuba
ndop were arguably the first certain exceptions to the rule that African
naturalism had to have an external source – another, Nok culture, was of
course yet to be described.

Gaudier-Brezska was an influential member of the Vorticist group, a
loose alliance of artists and writers which emerged in Britain just before
the First World War (in which context the reasons for the inclusion of his
work among that of the Primitivists are not perhaps unambiguous). Their
manifesto was the journal *Blast* whose leading lights included Ezra Pound
and Wyndham Lewis. Their principal meeting place was the British
Museum, and a nearby café frequented by artists, writers and Museum
staff. In the words of one commentator on the Vorticist movement:

> The British Museum, itself, was a center and meeting place for artists and
> writers who had spent a few hours in the great domed reading room, or
> among fragments of Grecian, Egyptian, Assyrian, Chinese, Oceanic,
> African, and other ancient and modern cultures of east and west. Artists
> were known to secretly check on each other's movements in the ethno-
> graphic rooms, like prospectors jealously guarding their "finds". (Wees
> 1972: 47)

They were all certainly aware of the much-heralded Kuba collections
gradually being put on display from 1909 onwards.

The hallmark of the Vorticists was not so much their adherence to any
specific visual formula, as a commitment to thorough-going eclecticism
allied to an interest in something much less readily defined – the creative
energy which lay behind artistic creation. Lewis himself later described
Vorticism as "this strange synthesis of cultures and times ... the first pro-

jection of a world-art." He, like the other Vorticists, was both well versed in Classical and non-Classical tradition and widely read. Anthropology was one of their constant resorts. Of Gaudier-Breska's conversation, Pound wrote: "a flow of remarks jab the air . . . It might be exogamy, or the habits of primitive peoples, or the training of African warriors, or Chinese ideographs or the disgusting 'mollesse' of metropolitan civilisation, or abundant chaff, or aesthetics" (Pound 1916: 35). Pound, for his part, later recommended access to Frobenius' writings as the main reason for learning German; whilst Lewis, in addition to visiting Africa for himself, also wrote essays commending the work of Elliot Smith and Jane Harrison (Michel and Fox 1969). Meaty tomes of academic learning were very much to their taste. Indeed Pound, anticipating criticism of the intellectual and scholarly resources assembled by the Vorticists, remarked that it is simply "another sibboleth of the artistic-slop crowd" that art is above intellect (1916: 124). "If our detractors," he continues, "are going to talk about art in terms of the 'Pears Soap's Annual' and of the Royal Academy, one dismisses the matter" (1916: 127).

This eclecticism was aimed at synthesis rather than at imitation. No single artistic tradition was selected as an especially rich model for modern art to follow. For this reason the primitivist game of comparing works of Western art to so-called "Primitive" prototypes cannot be played with this phase of the British modernist movement. "There is," Wyndham Lewis wrote, "no such thing as the *born Primitive*. There is the *Primitive* in point of view of date, the product of a period. And there is the *Primitive voulu*, who is simply a pasticheur and stylist; invariably a sentimentalist, when not a rogue" (Michel and Fox 1969: 148). The aim was a somewhat mystical one: to get behind the circumstances of any particular tradition of artistic creation to the imaginative sources of creation itself. It was these which needed to be tapped, rather than any individual artistic formula. Words such as "energy" and "vitality" are a consistent part of the vocabulary of Vorticism. (Lewis, indeed, was described by T. S. Eliot as having "the thought of the modern and the energy of the cave man.") In this scale of things contemporary, non-Western cultures were already remote from the ultimate sources: "The artist goes back to the fish. The few centuries that separate him from the savage are a mere flea-bite to the distance his memory must stretch if it is to strike the fundamental slime of creation." (Lewis, *Caliph's Design*, 1919; quoted Michel and Fox 1969:

152). In the studios of Paris – no doubt in part for polemical reasons – the primitive remained firmly a vestige of the first steps taken towards civilization, something basic and prior. In Britain, however, a significant element in the artistic community was beginning to rejig the evolutionist hierarchy, granting in the process a different standing to African art in particular. Lewis included Central African art with Egyptian and American Art as "the grandest and most majestic art in the world" (Michel and Fox 1969: 71).

Here imitation, or the lack of it, is no guide to influence or approval. Copying, crawling into each other's skin, let alone that of another culture, was contrary to Vorticist ideas. Even so they discussed non-Western art and culture avidly, studied it, read about it, absorbed it. The significant influence in the end was not Art as such, but the perception it offered of the possibilities of human culture. In the context of Africa, it was not so much individual works which provided inspiration, but an *idea* of Africa and its cultures – an idea, furthermore, that cannot be isolated from a broader conception of the place of Africa within a roster of other historical cultures. Kuba art was constantly compared in professional and popular literature alike to Celtic Art – not quite in the Classical tradition perhaps, but a worthy sub-species. Arguably this view of the integrity of Central African culture, which emerged in the discussion of Kuba art and culture, has in its quiet way been as significant in promoting the study of Africa's artistic heritage as what was emerging from the studios of those who had gone native in Montparnasse.

ACKNOWLEDGMENTS

I would like to thank those who were in touch with me following the American Natural History symposium at which this paper was presented on my behalf.

The text draws in part on my book *Emil Torday and the Art of the Congo 1900– 1909*. I am grateful to the publishers, British Museum Publications, for permission to include elements of the argument, especially from chapter 5, which are developed here.

NOTES

1 References to Emil Torday's letters refer to documents held in the archives of the British Museum's Department of Ethnography.

FOUR

Curios and curiosity
Notes on reading Torday and Frobenius

JOHANNES FABIAN

(6)

When the chips are down, we talk of objects as we reflect on collected art from Congo. Their mere presence in our museums provides food for thought. Exhibitions make that food into a cuisine; and like a cuisine, exhibitions need critics as well as consumers. Not being a certified expert nor an ardent visitor of museums, I must ask for indulgence when in these notes I dare to make pronouncements about collecting objects I have not seen, let alone touched or smelled, but only read about. Furthermore, not only am I going to talk about objects "once removed," as they exist in written reports and a few illustrations. I shall be concerned, as it were, with objectness itself. No *Ding an sich* looms behind this approach, just an attempt to understand a few of the conditions that had to be met in order to make collectible objects out of things.

How I came to ask such a question requires some introductory remarks regarding the larger project for which I have been preparing myself. After that I shall formulate my general understanding of the role of collecting in ethnography. I then turn to my sources and note some observations on expeditions and markets, as well as on object collecting and ethnographic knowledge. I will end with a conjecture on what turns curios into "art."

THE LARGER PROJECT: "ECSTATIC" ETHNOGRAPHY

For years I have struggled with epistemology *tout court* – the Kantian "conditions of possibility" of anthropological knowledge. I do not for a moment believe that I have exhausted the topic but, as I found myself adding more and more written sources to my ethnographic research, I began to feel the need for a kind of historical epistemology. I want to understand the historically determined and therefore changing goals, conditions, explicit rules, and implicit assumptions of emerging specialized knowledge about other cultures and societies. This is a vast area which I try to limit in time and space by concentrating on the period of exploration and early ethnography in Central Africa (c. 1850–1910).

Because I have a polemical mind I plan to begin by debunking a myth: the notion that the practice of knowledge gathering/production that was part of Western imperialist expansion was guided, only or mainly, by natural history methods, such as observing, measuring, collecting, classifying, and describing. This was (is?) a powerful myth because the immensely popular story it told about the quest carried out by the intrepid explorer and traveler served to justify the practices of exploration and scientific travel as intrinsically rational, that is, not guided by obviously ideological or doubtful moral motivations. Only sport – essentially big game hunting for the hell of it – was considered an admissible diversion from the labors of research.

I want to show that exploration and scientific travel had elements, aspects, and conditions that were anything but rational in the sense of being self-controlled, planned, disciplined, and strictly intellectual. There was a dimension to that practice of exploration and early ethnographic investigation that I call "ecstatic." By which I mean everything that corrects the image of the self-contained observer who contemplates from a distance, calmly records, and objectively reports. Much of what there was to know, and what explorers actually got to know, could only be attained by their being outside, if not beside, themselves.

When one begins to consider such questions one quickly realizes how much knowledge of the other – at the time and in the area to which I am limiting myself – was conditioned by preconceptions and prejudices, as well as topoi such as cannibalism and other forms of savagery. All of these were brought along and hardly controlled by their carriers. Gathering of knowledge was also affected by many circumstances that tend to be overlooked: illness – most often reported as fever – and its supposed treatments such as alcohol, opiates and other drugs; fear and fatigue; sex and its suppression or sublimation; physical violence and brutality.

Notice that all of this involves the body. Acknowledging the body's role in African exploration leads one to pay attention to other, less somber mediations of knowledge that, nevertheless, are what I called ecstatic: the experience of music [1] and dance, the appreciation of pomp and circumstance, in short, of all sorts of "performance" that more often than not marked early encounters between Africans and explorers/ethnographers. We should add to this list food and drink creating or impeding conviviality and, above all, the significance of objects in establishing relationships, objects that create (or fail to create) conditions for communication. These objects included presents, trade goods (commodities), weapons and all sorts of things from camping equipment to phonographs.[2] And there were, of course, collectibles (curios in English reports), that is, objects apt to arouse curiosity in the field as well as at home, or to serve as mementos and proof of having been there. It is as mediations of what I call the ecstatic aspect of ethnographic knowledge that objects will figure in my project. Here I shall concentrate on their collection as part of ethnography.

I began my reading,[3] or re-reading, of sources for the larger project at the end of the period I planned to cover, namely the first decade of this century, and with two well-known figures: Emil Torday (with Melville William Hilton-Simpson),[4] and Leo Frobenius. A third traveler, Samuel P. Verner, will be mentioned only occasionally (see Schildkrout's discussion in chapter 7 of Frederick Starr, who accompanied Verner on one expedition and was actually the only professional anthropologist of the group). These figures represent the end of a line of development that ran from explorer to professional traveler to traveling professional anthropologist. Most of the quotations come from their published reports.[5]

Before I get to Torday and Frobenius I should like to end these introductory remarks by illustrating my observations on ecstatic mediations of knowledge with a passage from an account written by one of their predecessors. In 1881, Hermann Wissmann and his mentor, Paul Pogge, reached the neighborhood of what later became the post of Luluabourg and is now the city of Kananga, a center of the Kasai region of Zaire. There an eventful encounter took place that was to transform their enterprise. The Chief Tshingenge arrived in a grand procession, together with about a hundred people, some of them armed. They were accompanied by drummers, dancers, and sundry merrymakers. The usual greetings, compliments, and gifts were exchanged. The not so usual occurred in the evening when these Bashilange, as Wissmann labels the people, organized a "Riamba-Fest" (riamba or dyamba, the Luba term for hemp). "Soon the curious group was enveloped by a screen of sweetly malodorous smoke from which there resounded huffing and coughing and protestations of friendship with the white man inspired by the narcotizing effect of hemp." He goes on to describe the drumming and dancing and then notes, "To us this curious orgy was new and exciting, the ear was deafened by the half-melodic hellish din that spoke of the narcotic effect, the eye enthralled by their fixed stare and the contortion of their limbs, the sense of smell offended by the repugnant vapor" (Wissmann 1889: 71–72).[6]

Wissmann figured out what this was all about: the Bashilange were celebrating the end of the monopoly that the Bangala and Tshokwe, by controlling regions between this country and the Atlantic coast, had held on contacts with Europeans (see also Frobenius 1907: 3).

It is hard to resist giving more fascinating detail on this encounter and on the eventual incorporation of Pogge and Wissmann into the hemp cult but this is not the place.[7] Let me just spell out what connects this case to the argument regarding ecstatic knowledge. While it seems that Wissmann, with certain ceremonial exceptions, did not take to hemp smoking himself, he acknowledges that his integration into the hemp cult was decisive in establishing the communicative and logistic conditions that allowed him to carry out his scientific and political assignments. It may be difficult to determine specifically how ecstatic (and in this case, ritualized) experience determined the content of knowledge he produced; but it is undeniable that it influenced his perspective on African culture and politics when he made pronouncements on topics ranging from music and dance to trade and regional politics.[8]

COLLECTING CURIOS AND DOING ETHNOGRAPHY: SOME
GENERAL CONSIDERATIONS

So far, my reading of the sources and of at least some of the secondary literature has led me to formulate the following basic assumption: collection of objects (some or most of which only later became classified as African art) was the most important concern of early professional ethnographic research, perhaps not in the hierarchy of scientific or political values, but certainly in terms of the logistics of travel: acquisition of trade goods for barter; decisions on routes, stops, lengths of stay; time spent on negotiating sales; labeling and cataloguing of articles; packing and shipping; and other expenditures of time and energy, including inquiries related to function, meaning and context of use.

The importance of objects is usually attributed to the fact that expeditions/travels were financed by museums. There is some truth in this but, for Torday, Frobenius, and Verner, this needs qualification. T. A. Joyce, Torday's collaborator on several major publications, noted in the obituary for Torday that the latter's expedition to the Kuba was first to be sponsored and financed by the Royal Anthropological Institute, "but owing to the strong opposition of certain members of the Council (on the grounds that the Institute was a publishing organization, and not concerned with fieldwork), the offer was withdrawn, and the expedition was sponsored by the British Museum" (1932: 48). In Frobenius' case, museum sponsorship came only after the fact. When he discussed the financing of his 1904–06 travels in the Congo Free State he mentioned grants from foundations, personal gifts, his own funds, 2000 MK from Mrs Krupp for weapons and hunting gear, as well as goods donated by about a hundred major German manufacturers. After completing the expedition (and evidently before publishing his report), he received funds from the ethnological museum in Hamburg which bought (part of?) the collection (see Frobenius 1907: v–vi).

That so much of early ethnography focused on collecting objects is not sufficiently explained by its institutional support in the metropolitan countries. There were other reasons which made objects the target of undertakings that defined themselves as contributing to scientific knowledge.

First, early traveling ethnographers operated in economic and political situations in which contact with other cultures was crucially linked to exchange and circulation of trade goods, that is, of commodities in existing (sometimes emerging, sometimes expanding) markets. In other words, travel (involving access, movement, communication) and economic transactions were not only means but also aims of exploratory expeditions. They were to demonstrate to rulers, investors, and the European public at large the potential of Central Africa as a target of imperialism. Although much of their content is descriptive of populations and their customs, none of the reports I am considering here announces itself as "ethnographic." Frobenius uses a subtitle designed to give weight to his travelogue but it is "Inquiries and Observations in the Fields of Geography and Colonial Economy." In the perspective opened up by such guiding interests, it was a stroke of genius to make a commodity of that which only facilitated the major goal and to sell objects obtained in trade transactions as collectibles in Europe. In sum, there is a way of showing the importance of object collection almost deductively, as deriving from the logic that governed exploration and early ethnography.

Second, there were of course also epistemological, methodological, and aesthetic reasons for assigning to objects the central place they occupied in early ethnography. Objects became objects of desire, not only because they offered prospects of profit but because they were, to use an expression coined by C. Levi-Strauss (for the use of myths), "good to think" – good to label, classify, judge, attribute to, serve as evidence, in short, to carry out all those operations by virtue of which information becomes knowledge. For many kinds of information gathered by explorers (for instance, astronomic, meteorological, horo- and hydrographic observations, and securing zoological, botanical and mineralogical specimens), systematic frames of knowledge pre-existed, capable of assigning specific tasks in great detail. Aside from contributing to evolutionary narratives and filling lists of queries devised in armchairs, ethnologists were expected to put their discipline onto empirical foundations. Such a task meant that they often had to formulate their questions, as it were, after they had encountered the answers. Palpable, manipulable objects were well suited to this kind of paradoxical undertaking; each of them was the answer to a question yet to be asked. Lack of time, of linguistic competences, and of advanced techniques of recording, combined with the vicissitudes of travel, severely limited the accumulation of "hard" social and cultural data. Collecting material tokens of other cultures permitted these travelers to establish a record that could be transported in space as well as in time. After all, the future destined for collections of objects was to serve the appropriation of the African past.

EXPEDITIONS AND MARKETS

Chronologically, our sources lead us to concentrate on the first decade of this century. Frobenius traveled between February 1905 and May 1906. This overlapped with Torday's stay but there is something suspiciously unclear about the chronology of Torday's travels as it appears in his pub-lished writings.[9] At any rate, we know that Torday and Frobenius met on May 19, 1905, while the former was a Compagnie du Kasai agent doing some collecting and ethnography on the side. Incidentally, from reading Torday's *Camp and Tramp* (1913a) it is impossible to tell that he was an agent of the Compagnie du Kasai (although he does mention that he was employed by the Comitée Spécial du Katanga before 1904).

Geographically these travelers covered a vast area, including forest as well as savanna, along the Kasai river and its tributaries (the old divisions known as Kwango, Kasai, and Sankuru, north of the Angolan border). The populations gave, or were given, names that changed even as explora-tion was in progress. In modern terms, the major groupings were chiefly the Kuba and related groups, Yanzi, Yaka, Lulua, Luba, Tshokwe, and a host of smaller units. For us this tangle of labels is significant mainly as one of the forms of chaos into which order was to be brought by means of the collection of objects.

Instead of repeating biographic information on Torday and Frobenius provided elsewhere in this volume or otherwise easily available, I should like to introduce our protagonists through a few entertaining quotes. Albeit obliquely, these will show that the year 1905 was indeed a season for collecting and that collectors began to define themselves (and their activities) vis-à-vis each other.

Here first is what Torday has to say about meeting Frobenius and his companion, the artist Hans Martin Lemme:

I was informed by the captain of the Marie that I was to be honoured with a visit from a distinguished personage, a very great man indeed. He was coming down by the next steamer, I was informed, so some four and twenty hours before I began my preparations. I took out my gun and brought down a couple of birds. Then I went into my kitchen, and with my own hands I prepared various dainty cakes, knowing full well how much a European who has been deprived of his ordinary fare appreciates such luxuries. In due time the steamer arrived. Two exceedingly Teutonic looking gentlemen stood on the deck. One of them was as fully armed as Tweedledum and Tweedledee; his cartridges filled at least four pockets and his waistbelt, and his armoury consisted of a revolver and a gun, with other weapons in the background. I went on board and invited him and his companion to lunch. After consulting two watches, he deigned to accept my invitation. We went up to the house and found that the cakes and other hors d'oeuvres were ready. Before we began our meal a man of the village came up to me, and begged me to reassure the foreigners he and his fellow-villagers really had no bad intentions, and it was quite safe to lay aside the paraphernalia of war. Fortunately my visitor did not understand.

My refreshments were greatly appreciated by my guests, especially as they had, according to their own account, just quitted a land where snakes and monkey were the only food obtainable. They had, in fact, just come from Michakila, where ordinary mortals find abundant supplies of goats, fowls, and pigs.

They inquired on how long I had been in Africa, to which I replied by saying that I had been in Kongo [that is what Torday calls the region around his post] about a month. The martial gentleman was good enough to give me some advice as to the rules which it was necessary to observe if I wished to enjoy good health, as he had spent fully four months in the Congo. I accepted his suggestions with gratitude and humility. It was only after a flow of words, uninterrupted for ten minutes, that the captain remarked that I had spent more years in the Congo than my nestor had spent months, and that possibly I already had some knowledge of the questions on which he was laying down the law.

Years later I read a book, published by the very same traveller, in which he described how he had fired a village, how he had tried a new rifle on the inhabitants, and how he had flogged a woman who had displeased his servant. Later still I learned that he had gone, on the pretence of scientific research into an English colony, and had there robbed the natives of their most sacred relics. Well, perhaps it was better for him and for me that I did not know then his real character; there might have been trouble in store for both of us.

What is to be deplored most with people of this kind is that they bring undeserved discredit on their profession and on their country, and I needs must state that he was not a typical scientist. (1913a: 74–76)

It is both easy and hard to recognize the great Africanist Leo Frobenius in this caricature (and I see no need to defend a person who showed himself in many respects a despicable character even in his own writings, see Fabian 1992). Nevertheless, this dogmatic gentleman had just prior to the meeting with Torday noted the following reflections that show him in a different light:

For a scholar, grown up with his studies at home, the first months during which he begins the work of exploration in Africa are decisive. It is the time when he must settle the accounts between expectations he brings along and the facts. Theory and practice struggle with each other and in the first months of African explorations he lays the foundations for later intensive and comparative work. (Frobenius 1907: 176)

Later on the same page, Frobenius describes the meeting with Torday during the few hours when his steamer stopped at Kongo:

At that time, a curious fellow stayed there. He very kindly sent a glorious roasted bird for our lunch to the steamer. Besides working as a trader he had ethnological aspirations of the English kind and he kindly deigned to introduce me to the necessary anthropological theories. He was the real Congo type: Hungarian by birth, an Englishman by education, a writer by profession, presently a rubber trader in the Belgian Congo. But, all in all, apparently a capable man. (1907: 176–77)

There are discrepancies between these texts that could be submitted to closer reading. It is more important to note that the squabble among these two largely self-taught men over theories, methods, and ethics documents how much the professionalization of ethnological travel had advanced by the turn of the century.

There was at least one other major expedition traveling through the region. Frobenius met its "manager," a Mr. "Werner" (1907: 249). This must have been Samuel P. Verner, known as the importer to the United States of a group of pygmies for exhibition.[10] Frobenius notes his convivial relations with Verner. On June 5, 1905 – a few weeks after his meeting with Torday – he welcomes him as a guest at a dinner party (1907: 186). Later he visits Verner at his "station" near Ndjoko Punda (at Ndombe?), a steamer stop on the Kasai where they share a meal and some palm wine (1907: 249). As far as I can see Frobenius says nothing derogatory about Verner. Their feelings, however, were not mutual. Verner was convinced that Frobenius – "nominally commissioned to make ethnic collections for the Berlin Museum" – used these activities as a cover for his real assignment which was to gather intelligence for the Germans on the economic potential of the region.[11]

Apart from adding an entertaining Rashomon-touch to our story these diverging reports definitely dispose of any simplified ideas we may still hold about the political and academic innocence of object collecting in the Congo around the turn of the century.

IN THE BEGINNING, THERE WAS THE MARKET

The ethnographic expeditions we are considering here were conceived, sponsored, and organized as collecting trips that were buying trips. Because we call what eventually got to museums or private owners "collections" we do not think twice when we refer to the activities involved in assembling objects as collecting. In fact, collecting is one of those terms full of connotations and hence replete with unreflected ideological presuppositions.[12] Semantically, collecting has an aura of innocence – just picking up things that are there for the picking. As collecting, the acquisition of objects evokes the leisurely pursuits of connoisseurs on the one hand, and the disciplined filling-in of taxonomic pigeon holes carried out by naturalists, on the other. The latter, apart from advertising its scientific legitimacy, also suggests epistemic analogies between gathering specimens "from nature" and assembling tokens of culture. How much there is wrong with this analogy has been the object of many a critical disquisition in anthropology. What is considered less often is the fact that, in the situations we are looking at, both kinds of collecting were always mediated by, among others, political and economic relations. Perhaps it is not always easy to demonstrate that power and a market were involved in botany and zoology; there can be no doubt that almost all ethnographic objects were acquired by transactions that may have included "gifts" but mostly involved sales and hence the prior constitution of objects as goods, if not commodities.[13] Commodification – at least some form of it – is not so much the result of collecting than its prerequisite.

A test for this assertion is provided by cases where, in the midst of "brisk trade," individual owners negated (or suspended) the commodity character of objects, either by refusing to sell them because they were currently "in use" for their magical qualities, or by insisting on giving them away as presents. Because such refusal to sell was, as far as we can tell from the reports, incidental and exceptional it cannot be taken as evidence of a prevailing traditional pre-market frame of mind. A better candidate for such an explanation would be an incident reported by Hilton-Simpson.

Once again the context is a "roaring trade in curios" (1911: 168), this time among the Tetela:

> The people, as a rule, were perfectly willing to sell their belongings (at their own price!), and only upon one occasion did we meet with a Batetela chief who declined to sell curios . . . [Instead, he said] that he would allow his drummer [to] perform for us while we sat at dinner in the evening! This honour we declined; we had all the native music we required when in the forest without accepting it as a favour from the chiefs. Very often upon our arrival in a village the local natives would organise a dance, in which our porters . . . used to take part. (1911: 176–77)

Yet, the clash of views that occurred here was most likely not one between pre-market and market orientations but simply between different conceptions of what constitutes an object.[14] There are numerous instances that document how firmly African objects were, in the minds and practices of their users, embedded in performance. Here is just one observation noted by Hilton-Simpson: "The local Basonge chief [at the Kasai Company factory in Batempa], having heard of our presence and our desire to purchase articles of native manufacture, came in one morning bringing a large number of interesting objects for sale, and accompanied by his professional dancers and orchestra" (1911: 35).

Just how conscious Africans were of the market aspects of collecting is illustrated by incidents where ethnographic objects appear to be contrasted with the chief commodities of the time, rubber, slaves, and ivory. These may at a first glance appear to weaken my case for the commodity character of ethnographic objects. But, as I read it, the contrast is established among objects of the same kind and therefore confirms our observations on the presence of the market as an economic institution as well as a cognitive frame.

Hilton-Simpson reports one occasion when the Torday expedition was introduced to a Pende chief by an agent of the Compagnie du Kasai, a certain Bombeecke. Bombeecke informed the chief of the expedition's intentions, insisting that they were big hunters but adding "that we wished to purchase all manner of object such as the natives had never previously had an opportunity of selling, and that we had not come in search of rubber, a commodity with which he well knew the Bakongo would have nothing to do" (1911: 284).

The key to this observation is that the Kongo refused to be drawn into the rubber trade because they resisted control by the Congo Free State; and they presumably thought that trading objects should be avoided for similar political reasons. Earlier in the book, Hilton-Simpson had already noted a case that points to political motives, albeit in the opposite direction. The Bambunda, he tells us, were not eager to sell objects and were "extremely reticent upon all matters connected with their tribal customs and beliefs" (1911: 266). Instead they wanted to sell rubber which in this region serves as a currency. Torday and Hilton-Simpson nevertheless tried to prevail upon chief Mokulu, with the help of some presents, to see to it that his people put up objects for sale (Hilton-Simpson mentioned "carved wooden cups, embroidered cloth, weapons, &c."). Mokulu stalled and repeatedly asked for more presents, but "whenever we mentioned the subject of curios to him, he simply laughed and looked at us with a twinkle in his eye, and not one object could we buy in his village" (1911: 268).

Hilton-Simpson went on to say that they should not have given Mokulu presents in the first place. "[We] speculated, and lost; and I think that Mokulu was far more pleased at the knowledge that he had cheated us than he was with the goods we had given him" (1911: 269). Later, among the Bapindji at Bondo village, Torday paraded his famous clockwork elephant. The chief wanted to buy it and Torday, hopeful to obtain some unknown fetish in return, began negotiations, but these were broken off when only ivory and slaves were offered (1911: 270–71). The point is, of course, that Torday counted on his toy elephant being classified as a fetish, thus making it an object that could be bartered against another one of its kind. The Africans (who may or may not have been ready to sell the object desired by Torday) preferred payment "in cash" over barter.

The market did not only become operative when objects were actually bought. The "currency" or trade goods an expedition carried largely determined its course and success: where to acquire the goods destined to use for purchases, how to transport them, how much to acquire; what populations to contact; the need to protect all that walking capital (weapons, hence the need for ammunition, and paramilitary escorts); the logistics of packing, transporting, conserving and shipping acquired objects – all this occupied by far the largest part of the time economy of these expeditions and their leaders.

It is not surprising that Africans met these buying expeditions as sellers, something that did not fit the image of savages who may "barter" or incidentally part with their objects but are not expected to have mercantile ambitions. Let me quote a few illustrations from the many that can be found in the reports of Torday, Hilton-Simpson, and Frobenius. In *On the Trail of the Bushongo* (1925), Torday recalls one situation where he had stepped up his buying for the British Museum among the Bushongo/ Kuba. He gives some detailed anecdotal information about the market, including the operation of such classical principles as supply and demand. "Trade was brisk for a few days, and some Bushongo who had held back their treasures in the hope of rising prices were now disposed to sell them at a discount" (1925: 201).

Hilton-Simpson reports a remarkable situation illustrating the role of specific trade goods. Whilst among the Kongo the expedition had run out of iron bars and knives. European cotton textiles proved useless because the paramount chief had issued a "decree announcing that any one of his subjects found wearing material of European manufacture would be instantly put to death" (1911: 310). This is a remarkable case of economic-political resistance – as well as of *authenticité, avant la lettre* some sixty years before Mobutu decreed his "authentic" dress code.

The following passage from Frobenius provides concrete and explicit illustrations for several of the points made so far:

> Slowly the tall sons of the Lukengo State approached and offered their ethnological stuff [ethnologischen Kram] for sale. I had sent my people into the country to invite the Bakuba and they came. But when they sell, the Bakuba are truly the worst Greeks. They begin by asking prices that are unheard of and don't bargain much. Then someone brings the same object and haggles over it such that the Ethnologist needs all his patience and passion for valuable collections in order to endure this ordeal. But in order to be able to acquire more I first had to pay higher prices and initially had to let much blood. (1907: 238–39)[15]

THE CURIO MARKET WAS PART OF THE WORLD MARKET

It would be wrong to entertain idyllic or heroic images of the early traveling ethnographers as connoisseurs of fine and interesting objects, as if scientific pursuits and aesthetic judgments could have existed outside a context of political economy. Both Torday and Frobenius (and to a lesser extent Verner) traveled, acquired their trade goods and much of their knowledge about markets, made their contacts and bought objects in regions within the sphere of influence of the Compagnie du Kasai, an agency set up for the "collection" of rubber. The extent to which populations were drawn, through rubber and other commodities, into the world market determined their accessibility for the ethnographer-collectors. Both Torday and Frobenius confirm rather than invalidate this observation whenever they point to their success in contacting populations that, so far, had resisted the Congo Free State and the Compagnie du Kasai.

Torday was, of course, a rubber collector before (and while) he collected for the British Museum. Commercial intelligence gathering was quite likely Frobenius' ulterior purpose.[16] But even more to the point is that others had, before them or at the same time, recognized the world-market potential of ethnological collectibles. Torday, Frobenius, and Verner were not only competing among each other.

At a place in Compagnie du Kasai territory called Bena Makima, Frobenius came into conflict with a company agent who doubled as a collector of objects (and may even have acted for the Compagnie; the affair was never sufficiently cleared up): "Mr. Oeyen was a passionate collector of ethnological objects and sent these for sale to Europe . . . With my similar enthusiasm for ethnological objects I was getting into this gentleman's way. When, naturally, I paid for the things whatever the value was they had for us Mr. Oeyen very soon declared that I was spoiling the prices" (1907: 202).

This led eventually to open, violent conflict. Oeyen claimed that he did his collecting for the Compagnie du Kasai. He beat up Frobenius' porters, some of whom deserted, and closed his station to Frobenius. His superior, a certain Cassart, intervened and promised to settle the conflict. But it remained no more than a promise. The same thing happened when Frobenius took his complaint all the way to the "direction générale" of the company in Europe (see Frobenius 1907: 202–03).

COLLECTING AS A POLITICAL ACTIVITY

Because the presence of the State in this area was still very tenuous (after twenty years), other agencies, such as the missions, traders, and the para-

statal companies, arrogated to themselves political, that is, coercive judi-
cial or military functions. Expeditions could not but follow that pattern
although, as we shall see, they differed in the means. The early collecting
of objects was backed up by the exercise of some kind of authority and
often by real force.

Torday prided himself on never having had to use force.[17] Nevertheless, he took political initiatives and responsibilities as a matter of
course. When he traveled among the warring Yanzi, for instance, he
spoke of his expedition as being on a "peace mission." He acted as a
peacemaker and political broker, much like Francis Galton did fifty years
earlier, with more success, when he single-handedly imposed his "pax
Galtoniana" on enemy groups in what is now Namibia.[18] Torday stated
that all colonization is "in itself an injustice" (1913a: 243). His tact and
compassion, and his willingness to understand the other side on its own
terms certainly made him an exceptional figure. He nevertheless profited
from "the powers that be." Hilton-Simpson acknowledged that his
expedition traveled under the protection of the government, represented by troops who were always in the proximity of his route (1911:
115–16).

Frobenius, because he was personally a rather violent character and
perhaps because he could not be sure of protection by the Congo authorities, used force and coercion whenever he felt they were needed. He was
proud of his "police soldiers," a uniformed private military escort carrying twenty modern rifles and he marveled at the sense the natives had for
weapons (see 1907: 193–94). He freely administered beatings when he did
not get his way, especially when he met with insubordination or refusal to
provide porters and provisions for his expedition.[19]

Finally, collecting also was political in the sense that it involved international politics. Our three protagonists each represented a different
national interest: Germany, Britain, and the United States.

COMMODIFICATION AND DISTINCTION

To insist on commodification being a prerequisite for ethnographic collecting does not mean that ethnography is being equated with trading
nor, for that matter, that curios were a commodity like any other.
Collecting African objects was distinguished from rounding up supplies

of rubber. Why that should have been so cannot be explained in market terms alone. While collectible curios were being produced under the very eyes of the collectors they nevertheless regarded them as a non-renewable resource. When Frobenius once was forced by the rains to stay in one place, he observed that Africans were carving objects. Some of these he bought if he considered them good enough (1907: 83). But almost in the same breath he lamented the corruption of African crafts under European influence. It is as if attestations of threatened tradition and almost vanished originality were required as the finishing touches on the patina of collected objects.

If curios were, unlike rubber, a commodity of distinction because threatened by extinction, this did not remove them from the sphere of markets and commodities. Scarcity, real or manufactured, increased demand (and of course production). Still, from the beginning, authenticity was only interesting if it was backed up by quantity. After all, if you want to create and maintain a profitable market for unique pieces you must keep them in steady supply.[20] At one point, Frobenius, not bothered by the contradiction it implied, ended one of his laments about the disappearance of traditional crafts with the (prophetic) proposal to train Africans and "get a steady supply of products from these schools onto the world-market" (1907: 235).

I also think we are entitled to surmise that African owners and producers of curios recognized links between authenticity and scarcity as being important to their customers. Some cases of refusal to sell, or to sell at a given moment, may have to be interpreted as market-guided behavior. In fact, one may even have second thoughts about what exactly happened when Torday convinced the Kuba to part with their royal statues. He took the king into his confidence, we are told, and "he pointed out how many of the native arts were dying out" (Hilton-Simpson 1911: 193). When the king agreed to part with the figures, Torday counted this as a major feat of persuasion and was convinced he had acquired something uniquely valuable. But from everything we know of African conceptions regarding these and similar objects – and much of that can be learned even from sources that were written from a rather different perspective – it is unlikely that for the Kuba these carvings could have had the status of unique objects doomed to disappear when their material embodiments decayed or were lost due to some other circumstance. Who was outwitting whom in these deals? Economically the answer seems clear (and is getting clearer with every decade that passes) – but intellectually, culturally, aesthetically? Even the political implications are worth pondering. After all, Torday reported that one of the arguments that convinced the king to give him the statues was that they would be exhibited in the British Museum. The ruler must have interpreted this as a way to establish a real presence of Kuba political power in one of the centers of imperialism.

In fact, the situation was even more complex. Both Torday and Frobenius knew that it was not political domination as such that doomed traditional culture to disappearance, but the expansion of a market that was to have its local effects largely as a labor market. Hence the topos of depicting African workers in towns as degenerate, uprooted, unauthentic, and ridiculous, and opposing all this to the nobility of traditional culture embodied in genuine objects.

In other words, the chase for the disappearing object was to a large extent an ideological construct that served to camouflage gross commercial and often doubtful political aspects of collecting. In the sources I am examining here, the collectible objects shared their essential quality with the object of anthropology at large: they were deemed doomed; although present – otherwise they could not have been bought – they were really past. That is what constituted their scientific interest.[21]

One final question remains to be asked regarding the limits of collecting – not the ones imposed by the limits of the buyers' means to buy or the sellers' willingness to sell, but some sort of restraint that we would today qualify as ethical. As far as Torday is concerned, a concern with tact and respect for African values pervaded his reports. Frobenius usually cannot be credited with such qualities. Yet even he acknowledged limits. Here are two interesting instances. In one case, a young man whom he asked to sell his kiteki (a protective object) answered: "Go away, Tata Boka [Frobenius' African name]. Leave the kiteki alone. What am I going to do when my wife gets sick? Who wants to think of a museum in such a case?" (1907: 59). In another case, Frobenius walked through a village and saw a carved door that aroused his interest. He was told that in the hut behind that door a woman was dying. Rather sanctimoniously he stated: "And the ethnologist's passion for collecting (*Sammelwut*) stops at the door of death" (ibid.).

CURIOS AND CURIOSITY: OBJECT-COLLECTING AND
ETHNOGRAPHIC KNOWLEDGE

Object and method

The fact that ethnographic collecting as exemplified by Torday and
Frobenius was embedded in a market and conditioned by commodification does not mean, of course, that it was devoid of intellectual significance. After all, our travelers did think of themselves as ethnologists.
Frobenius, for instance, stated that the market was not just a circumstance of collecting, an opportunity or a nuisance, as the case may be:
"The scholar concerned with ethnological problems must in these countries be practical and pay attention to commercial problems ... The point
is not whether one buys dearly or cheaply, but rather whether one is able
to gain access to the natives and actually gets the object" (1907: 358, see
also 355).[22]

The transaction itself is important but objects, despite commodification, remain objects. As such they are products of objectification, that is
of processes in which complex ideas are given material existence. In the
ethnographic situation – where we strive to understand other peoples'
intellectual life without having direct access to it, objects, much like language, are mediations of knowledge. Both our protagonists were aware of
this. As a matter of fact, when we get the impression that the collection of
objects came first, followed by the collection of ethnographic information, we cannot be sure what dictated that order of preference – the
market conditions we outlined above or certain theoretical views regarding the nature of anthropology (epitomized by "diffusionism"). Or is this
a moot question? Should we perhaps see in the latter a reflex of the
former?[23]

Among the uses to which objects were put right on the spot, before
they were shipped to the sponsoring museum, was to serve as proof (or
disproof) of cultural and historical connections. Already at the beginning of his trip, Frobenius anticipated his later "morphological"
method when he derived the cagey personality of forest people from
their use of the bow and arrow and contrasted this with the open
aggressiveness of savanna dwellers who used the spear (1907: 80). At
the time we are covering here, establishing ethnic boundaries, migra-

tion routes, determining "races," their degrees of mixture (or purity), locating centers and peripheries of diffusion was an urgent task. This was not merely an academic problem; the state and the large companies needed such information in order to establish administrative units and boundaries and, above all, to plan labor policies (regarding potential recruitment, location of production sites, etc.). Both Torday and Frobenius observed that the colonial agencies had succeeded in creating Luba ethnicity with the help of criteria that defined people as actual or potential wage earners in the emerging colonial economy.[24] Both helped to explain resistance to colonial rule among certain populations, for instance, by demonstrating a Bushongo-Kuba cultural sphere whose principal common identifiers were art and material culture.

Objects and knowledge

Although it is easier to tell from Frobenius' account than from Torday's, both men aspired to scientific knowledge. They claimed certain privileges (or made excuses for strange behavior); they set the terms of getting to know the natives, convinced that their intrusive curiosity[25] was sanctioned by science. Obviously, the scientist's or naturalist's stance was most easily maintained with regard to objects one could point to, acquire, and later manipulate, examine, compare, store, ship, etc. By projecting it on the African, Frobenius (taking another contradiction in stride) revealed his own image of such object-oriented science: "I studied this point thoroughly, first theoretically, then long enough practically ... Trading in ethnographic stuff is, as it were, the highway that leads us to a community of interests and to agreement with the negro. One should never forget that the negro is a thorough materialist and a positivist of the worst kind" (1907: 355). We get a rare glimpse of the semantics of collecting when Frobenius expands on this statement and reports the expression *Tschintu* (the native's thing) as their term for collectibles (1907:357).

That object-collecting was part of his methodological strategy becomes clear whenever Frobenius was able to do what one may call stationary ethnography. This is how he described his work at Luebo where he stayed for a longer rest:

many a small column of my messengers roamed the country under the
well-tried direction of old people. Their task was to call the natives
together and to get them to bring along their sacred stuff, their knowledge of religious matters, and other things. Nengengele and Palia Messo
were the leaders of these small enterprises, as a result of which black citizens almost daily hurried to come to us. But I also had other people who
served as touts [*Schlepper*][26] in order to attract knowledgeable men.
(1907: 351)

Objects and objectivity

While material objects were most easily studied objectively, matters were
different, or should have been different, with other kinds of knowledge
that demanded linguistic competences and, above all, participation in
performances and thereby submission to rules governing such performances. Torday and Frobenius knew that almost everything they collected was embedded in contexts that involved performances or actions.
Yet again and again one gets the impression that these ethnographers
wished that all of culture came in the form of "curios." It is now that we
recognize one of the functions of that concept: it allowed one to separate
material objects from their often equally material context.

When modern critics denounce the decontextualized form of earlier
collecting they seem to have in mind mainly the separation of material
objects from cultural, that is, symbolic or ideological contexts. But the
more thorough separation that had to be achieved by those who pio-
neered ethnographic collecting was the separation of the material object
from its material embeddedness: from sound, movement, smell, space,
time and timing, and so forth. At any rate, these ethnographers-collectors
sought to create situations where they could observe and record without
being involved.

Before ending *Camp and Tramp*, Torday states that "having told what I
had to say about the natives, I shall now give them a chance of speaking for
themselves" (1913a: 269). He remarks on the importance of authentic
folklore and says that the texts that follow were "overheard when I was a
concealed witness of their talk round the campfire" (1913a: 270). While
this is not at all characteristic of Torday – he always sought the company
of Africans and tried to engage them in conversation – it does reveal his
occasional desire to be a detached scientific observer.

Limits on interaction and involvement were also set by the time economy of these expeditions. A story, myth, proverb, genealogy, or some other kind of text could be bought rather quickly. Transactions of this kind are too numerous in our sources to be reported here. They presupposed, of course, another kind of commodification – that of knowledge and information. As in the case of objects, this was a process that involved both the ethnographers and their African "informants." When Torday set about to collect a Yaka vocabulary he devised an ingenious procedure:

> In order to stimulate public interest I provided myself with a packet of sewing-needles; and when I asked in Kimbala the Bayaka name of some object, the first man to give it received a needle; if, however, he told me a wrong word, he had to surrender one of those previously earned, and the reward went to the man who corrected him. Thus I accumulated my vocabulary at a cost of about twopence. (1913a: 145)

Waiting around until free information came along was seldom possible. Incidentally, this explains perhaps the emphasis on rituals as privileged objects of ethnographic description. Rituals were events, or action sequences, short enough to be observed, although it took Frobenius almost nine months to see his first masked dancer in action (1907: 256).[27] By that time he had sent collections home that needed, in one case, a caravan of sixty-seven porters. He had by then also completed substantial parts of the manuscript of his published report.[28]

CURIOS AND OBJECTS OF ART

To be exact Torday described himself as buying curios; Frobenius did not buy *Kuriositäten* (he described ethnographic objects as *ethnographischer Kram*). Torday identified objects either by general labels, or descriptively. Frobenius pretended most of the time to base his classification of objects on native terms (at least as regards the principal objects of desire – statues, fetishes, fabrics, and so forth). Both traveled with artists who, among others, prepared artful renderings of collected objects. But neither Torday nor Frobenius were inclined to call them art. In view of the fact that the aesthetic reception of things African seems to have been in full sway in the metropolitan countries, certainly by the time our sources were published,[29] this is rather surprising.

THE AESTHETICS OF COLLECTION

Both traveling ethnographers liberally dropped judgments regarding relative quality, beauty, and authenticity, not just with regard to objects but also to music and dance, speech, bodily appearance, and village architecture. In fact, distinction – the demonstrated ability to tell one culture from another, one expression from another, and to see all this arranged in a hierarchy – was a fundamental instrument in establishing intellectual control.

Torday, who collected the pieces that are now considered the most exquisite, mentioned "arts and crafts," [30] but both the plural and the juxtaposition are significant. The same goes for statements by Hilton-Simpson such as the following: "Music and dancing are the arts in which the Basonge chiefly excel, and we were unable to find any traces of the carver's art to compare with the specimens we were later to secure from the Bushongo" (1911: 36). Art may be used ironically, such as when he tells us of the Bankutu that "with the exception of the building of huts, the only art that has been developed . . . is the art of killing their fellowmen by stealth" (1911: 133). Frobenius did speak, not so much in the text but in captions to illustrations of carved cups and pieces of "velvet," of *Prachtstücke der Kubakunst*, splendid specimens of Kuba art.[31] But he too classified given objects as *Kunstgewerbeartikel*, craft articles (1907: 248).

On the whole, it is clear that what they collected did not evoke to them Art with a capital A. Yet both ethnographers took first steps in that direction when they talked of styles (although not actually using the term "Art", as far as I can see), or pronounced on degrees of purity (when they regret European influences). A clue, however, may be taken from the fact that both Torday and Frobenius grew eloquent and somewhat solemn when they linked the production of certain objects to political structure, especially the Kuba "royal court." My hunch is that the transformation from curio to object of art began (but may not have been completed – for that, it took other processes in the metropolitan countries) when the mechanism of distinction mobilized political and ethnic categories: that is, when the products of certain groups (people near the court, or certain ethnic groups of "nobility") were praised as pure and refined. Aesthetics and politics mesh. There is an interesting corollary to this. Frobenius makes a lot of the fact that the "Baluba" are great story-tellers and talkers but not great producers of exquisite objects[!] (see 1907: 197–98). Because the Baluba are consistently depicted as the most "uprooted" among these populations his observation fits ideas regarding authenticity which he and Torday shared. In the logic of ethnographic collecting, they express the premiss discussed earlier: objects are collected that are doomed to disappear because they really belong to the past, a past in which the peoples of Africa had to be placed if the schemes of science and imperialism were to make sense.[32]

But this can be read as a verdict only if we were to forget how we started: objects were to be appreciated as mediations of "ecstatic" knowledge. They remain outside shallow rational schemes, even a hundred years on, and challenge us to step outside our self-complacent views of history, that of Africa as well as that of our disciplines.

APPENDIX TO CHAPTER FOUR

LEO FROBENIUS, ON THE ETHNOGRAPHY AND

ECONOMICS OF COLLECTING

The following is part of chapter 20, Nochmals zu den Bakubavölkern *(Once again to the Bakuba peoples), in Leo Frobenius'* Im Schatten des Kongostaates. *After a passage discussing the basic distrust with which Africans meet European explorers and ethnologists, Frobenius gives this summary of his experiences. Original page numbers have been added in square brackets; the translation is by Johannes Fabian.*

Now, there is one means to overcome this mistrust very quickly: one must create in the Negro the conviction that one wants to extract from the country everything he [i.e. the ethnologist] values. *Tuschimuni*, the stuff made of legends and pieces of traditional history [*Legendenkram und Histörchenüberlieferung*], cannot, according to his view, possibly be valuable, because the Negro is not accustomed to have these things paid for. They are not real objects. That the European buys rubber, this the Negro understands, it is something palpable. Therefore, dear ethnologist, if you want to be understood by the Negro, if you want to overcome his mistrust, you must confirm his conviction that you want to profit from him. This is very simple. You tell him that he has indeed something that is useful to you, namely the ethnographic stuff (*ethnographischen Kram*) which is valuable in Europe.

Trading for ethnographic objects, furthermore, causes for the Negro a pleasant sensation. The Negro definitely does not like the rubber trader because rubber first has to be tapped, and tapping it means work,[357] a lot of work, and work is for him always something he detests. On the other hand, the Negro approves of the ivory trade, because ivory does not need to be worked on, it is just there. The same is the case with ethnographic stuff. Ethnographic stuff is there, it does not have to be made. Therefore, dear ethnologist, you will immediately be sympathetic to the Negro, as soon as you give him the opportunity to earn something valuable without working.

In sum and generally speaking, ethnographic trade will always gain the Negro's comprehension. Now, when the white man comes and the Negro sees that he wants to buy the *Tschintu* ("the native's thing") he will be somewhat surprised that the European, who can make for himself so many things that are more beautiful and better, has a desire for such things, but he can approve of the matter. The second question is now, whether he wants to occupy himself with it. As a practical trader he likes to wait and see before he will strike a little deal, and to determine how much another person gets. Therefore the beginning is difficult because everyone always waits until someone else has made the test. Once the beginning is made and once the first buyers have been satisfied, the offer usually grows very fast and the mass is gripped by a kind of selling rage. The first ones hesitate, all others cannot be satisfied fast enough. Then the crowd is overcome by a kind of furor. I want to go into this in a little more detail:

Often there has been talk about the prices that have to be paid and, strangely enough, in circles of colleagues even today it is believed that the European makes the prices; the right word has, therefore, not yet been spoken. In the ethnographic trade with natives such is not the case. In these countries, when the Company or the State prescribes the prices for the rubber trade, the traffic in ivory, or the recruitment of labor, this is possible only because they are without competition in their concessions and can claim a supremacy which definitely amounts to absolutism. Although in some sense justified, this is a rape, rape because the native really has his price for everything. It is altogether wrong to believe and maintain that a musical box or an umbrella can work wonders. It will be accepted as a present, but not as a trade. I want to stress that every object, from the simplest calabash to the most valuable spear, from a palm tree to a piece of rock, from a hut to a bunch of straw, has its fixed price. What is at stake here is the important and difficult question how to find out the price. Perhaps one arrives with a standard of value that, so far, the native does not know, for instance, with copper bracelets or beads, and so forth. But as soon as these objects are put onto the market they immediately, in less than five minutes, have an exchange value [*Börsenwert*, literally "stock exchange value"] for the native [358]. The value is decided on by popular taste or by need. Thus the new merchandise is integrated into the system of existing values. My dear colleagues, therefore, [should] realize that the scholar concerned with ethnological problems must, in these countries, be practical and pay attention to commercial problems. This is not pleasant but it is necessary. The point is not whether one buys dearly or cheaply, but rather whether one is able to gain access to the natives and actually get the object. Because of this question, which is a fundamental question, the ethnologist must be concerned with these matters.

In order to have a clear understanding of the market situation it is most practical personally to apply some care to these things. Among the boys you must have people you can trust. The black youths are intelligent enough and able to learn after a few weeks what is at stake for the European. One should not personally go to the market and buy; rather let the youths do the bargaining. One should check from time and will soon realize 1) the value which the desired objects have among the natives and 2) the value which the natives ascribe to the objects one brings for them.

To be sure, the ethnologist always must be watchful. He must, as it were, participate unseen in the buying transactions. These [359] black buyers are always ready to refuse an age-old, broken object simply because it can no longer be used. Because you must never forget that the Negro cannot comprehend that we Europeans have the "lack of understanding" (as he calls it) to store such things in museums. The Negro assumes that we use the make-up box to put our make-up in it, the bow to use in war, the ancestral effigies for religious purposes, and so forth. Thus the Negro will never really understand why an ancient broken object is more valuable to me than one that was made recently and shows no traces of wear.

As I said, the beginning is almost the most difficult thing, that is, the setting up of ethnological trade in a newly opened region. For that, too, I thought up a new recipe in the Pianga region. If at all possible, one should begin by establishing friendly relations with the women and, as is well known, this is accomplished most quickly among all female beings of this earth through their offspring who roam the village street. Present a six-year-old girl, following after her mother, with a few beads. Flirt with the baby who rides on the hip of his mother, give a little boy a toy trumpet or a box of tin soldiers, this is always the best means to make contact, in Europe as well as in Africa. Most of the time the mothers are touched. You approach the houses and first, naturally, you look into them from the outside. Then have them offer you one thing or another only to give it back immediately. Because everyone is watching to see whether the white man is honest or whether he simply keeps the object. Every native potentate who amounts to something takes from his people whatever pleases him. Naturally, they fear at first that the Europeans will do the same thing. When you praise the first object you see and then return it, and repeat this several times, a certain calm descends on the whole assembly, a feeling of trust. Now the people already know that the white man does not rob. Then you take another object and ask for the price. This other object, the one that is to open up trade, must by no means be valuable to the natives or everything is lost. For this [opening gambit] one must choose a relatively worthless thing and always something that belongs to a woman.

Initially, the men are reluctant and think they can make a killing with the most simple stuff they offer. Everything owned by men should at first be ignored and one should select baskets and pots or any objects that do not have an individual value but can be bought by the dozen on the market. With the selected objects and the woman who owns them one should first go to a place where the further trade is to be initiated, a [360] place, if possible, that is in the shade and near the working table of the white man.

Then you pay for the first object but not much more than what it is worth for the natives; what that is one has to have previously found out by his native youths. But one should give a nice present emphasizing that this present is only given in the beginning. Immediately, general content will settle on the faces of all onlookers. The moment must be used, you make your wish known and leave the rest to the boys. Usually the women give their things to the men to haggle about and finally the men also come with their own possessions. Naturally one must wait for the right moment, until there develops a longing to sell even the ancestral and sacred images, and especially the masks that are so difficult to get. Sometimes eagerness grows very fast and gets so intense that everyone is ready to sell everything he owns. But equally quickly the mood subsides and is replaced by a "cooler" market that cannot be revived that easily.

Dear colleague, if you read this you may find it rather dry and boring. But believe me, if you want to bring home comparative material, if your aim is to establish a thorough collection representing the extant forms of what the people own [des Völkerbesitzes], [361] you must take upon yourself the rather unpleasant and uncomfortable work of trading. The theory, by the way, is much easier than the practice and among different tribes you will have to proceed according to their peculiarity. But since I have been the first disciple of our science to visit the interior of Africa guided by ethnological tasks I consider it my obligation to speak about the matter, with an emphasis on the conditions that I met with. The matter is easily tiring and often quite boring. Furthermore, it is exerting because it calls for constant control of the assembled crowd and of that which is offered for sale. But if you carry out the work, you will have nice results. So, it is quite all right if you first practice the theory and then do the practical work.

In this manner, with the help of collecting and through my black collecting buyers [Sammlungsaufkäufer], I succeeded in building the best relationship with the Pianga. Two birds were thus killed with one stone. I got my museum collections and acquired the friendship of the people.

NOTES

1 Perhaps one should put this more generally as the experience of "noise" which in accounts of African travel always seems to mark the beginning, later to be transformed into sounds that are meaningful and evocative.

2 For a most original and incisive account of the "exchange" of objects in early colonization (in this case of the Pacific) see Thomas 1991.

3 The reading for this paper was made possible by a stay in 1990–91 at the Getty Center for the History of Art and the Humanities in Santa Monica, California. Its support is gratefully acknowledged. I also thank my tireless research assistant, Elisabeth Cameron, and colleagues at the Center, especially Suzanne Preston Blier, for listening and responding to an earlier version.

4 On Torday see the essay by John Mack (1990), written to go with an exhibition of his collections in the British Museum. Hilton-Simpson's account of his travels with Torday (1911) offers us the rare case of an observer observed. However, his account covers only the expedition led by Torday between 1907–09.

5 This essay cannot be burdened with the critical literary and philological analyses that would be required to answer questions regarding reliability, relative weight, and rhetoric authority. Let me just note that the four major sources from which I shall be drawing, two by Torday (1913a, 1925), one by Hilton-Simpson (1911), and one by Frobenius (1907) range from adventure story to monograph. None of them is "pure," often genres are mixed within one and the same chapter.

6 All translations from the German are my own.

7 It should be noted however that the hemp cult does have a bearing on our principal topic. As an anti-fetish movement it seems to have caused the destruction of much precious "Luba" statuary, see also Szalay 1990: 21, with further references to the literature.

8 On the other hand, Wissmann also typifies the turn I believe to have been constitutive of modern anthropology: eventually, coeval experience is denied in a distancing discourse. A few years after the initial encounter he actually used the hemp cult in effectively bringing his friends under colonial rule; in fact, by the end of the book from which I have been quoting he had formulated some thoughts on how hemp smoking might be used in civilizing African savages (1889: 254). After all, as *von* Wissmann and governor of German East Africa, he became one of the chief architects of a colonial regime.

9 In the preface to his scientific monograph (Torday and Joyce 1910: 5), Torday says that his Kuba expedition took from October 1907 to September 1909. He also mentions "huit années de séjour antérieur dans l'État du Congo" which would place his first arrival in 1899 or 1900. In *Camp and Tramp* Torday tells of his African adventures from 1900 to 1907 (1913a: 17), and says that he first

arrived in Boma in March 1900 (p. 19), then in Matadi for the second time in 1905 (p. 57). He returned to Europe in 1907. The starting date is confirmed by Hilton-Simpson (1911: 1). According to Joyce's Obituary (1932) Torday made two visits to England, one in 1904 (when the contact with the British Museum was made), another in 1906, after he had left the service of the Compagnie du Kasai. Should that be 1907?

10 On Verner see the contribution by Schildkrout (chapter 7 in this volume); Bradford and Blume 1992; Gordon Gibson's unpublished paper on Verner 1990; and Schildkrout and Keim 1990a: 48.

11 Stated in a letter written much later (1936) and quoted in Gibson (1990). It is more than likely that Frobenius did intelligence work but the Berlin Museum was not the sponsor of his trip (see above). Gibson (1990) also noted that Verner "directed Frobenius to the country of the Bena Mbindu (Bindundu) where they expected Frobenius' party to lose its way." Apparently Frobenius was not taken in. He was, incidentally, aware of being suspected as a spy – for the English, or the Congo Free State, or the Germans (1907: 274).

12 It does of course have a long history. See the interesting work by Pomian (1990). I wish to thank Luisa Ciammitti who brought this book to my attention.

13 I do not recall having found in my sources evidence of yet another possibility – requisitioning, or whatever euphemism may be used for the seizure of objects. It is, however, likely that, for instance, Frobenius' African "scouts" (see below) were not squeamish about how they got their objects together. For a thorough critique of the notion of "exchange" in connection with objects see Thomas 1991.

14 See MacGaffey's essay in this volume (chapter 9); notice also that the Tetela chief anticipated Robert F. Thompson's views on African art and motion by more than half a century (Thompson 1974).

15 Frobenius also uses variants of this expression, such as *ethnographischer Kram*, ethnographic stuff, if not actually "junk," bric-a-brac (1907: 355) and *heiliger Kram*, sacred stuff (1907: 351).

16 To be accurate, information about a potential African labor force was at least as important. Frobenius states this at the very beginning of his report (1907: 2) and subsequently reports amazing experiments in what would now be called the applied anthropology of work (1907: chapter 6).

17 At least not in connection with collecting objects. But he did report on beating up a Muluba who was about to sell his wife as a slave to the Tshokwe (1925: 277).

18 Torday (1913: chapter 10). On Francis Galton, who as an early traveler and author of a successful handbook (1972) had a great influence on the professionalization of travel, see Fabian 1987. Torday, incidentally, recalled some personal advice he once got from Galton on dressing up when negotiating with natives (1925: 138). Frobenius also reported that his services

as peacemaker were sought in a conflict between the Independent State and the descendants of Wissmann's friend Mukenge Kalamba of the "children of hemp" (1907: 257).

19 See especially the chapter reporting on his trip through Pende country (1907: 267–68). He then recounted that once "friendship" was established he could hardly manage to take down all the ethnographic information and buy all the objects that were offered (1907: 271). Photographs of his *Polizeitruppe* are reproduced in 1907: 270–1.

20 How well Africans always seem to have been aware of the supply side of the market – and the doubts that this creates about the recent origin of "tourist art" – has been noted for some time. See, for instance, Richter 1980: 3–4 and especially the exhibition catalogue pertaining to northeastern Congo by Schildkrout and Keim (1990a). See also Schildkrout, chapter 7 in this volume.

21 This argument was developed in Fabian 1983: 95–96. The topos of spoiled authenticity/originality is open to yet another interpretation. In the context cited earlier (Frobenius 1907: 83–84) Frobenius thought about instituting certain controls as regards collecting objects. We may have here the methodological prototype of what later was often called "data control." The point is that data control is not aimed at that which is given but at those items/objects that are admitted as data. As an expression of discipline it really is control of the objectives and purposes of a scientific activity.

22 Because of its extraordinary lucidity and great interest for the topic of this paper a portion of the chapter from which this quotation was taken is reproduced in translation in the Appendix.

23 Perhaps it is time that much maligned diffusionism – which never ceased to be useful when the only things to go on were objects and their distribution in space (see Hodder 1978) – should be appreciated historically, especially in histories of anthropology. Was it not an outlook that imposed itself when mercantile expansion set in motion processes of globalization?

24 See also the long passage on this topic in Hilton-Simpson (1911: 72–75).

25 On the historical and philosophical background of the notion of curiosity see Pomian 1990 and, as related to the subject at hand, Thomas 1991: 126–27.

26 A surprisingly modern term, now used for entrepreneurs specialized in illegal laborers or immigrants.

27 Later he was not above having the greedy Tshokwe put on masked initiation dances for *matabishi*, payment (1907: 327, 331).

28 Frobenius recommends his method of "writing up" in the field (1907: 352) and promises that a more ethnographic volume is soon to follow. It never was published during his lifetime although we now have an edited collection of his Congo fieldnotes prepared by H. Klein (1985).

29 See the contribution by Mack (chapter 3) to this volume.

30 See 1925, in the heading of chapter 19, that is, many years after he had done the collecting.

31 See for instance the illustrations in 1907: 234–35, 253–56.
32 Torday as well as Frobenius accepted, and contributed to, this colonial image
 – or rather mirage, because of a population that existed largely as a colonial
 artifice one could not have an image – of the Baluba as the Jews of the
 Congo. Torday notes some rather general analogies, such as their being
 "scattered all over the Land" (1925: 40). Frobenius obviously relishes the
 occasion to vent his anti-Semitic feelings. At one point he tries to get a
 particular "Luba portrait" because it shows a *"Semitentypus"* (1907: 62).
 Note, however, that this colonial topos had the function to classify, by
 designating them as "Jews," at least one category of Africans as
 contemporaries.

FIVE

Artes Africanae: *The Western*
discovery of "Art" in northeastern Congo

CURTIS A. KEIM

✦

Shortly before he crossed the Uele River in 1870, the explorer Georg
Schweinfurth saw and sketched a Zande harp which had a carved human
head on the end of its neck. The sketch provides the earliest record of the
well-known "Mangbetu" anthropomorphic harps, for Schweinfurth
noted on it that it portrayed the great Mangbetu king, Mbunza. And
because he noted no such harps among the Mangbetu themselves, the
sketch also provides our best clue to the origins of Mangbetu harps.
Apparently the first such harps were portraits made by neighbors.[1]

More remarkable than the sketch and its clue, however, is the fact that
Schweinfurth portrayed Zande harps only twice in his works and he never
discussed their anthropomorphic necks. Schweinfurth published two
small drawings of the harp portraying Mbunza in his *Artes Africanae,* a
catalogue of the material culture of the peoples he visited, but he failed to
mention that it was a portrait of Mbunza or even where he saw it (1875:
XIV: Figs. 6 and 7). We only know about the connection with Mbunza
from one of Schweinfurth's unpublished drawings found in the
Frobenius Institute (Schildkrout and Keim 1990a: 238). The explorer also
portrayed a similar harp, again without comment, as part of a drawing of
a Zande "minstrel" in *The Heart of Africa* (Schweinfurth 1874a: 444) (see
Fig. 5.1). In Schweinfurth's time the Zande were known as the Niam-
niam.

Something seems out of place. Why would Schweinfurth, an admirer of
African art, fail to make more of this harp, especially considering the
importance of figurative art in nineteenth-century Europe? This question prompts a closer consideration of the accounts of all the Europeans

5.1 Sketch by Georg Schweinfurth, "A Niam-niam minstrel."

who visited the Mangbetu in the nineteenth century. Is Schweinfurth's neglect of the harp unique, perhaps an oversight? Or is it part of a wider pattern of neglect in which the figurative objects that we value today were not then considered extraordinary? If so, why? And what eventually prompted Europeans to take an interest in art depicting the now well-known Mangbetu head?

Careful reading of the explorers' texts reveals that in general they did not value African figurative art. This confirms, in a sense, what we already know about nineteenth-century Western disregard for African art as well as twentieth-century reappraisal of that art. But the texts also provide greater insight into how various Europeans tried to reconcile their different hierarchies of race, social organization, and art. Moreover, they show that at least some of the story is local and personal, and independent of attitudes in Europe.

THE EXPLORERS: GEORG SCHWEINFURTH

Schweinfurth, a German botanist and academic, penned the most famous account of the region now known as northeastern Congo. A lively writer and superb illustrator, Schweinfurth described his three-week visit with the Mangbetu people in glowing terms and frequently employed words that have been translated as "elegant," "artistic," and "masterpiece" for the whole range of Mangbetu artistic culture that he observed – music, dance, dress, architecture, metallurgy, woodworking, basketry, and pottery.[2] Indeed, he believed he had found an African civilization so much more advanced than their neighbors that they deserved a special place in African ethnography. Others agreed to the extent that all visitors to the Mangbetu until the middle of the twentieth century accepted Schweinfurth's opinion and felt obliged to either confirm it or explain why the culture had declined. Even among those who had never visited the Mangbetu, Schweinfurth's descriptions and opinions were rarely, if ever, questioned.

Schweinfurth's favorable judgments of Mangbetu material culture rested on several European standards of artistic value – symmetry and order, care in manufacture, originality of design, and value of materials. He states, for example, that Mangbetu pots were better than those of other African peoples due to their symmetry. He admired their ceramic water bottles because they "rival in symmetry the far-famed examples of Egyptian art" (1874a, II: 116). In manufacturing, Schweinfurth praised the "great care" of potters and the hard work of blacksmiths (1874a, II: 109, 116). He appreciated the "superior finish to details" in wood carving and "neatness of finish" in iron working (1874a, II: 111, 109). In an often-cited passage, Schweinfurth remarked that the reason for the superior work of Mangbetu carvers was the control afforded by a knife peculiar to their culture. The knife has a long handle which rests in the crook of the elbow and the blade is angled to present the cutting edge where it can be easily controlled with the fingers (1874a, II: 111).

The explorer also evaluated Mangbetu art on its inventiveness (1874a, II: 109). He felt that the artists went beyond both mere utilitarianism and slavish duplication to create objects which somehow illustrated individual creativity, an important indication to Schweinfurth that the Mangbetu civilization was advanced. Finally, Schweinfurth was impressed by work in rarer materials. Although he seemed disappointed when a silver plate he gave to King Mbunza was relegated to the category "white iron," he greatly appreciated Mangbetu iron work. He stated that in the "judgment of connoisseurs" many Mangbetu iron chains were masterpieces which vied with the best steel chains of Europe – perhaps the ultimate compliment (1874a, II: 47, 109).

For all of his enthusiasm for African culture, however, Schweinfurth still maintained that even the best African art was not equal to European art. This was not fine art, not real art, but *Kunstfertigkeit* (industrial art) or *Kunstfleisses* (handicraft). The subtitle to the English edition of his *Artes Africanae* is "Illustrations and Descriptions of Productions of the Industrial Arts of Central African Tribes." Indeed, the term "handicraft" seems to have been implied even when the word *Kunst* (art) was employed to describe African appreciation of beauty (as in "instinctive love of art") or to African skill (as in the "art of joinery") (1874a, II: 29, 113; 1918: 303, 350). Thus Schweinfurth qualified his enthusiasm for African material culture and was able to state that in Africa it was possible to speak of "culture, art, and industry in but a very limited sense" (1875: VII).

Enid Schildkrout and I have discussed elsewhere how Schweinfurth's European views led him to categorize Africans according to two coincidental hierarchies, one racial and one political. He saw Africans as spread across a racial spectrum which ranged from the least to the most biologically evolved, and he believed that Africans such as the Mangbetu who had the most centralized political structures were the most evolved (Schildkrout and Keim 1990a: 29–34). We can see in the above passages that Schweinfurth also applied this line of thinking when considering African material culture. He concluded that African material culture could be hierarchized, with the best being called craft, a respectable category. By categorizing Mangbetu art as craft – good art, but limited – he reinforced his idea that the Mangbetu were racially superior to other Africans but inferior to Europeans.

Schweinfurth was, of course, reflecting ideas that were current in contemporary European and German thought. He believed, for example, in evolution and in Franz Josef Gall's phrenology, and he collected skulls in Africa for (pseudo-) scientific research. He also visited Africa at the very moment when an industrializing Germany was forming its national, political, and racial self-consciousness. Sponsored by the Prussian Royal Academy of Science and the Humboldt Institution, Schweinfurth was proud to raise a German flag over his camp at Mbunza's court (1874a, II: 7). And his broader sense of a relationship between race, politics, and material culture reflected the growing German interest in folk culture as a feature of German national and racial self-consciousness.

But Schweinfurth failed to follow his arguments about African art to what in the 1920s and 1930s became a logical European conclusion, that African figurative art represented the highest form of African art. For him figurative art seems to have remained mere craft, like pots, tools, baskets, and buildings. Thus we cannot even be sure that Schweinfurth did not see considerably more figurative art than he wrote about. It is primarily because he was so clearly attracted to visual phenomena and such an excellent observer that we surmise that he must have remarked on whatever figurative art he saw. He must also have had an unconscious Western attraction to the human form.

What prevented this visually oriented explorer, one of the first Europeans to take African material culture seriously, from considering African figurative art as more than craft or at least as a high form of craft? Perhaps one could answer that Schweinfurth had already taken a giant step in asserting that some African material culture was beautiful and technically equal to European craft. Furthermore, he had recognized that much of Central African figurative art was secular, not sacred. While visiting the Bongo, Schweinfurth discovered that their funerary figures were secular portraits rather than idols. Surprised, he noted that other such wooden carvings collected in Central Africa might be similar (1874a, I: 286). This recategorization from sacred to secular was a significant theoretical step, one that is still working its way into popular Western consciousness and one that allowed the explorer to group figurative art with craft. Ironically, this regrouping probably made figurative art less interesting to Schweinfurth because it no longer served as a window into the African religious mind which so fascinated Westerners. But to have gone the next step and assert that it was superior craft or even real Art would have perhaps been too great a theoretical shift at one time.

There is, however, an even clearer reason why Schweinfurth did not distinguish figurative art from other sorts of craft. To have done so would have challenged fundamental Western theories of hierarchies of race, social structure, and art. This is because the Mangbetu, whom he considered the most advanced of Africans, had little figurative art while their supposedly inferior neighbors had much more. In fact, it is probable that Schweinfurth did not see figurative art during his brief visit with the Mangbetu. He saw the "Mangbetu" harp mentioned above just before he entered Mangbetu territory, among neighbors who were portraying the Mangbetu king, and among the Mangbetu he specifically noted that there were none of the "pretty little mandolins" of the Azande (1874a, II: 117). In fact, if the Mangbetu employed figurative art at the time of Schweinfurth's visit, it was infrequently because most of what we know as Mangbetu figurative art developed in the early colonial period (Schildkrout and Keim 1990a). Had Schweinfurth stated that figurative art was superior to mere craft or was a superior form of craft he would have had to account for its greater presence in the supposedly inferior cultures of the Mangbetu neighbors.

Perhaps he could have solved this problem through some mental gymnastics. He was, after all, able to justify his assertion that the Mangbetu were the most cannibalistic people in Africa by stating that Mbunza hid evidence of his voracious cannibalism and that cannibal tendencies increased with racial evolution (up to a point) – the higher grade of humans ate their blacker neighbors while the lower grades were not cannibals (1874a, II: 92–94). But Westerners were intensely interested in

African cannibalism and Schweinfurth was obliged to address the question. Asserting that figurative art disappeared in the middle of the racial hierarchy, by contrast, would have involved more tortuous reasoning, especially considering that Schweinfurth had little firsthand evidence. Moreover, he would have been theorizing about something Westerners were only vaguely interested in at the time.

One indication that Schweinfurth was still working out categories of how the hierarchies of race, social organization, and art interarticulate is his lack of clarity on the origins of differences in art and social organization. He could not decide whether the superior Mangbetu rulers and artists evolved locally or descended from "Semites" (1874a, II: 58, 92). He was also unclear about how biology and culture are intertwined and lamented that Arabs and Europeans would disrupt African societies and displace African art with industrial art without his indicating how African biological propensities for specific types of art could be transformed by cross-cultural contacts (1874a, I: 314; 1875, viii).

We can suppose that Schweinfurth did not clearly assign origins to cultural differences because Westerners had not yet achieved a consensus on the origins of biological differences. While evolution and racial hierarchy were widely accepted in Europe and America by the late nineteenth century, theories of exactly how diversity arose were still debated.[3] Westerners had not yet fully accepted Darwin's view of evolution so that there were competing theories of how humans evolved, how different races and sub-races were related, and how changes occurred in the biology of groups and individuals. Even within the growing Darwinian camp understanding of variation had to await the rediscovery of Mendel's genetic studies and these revelations did not get incorporated into more general understandings of race until the 1920s and 1930s.[4]

In sum, in Schweinfurth's texts we can see him trying to harmonize his own experience and enjoyment of Africa with the categories he brought with him from Europe. He felt that African art was art, but stopped short of equating it with European art. He was satisfied with the correspondence he saw between the three hierarchies of race, art, and social organization, but was uncertain about the origin of African art – whether religious or secular, biological or cultural. And he did not separate figurative and non-figurative art, probably because to do so would have presented difficult typological problems.

THE EXPLORERS: WILHELM JUNKER AND GAETANO CASATI

Wilhelm Junker and Gaetano Casati, together with Giovanni Miani and Emin Pasha, are the other European travelers who visited the Upper Uele region in the period before the Belgian conquest. The attitudes of these visitors are not as easy to analyze as Schweinfurth's because none was as interested in African material culture or in working out a hierarchy of African societies based on material culture. In fact, only Junker and Casati provide enough information to warrant discussion.[5] Like Schweinfurth, they saw figurative art in the region but hardly commented on it. Junker, a German–Russian academic, collected one of the earliest anthropomorphic harps from southern Sudan, but he failed to mention any figurative art in his accounts of his journey. Casati, an Italian cartographer who lived in close proximity to Africans, also saw figurative art, but his only comments on the subject concern the Barambo, close neighbors of the Mangbetu, about whom he noted: "A special industry gives an idea of [Barambo] talent – the art of making pretty little statues by woodcarving is theirs, and in this they excel all the other tribes. Handles of their barkboxes, the girdles which they use for dress, are all ornamented with carvings of human heads and small figures" (1891a, II: 194). As cursory as this passage is, it suggests, by contrast, that Junker ignored such art since he also spent several months among the Barambo and even met Casati there, never writing a word on figurative art.

Junker and Casati do make regular assessments of the quality of African material culture and consistently echo Schweinfurth's opinions. Junker used words such as "beautiful," "elegant," "dainty," "remarkable," "accomplished," and "fine." He praised symmetry, order, regularity, "pleasing proportions," and "elegant simplicity," and stressed that the best artists were those patient enough to pay attention to detail (1891: 245; 1892: 7). Likewise, Casati called African creations "splendid," "artistic," "inventive," "pretty," and "elegant." He too appreciated "workmanship" and "precision" (1891a, I: 126–27). And in the rest of his remark on Barambo art quoted above, Casati noted that in their wood carving "a certain regularity of design is united to clever and intelligent workmanship" (1891a, II: 194).

Like Schweinfurth, both travelers also complimented Africans on their work in rarer materials such as iron and ivory (Junker 1892, II: 46; Casati

1891a, II: 97). They also appreciated the high quality achieved with simple tools. "The elegance of all these objects," wrote Casati, "might suggest the idea that the tools used are perfect or nearly so; but it is astonishing to see how admirably these people can carry out the ideas which their inventive minds conceive, with such imperfect and primitive means" (1891a, I: 125).

Yet for all their compliments, neither Junker nor Casati believed that African arts merited equal status with European arts. While Junker, a self-conscious standard bearer for European civilization, thought that some "gifted races" such as the Mangbetu had evolved more artistic sense than others, he had little overall sympathy for African culture, material or otherwise (e.g. 1892: 132, 143). Junker wrote that "The adult black, with a generation of years behind him, is still, so to say, in his teens so far as regards his mental capacity" (1891, I: 154). Casati saw African art of all kinds as inferior to Western art because it was merely an expression of "instinctive" artistic ability and desire, without the "true reason" of the best Western art (e.g. 1891a, I: 62, 186–88). In this, Casati expressed a criterion of art not mentioned by Schweinfurth, but he does not make it clear what role reason played in European art or how he could tell it was lacking in African art.

Although the two explorers came to essentially the same conclusion as Schweinfurth about the origins of human diversity, they seem to have been clearer in their own minds about how to account for it. Thus, Junker wrote that while Africans were mentally children, they,

> like others, are diversely endowed, showing various degrees of quickness... They, of course, lack the training and education which give rise to so much difference in the mental capacity of our own social classes nevertheless here also the higher circles, princes and nobles, are the most highly endowed with intellectual qualities. This is doubtless due to the fact that, despite his limited sphere of action, the Negro ruler is still compelled to think and act in his capacity as judge, lawgiver, and captain, whereby his cerebral activity has more play than that of the common folk. (1891: 157)

Positing an African class system, this is a fairly clear statement of the neo-Lamarckian position that characteristics learned by an individual could be inherited by offspring, a position which was the most popular late nineteenth-century explanation for human diversity. Even Darwin himself, who first disputed nearly all of Lamarck's propositions, came to understand that his own theories of variation and natural selection were by themselves insufficient to explain the origins of life's diversity and began to adopt a neo-Lamarckian view in this regard.[6]

This use-inheritance view on diversity allows us to understand how Junker and Casati could state that African artistic ability was instinctive while also maintaining that it could be destroyed. That is, since any degradation in artistic skills could result in less skill being inherited by offspring, there was not only a danger to culture but also to genetic artistic capacity. Schweinfurth most likely employed a similar paradigm when he decried the destruction of African art under Arab and European influence. But Junker and Casati, on the eve of the European Scramble for Africa, drew different conclusions. They believed that Africans ought to be colonized and African artistic skills ought to be "improved" by contact with Europeans. Always unsympathetic to Africans, Junker thought that "compulsory labor" and "an intermediate educational stage" would be required "for generations" before Africans should be allowed to choose their own cultural practices (1891: 97, 385). Referring to a generic African, the gentler Casati wrote: "Taken from his savage habits and mode of life, improved by instruction, his moral and intellectual faculties developed by kind teaching and not by the tyranny of European superiority, he cannot fail to fulfill, by his conduct, the hopes now entertained of him" (1891a, I: 63).

In sum, except for Casati's brief description of Barambo art and their prescriptions for improving Africans, both Junker and Casati parallel Schweinfurth on all points concerning African material culture in general and figurative art in particular. The exceptions are insignificant compared to the clear general sense in all three explorers that African art, figurative or otherwise, was only craft and, despite its occasional brilliance, evidence of African evolutionary inferiority.

THE SOLDIERS

As a result of the Act of Berlin of 1885 Leopold II began to assemble the forces necessary to win a race against Britain, France, and Germany for northeastern Congo and, he hoped, for all of southern Sudan up to the Nile River. The first Belgian conquerors swept up the Uele River and in early 1892 they established a major post at Niangara, near the capital of King Yangala, the Mangbetu-Matchaga ruler who had conquered Mbunza's territory in 1871. During the next ten years a total of a hundred or more European officers, mostly Belgian, led their African soldiers through the region putting down resistance; recruiting soldiers and porters; gathering food, ivory and rubber; and generally attempting to establish a colonial order. While European–African relationships were often strained and violent during this period, from the very beginning there were exchanges of material culture.

Mutual gift-giving between the conquerors and local chiefs was common. In one of the earliest extant colonial letters from the region, for example, Emile Christiaens, commander of the Makua Zone (posted at Niangara, 1893–95), mentioned that on his first visit to Yangala's court he received gifts of war knives (MRAC, 54.95.71, September 2, 1893). Elsewhere he wrote that he gave the famous Nenzima, Yangala's wife and chief counselor, a bracelet that she was pleased to receive (MRAC, 54.95.71, October 15, 1893). The most common sort of exchange, however, was theft – as booty by both sides during skirmishes, as loot resulting from soldiers marauding for food, and as loads stolen by deserting porters and canoeists. Among the Mangbetu, at least, purchase does not seem to have been a large factor during the first years of conquest. When asked by the Governor General to provide objects and ethnographic information from the Mangbetu for the second Antwerp Exposition in 1894, Christiaens replied that he could send very little because he was completely occupied by war and because the Mangbetu were reluctant to sell their belongings (MRAC 54.95.72, November 15, 1893). In other circumstances Christiaens was willing to confiscate African objects, but he could not easily have done so among the Mangbetu around his post because they were his allies.

The earliest registration dates for figurative pieces from northeastern Congo in the collection of the Africa Museum in Tervuren, Belgium occur just after 1900.[7] This delay of a decade between the invasion and the first documented appearance of figurative pieces in Europe represents the period in which pieces were making their way back to Europe and in which the museum, founded in 1897, formally began its acquisitions. In other words, despite the delay, it is clear that from the beginning the conquerors were collecting figurative pieces throughout the Upper Uele region. It is striking, however, that while they were collecting them they were not describing them. Out of perhaps fifteen journal reports published by the officers; several collections of personal papers, letters home, and official correspondence; two books of memoirs; and an ethnography to which some of the officers contributed, there are only three brief references to figurative objects.[8]

One of those references is in the unpublished works. In a personal notebook of Emmanuel Muller, a soldier who served in the Uele District in the first decade of the twentieth century, there are rough sketches of Mangbetu heads on knife handles along with a list of Mangbetu vocabulary (Fig. 5.2). Elsewhere in the notebook Muller sketched a house painting he saw in a Zande village depicting the meeting of two Belgian officers (54.95.1). Emile Christiaens, one of the first Belgian officers in the region, makes no comments on figurative art even though his letters indicate that he collected material culture, especially weapons, and other sources indicate that he acquired a Bua mask in an 1892 skirmish on the Lower Uele. The mask is not mentioned in Christiaens' detailed log nor in his official or family correspondence, all of which have been preserved (MRAC 54.95.70: November 26, 1892; March 20, 1893). Christiaens likely feared that publicity would mean the mask would be claimed by Leopold's state, since a government decree of 1891 had ordered government agents to save for the King all confiscated "arts and crafts" (Salmon 1992: 182–83).[9] Nevertheless, Christiaens failed to mention figurative art even when he specifically wrote detailed reports on Mangbetu customs, as in a letter to the Governor General or in a paper presented to the Cercle Africain in Brussels (1896).

Turning to published writings from the conquest period, Guy Burrows' *The Land of the Pigmies* includes a photograph of two wooden "war masks" he labeled Mangbetu (1898: 87) and he acquired a skin "hunting mask" in the region in about 1900. These masks, now in the British Museum, bear little stylistic resemblance to the rest of the Mangbetu figurative tradition. They were likely either brought in on a temporary basis by healers from neighboring peoples or they were collected among peoples such as the Makere who speak Mangbetu-related languages but were not part of the kingdom core nearer to Niangara. What is most interesting here is that Burrows chose to illustrate such masks as Mangbetu while disregarding Mangbetu anthropomorphic

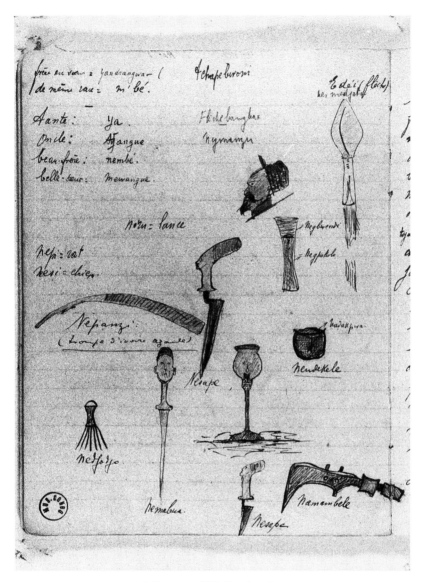

5.2 Emmanuel Muller, drawings.

knives, harps, and boxes. We might surmise from this that he was ignor-
ant of such objects, especially when we consider that a number of his
other observations on Mangbetu culture are patently false or lifted
directly from earlier travelers' accounts. Does this mean that the common
Mangbetu figurative objects were unavailable both around Niangara,

where he had succeeded Christiaens as commander of the Makua Zone, and at Yangala's capital for which he was responsible? Or perhaps, like Schweinfurth, he failed to notice African figurative forms in a secular context – decoration, commemoration, portraiture, and regalia – while focusing on the masks which he considered more noteworthy because they represented occult powers.

The other published account in which figurative art is mentioned by the conquerors is *Les Mangbetu*, by Cyrille Van Overbergh and Eduard de Jonghe. This is not exactly a conquest account because it was compiled and published in the first decade of the twentieth century (1909). The compilers did, however, ask specific questions of six Belgian officers who had served in the Mangbetu area since 1892. If one keeps in mind that the subjects discussed represent largely the concerns of early twentieth-century ethnographers, and that the officers' information results from memories sometimes nearly two decades old, then it is remarkable how closely the officers' views parallel those of the nineteenth-century explorers. When asked specifically about sculpture, for example, only one of the officers responded that the Mangbetu carved wood and ivory figures and animals (1909: 423–24).[10]

Like their predecessors, these soldiers praised the regularity of Mangbetu designs and noted that they were "agreeable to the eye and sometimes truly artistic." They believed that Mangbetu art was "infinitely more gracious" and "clearly superior" to that of their neighbors (1909: 405, 425). The Belgian officers also typify the Mangbetu as having "a certain degree of intellectual culture." Once again, however, theirs was not the art of equals. Concerning the figurative paintings on houses, the Mangbetu were said to have "true artistic sense" even though the paintings were "imitation and not imagination . . . the drawings of children naturally" (1909: 405–06).

The soldiers thus echo Schweinfurth: superior Mangbetu aesthetics parallel superior Mangbetu race and politics, but figurative art or lack of it is not evidence of evolutionary advancement. We know, however, that the soldiers did see figurative art among the Mangbetu and that they saw value in it because they took it home with them. Thus although figurative art did not yet appear in Western typologies, from the point of view of the Mangbetu and their neighbors, there was increasing demand for such art. Local peoples could not fail to notice that figurative art had utility in the tense cross-cultural exchanges that characterized the early colonial period. And since figurative art did not symbolize the key metaphors of any local world view (except perhaps for the few masks) but was created for non-ritual purposes, local artists found no reason not to respond with increased production (Schildkrout and Keim 1990a: 233–57).

THE SCIENTISTS

By 1902 the Upper Uele district was sufficiently "pacified" by Belgian guns that King Leopold began to permit scientists to enter the area, first along the river and then, by the middle of the decade, throughout the region. Of these, only three commented sufficiently on material culture so that we can analyze their texts: Herman Schubotz, traveling in the region for Duke Adolf Friedrich von Mecklenburg in 1910; Jan Czekanowski, sponsored by the Königlichen Museum für Völkerkunde in Berlin and visiting in 1911, and Herbert Lang of the American Museum of Natural History in New York who lived in the region from 1909–1915.

Czekanowski, a Polish anthropologist, spent several months in the Uele region in 1911, but did not publish a detailed academic ethnography until 1924. What is significant for our discussion is that Czekanowski made no comment on figurative art despite the fact that he obtained two statues, identified as Mangbetu in the collection of the Museum für Völkerkunde in Berlin. Had he discussed such art, however, we would probably still not know how he interpreted it because he adhered strictly to new "objective" and "scientific" standards which limited him to precise description. Of course, since the same standards also included efforts to be comprehensive, his failure to note any figurative art in the region would seem to mean that either he did not see such art or he considered it irrelevant because it was only made for sale to Europeans.

Each of these interpretations is possible. Czekanowski may have seen little "traditional" figurative art because after the disruption of twenty years of conquest and the purchases by other Europeans, little such art may have been visible in rural areas, especially to a somewhat transient researcher. Lang, who was in the region at the same time, bought much of his figurative art in the government posts of Poko and Niangara and especially at the court of Okondo, Yangala's successor. Czekanowski did not visit Okondo, a puzzling fact considering that everyone else did, and his only contact with figurative art might have been with recently created pieces such as the two he purchased in the Belgian administrative posts. These pieces he considered unworthy of comment, more like souvenirs than ethnographic data.

Herman Schubotz, a German natural scientist, made a brief, two-week visit to Okondo's capital in 1911. His account of the stay is revealing because it closely parallels Schweinfurth's account forty years earlier. Several passages of his chapter on the Mangbetu were clearly modeled on passages in Schweinfurth's *The Heart of Africa*, and even Schubotz's drawings look much like those in *Artes Africanae* (see Geary, this volume). Like Schweinfurth, Schubotz ecstatically praised the level of Mangbetu workmanship as well as their "primitive good taste" (1913: 43–56). In trying to claim for himself some of the glory of Schweinfurth and the Mangbetu, he reveals how little attitudes had changed.

Schubotz also published drawings of the Mangbetu figurative style. These drawings were not of the embellished harps, knives, and boxes which were the primary figurative tradition south of the Uele, but of anthropomorphic pots, a new form of Mangbetu art apparently modeled after Zande figurative pots (Schildkrout, Helman, and Keim 1989). Considering that Schubotz visited Okondo's court at virtually the same time that Lang acquired many different kinds of figurative art there, it is puzzling that Schubotz drew only these pots. As with others, however, Schubotz's stay was very short and it is entirely possible he saw no other figurative art. He likely purchased them at the Niangara post and chose to portray them because he had models to draw from.

Up to this point the perspectives of the so-called scientists fail to give a clear indication of changes in European classifications of African art. Both Schubotz and Czekanowski are collecting figurative art, but Schubotz still echoes Schweinfurth while Czekanowski makes no comments on African aesthetics. The situation is very different, however, with Herbert Lang, the German mammalogist who led the American Museum Congo Expedition to the Upper Uele. Lang was the first Westerner to take the figurative art of the Upper Uele seriously. Charged to collect for every museum department, Lang returned from the five-year trip with about 4,000 ethnographic objects and thousands of photographs. Much of what he collected was from the Mangbetu, and especially from the court of Okondo where he was on excellent terms with the King and with Nenzima. The exceptionally able Nenzima, sister of Mbunza and head wife of the late Yangala, acted as a sort of elder prime minister and chief judge for the Mangbetu-Matchaga during the reigns of Yangala (died 1895), Mambanga (died 1902), and Okondo (died 1915). She also encouraged the production of art works for Lang and other visitors.

Like others who visited the region, Lang judged African art by European standards. He was impressed by carving that had pleasing patterns, complicated designs, artistic features, symmetry, smooth and polished surfaces, minimalist expression, and unusually careful work with rudimentary tools. He also noted that older pieces were preferable and that ivory was especially suitable "for the expression of the beautiful" (1918: 527–28, 531–32).

Lang differed from all of the others, however, in that he separated Mangbetu figurative art from craft and, in an even greater theoretical leap, considered it to be equal to Western art. For the first time, a Westerner not only collected regional figurative art as art, but also encouraged it and advertised it to the West. By the end of his stay Lang was commissioning artists to create figurative pieces for the American Museum of Natural History. His article, "Famous Ivory Treasures of a Negro King," published shortly after his return to New York, and a companion exhibition provided the Western public with its first real look at Upper Uele figurative art.

One of the major factors that allowed Lang to see figurative art in a new way is that he associated it with political centralization. In the period between Schweinfurth and Lang, between 1870 and 1910, figurative art had become more common among the Mangbetu, at least partly due to European demand. Moreover, the Azande, who also had a centralized political structure and figurative art, had established themselves in the forest to the west of the Mangbetu. Lang, who spent five years in the region, got to know both Mangbetu and Zande kings and their artists, and although he collected figurative art outside these kingdoms, most of what he collected was purchased at kings' courts or in European posts associated with kingdoms.

However European and American ideas about the connection between race and culture still made it impossible for Lang to merely assert that African figurative art was real art. In order for him to make this claim he had to deal with the question of race. Specifically, Lang felt he had to justify his belief in Mangbetu artistic equality within the framework of eugenics, a type of evolutionism popular in the first half of the twentieth century (Lang 1915). Eugenics not only posited biological hierarchies of race and class, but also aimed to improve humans by consciously improving human breeding within various human groups (Kevles 1986). This implied that within any human population some people were superior to the rest, an idea similar to that used by Junker above when he stated that "princes and nobles, are the most highly endowed with intellectual qualities." This idea allowed Lang to support the widely held Western belief that Africans were inferior and still assert the equality of the Upper Uele figurative art. Thus Lang could write: "That the negro race produces a smaller number of superior men than other peoples becomes particularly evident in these regions" (1918: 529). While the statement is patently racist, to most contemporaries and to his predecessors in the Uele, Lang was a revolutionary for considering *any* Africans to be "superior men."[11]

Elsewhere in this volume Johannes Fabian hypothesizes that the process of Western recategorization of African objects from curio to art probably begins with the linking of objects to social hierarchy. This seems to be exactly what happened among the Mangbetu. Schweinfurth began the process by calling all Mangbetu material culture art in the sense of "highly skilled craft" and by linking it to a supposedly superior Mangbetu political system. Lang took the process an important step further by separating craft and figurative art and calling the latter art.

Furthermore, and this also supports Fabian's ideas, Lang equated African and Western artists without upsetting Western notions about African political hierarchy. The artists Lang was celebrating were specifically associated with the kings who represented the "most advanced" form of "traditional" African politics. This is easily seen in the title of his article which describes African artists as equal: "Famous Ivory Treasures of a Negro King." The word "famous" in the title seems strange since there could be little fame in newly made objects belonging to a little known king. But, if Fabian is right, Lang needed the objects to be famous because he needed them to be authentic "objects of distinction" that had existed in the precolonial era. These objects could prove that the great African peoples and kings were more biologically advanced than lesser peoples' kings, thus substantiating the Western belief that different

African political structures resulted from African racial differences. The implication was, of course, that European biology was superior to African biology because of Europe's more advanced political structures. Lang asserted that although the objects themselves were new, they were like those buried with the great King Yangala when he died. Traditionally, Lang said, artists created such objects anew for each Mangbetu king. We know from earlier observers of Yangala's court and from oral testimonies of Mangbetu themselves that Lang's claim is probably false.

Our understanding of Lang would be incomplete, however, if it rested merely on Lang's attempt to explain his observations in terms of the current Western theories of race. Why should Lang choose to apply the evolutionary argument in this particular way – by elevating African figurative art – when other eugenicists and other travelers had not yet done so? The answer is that while Lang himself may have had to justify his appreciation of African figurative art with racist theory he also had more personal motives for celebrating the art. Whatever his evolutionary bias, evidence suggests that Lang interacted with Africans on a far more equal basis than other Westerners in the region. His five years in the Uele was much longer than required by his contract with the American Museum of Natural History. Moreover, he spent a great deal of his time with Africans in situations in which he was not in command. He clearly liked being in Africa and later in his life settled in Southern Africa as a professional photographer, which raises another point, that Lang was visually oriented. The only other visitor to the Mangbetu who took their material culture as seriously was Schweinfurth, the illustrator, who was equally attentive to his visual world. Lang, the passionate photographer, must have seen and appreciated Uele art from the beginning in ways that other visitors did not.

That Lang liked Africans, stayed for a long time in the region, and took material culture seriously certainly accounts for the fact that he became increasingly fascinated by figurative art as his stay in the Uele progressed. This must have forced him to try to reconcile the stock racist model he brought with him with the evidence provided by artists themselves. We can imagine Lang trying to work out categories that fit both his immediate experience and the expectations of Western society.

Finally, we must also consider that Lang was attempting to find a place for himself in American society. We sometimes forget such personal motives while looking at wider historical themes, but here we must wonder whether Lang was as interested in his society's current paradigms as he was in his own position in that society. Lang, a German, was an outsider at the American Museum of Natural History and in American culture in general. If Mangbetu figurative art had become evidence of a new paradigm as Lang believed it should, Lang would have cleared an intellectual space for himself because the evidence was his evidence. In this too, Lang was very like Schweinfurth because no other visitors to the Mangbetu identified their own careers so closely with Mangbetu art upon their return. Perhaps this suggests that we can remake Fabian's model slightly: The creation of "objects of distinction" can also be taken to be an attempt to use objects and interpretations to create a place for the collector in society. We only have to look at Schweinfurth, Frobenius, and many modern scholars to see that careers are made on "ownership" of new interpretations of objects such as these.

Whatever caused Lang to believe that Mangbetu figurative art was real art and ought to be famous, his efforts did not succeed. Schweinfurth made himself and the Mangbetu famous, but after a few articles and an exhibition, Lang, his ideas, and his collection of objects and photographs were more or less ignored and have only recently been rediscovered. One must assume that his particular ideas about African art, his attitude toward artists, and his personality did not fit in with the American intellectual climate of the day.

In the Uele region itself, the arts of the Mangbetu and other peoples began a long deterioration after the departure of Lang and the death of Okondo in 1915. Within a few years the figurative pieces purchased in the region (with the exception of the pots) seem particularly crude and were not associated with chiefs' courts. As colonialism took hold it changed the structure of society by using the kings – now demoted to chiefs – to collect taxes and to organize local labor for producing cash crops. The colonial administration eventually encouraged the chiefs to decorate their villages with geometric designs and to put on folkloric dances for tourists who were visiting the exotic Mangbetu, but this "art" was not meant to demonstrate African artistic equality. The Dominican missionaries at Rungu began an artisan school in 1929 which could have revived Mangbetu sculpture. The main effort, however, was to "improve" Mangbetu taste and from 1930 until his death in 1954, Brother Marcolinus Meylemans, a sculptor, trained a few Mangbetu to sculpt in a Western naturalistic style (Lelong 1946, I: 218–20; Nys 1954: 71–72). Overall there was less and less place for the traditional arts and almost none for figurative arts. Agricultural work was paramount.

The attitudes of all the Westerners who came through the Uele region during the middle and later colonial period, seem closer to those of Lang's predecessors than to Lang. Therefore, Lang is significant today not for his ideas, which were ignored both in the West and in Africa and which today are out of date, but because he happened to be in the Upper Uele region at a propitious artistic moment and because he participated in, and documented that moment. That moment, surprisingly, was one of relative equality between Africans and Europeans. For all of the burdens of conquest, rubber collecting, porterage, and food production, by 1910 the impact of the colonial regime was still sporadic rather than systematic. Belgians had to rely on local rulers to maintain control, and cash cropping, missions, roads, plantations – the effects of the post-Leopold scrambles – were still to come. For Africans, traditions were still alive and there was still hope of being free (see chapter 1, this volume and Jewsiewicki 1983,1991 a, b).

These were fertile conditions for figurative art. Artists near colonial posts had easy access to styles and forms from across the region and from Europeans, and they had the patronage of both Europeans and a few African rulers who used it to enhance their prestige with both subjects and foreigners. The moment was an awkward one, for Westerners were still convinced of the superiority of their race and civilization, and African artists certainly understood that they were not considered real equals. Nonetheless, a small window of artistic equality opened and Lang's fortuitous configuration of abilities and weaknesses allowed him to memorialize it.

CONCLUSION

In the last twenty years a number of scholarly studies have investigated the ideas that allowed Westerners to treat Africans as primitives, a sort of sub-human species that both needed help and deserved exploitation (see chapter 1). Indeed, the violent "pacification" and colonization of Africa could only have occurred if Africa was considered to be vastly inferior to Europe. These ideas were so common in the West that it would be remarkable indeed if we found a Westerner in Africa who did not share them. Thus it is no surprise to discover that all Western visitors to the Mangbetu until perhaps the 1960s or 1970s considered Africans to be inferior. Even the most sympathetic visitors like Georg Schweinfurth and Herbert Lang framed their remarks with Western models of inferiority. For Schweinfurth the Mangbetu were better than all their neighbors, but still far from European standards. For Lang, a few Mangbetu were like Europeans, but very few.

Now that we are beginning to understand the tropes of imperialism it seems that we could profit from asking how individuals reconciled their personal beliefs, personalities, and experiences with those tropes. Or, to put it in other terms, we might ask how individuals diverged from or extended their seemingly monolithic cultural values. This is an important question if for no other reason than that we must live our own lives within our own cultures' forceful paradigms. In the case of Schweinfurth and Lang we might say that each had the unique experience of "discovering" African art. Schweinfurth was one of the first to call African material culture "art" and his view of Mangbetu material culture became a standard interpretation well into the colonial period. Lang was the first to equate Mangbetu figurative art with Western art and possibly the first to assert that Africa had real artists. While each one's "discovery" can be said to be both self serving and expressed through imperial tropes, both represent early, rare, serious, and personal attention to African material culture and its social context.

To understand these two "discoveries" of African art it is at least as important to understand the two visitors and their experiences among the Mangbetu as it is to understand either their search for glory or their imperialist ideas. Others shared their desire for glory and their ideas but did little to extend the West's understanding or appreciation of African art or any other aspect of Africa. If one is sympathetic to the two, and especially to Lang who spent years with the Mangbetu, one might even say that their personal experience of Africa was of foremost importance in their interpretation and that the meaning they attached to the objects went as far toward "Art" as was possible in the Western cultural context.

NOTES

1 Eric de Dampierre suggests that although Schweinfurth wrote "der Kopf soll den Sultan Munsa (Monbuttu) vorstellen" on the drawing it is in fact a drawing of a woman. If this is so, then the Azande or Arabs who informed him were probably making fun of him. It may not be so, however, because Zande men wore their hair in elaborate styles which might have been confused with the elaborate Mangbetu styles and portrayed as a composite. It is difficult for us to know what they meant by their portraits. In any case, such an interpretation does not negate the fact that Schweinfurth's drawing is evidence that the figurative "Mangbetu" harp existed just across the Uele River from Mbunza's territory, where the drawing was made. This point is more important here than whether the subject of the harp was Mbunza (1991: 24).

2 I use the English versions of the travel accounts, but have checked the German and Italian where specific words could make a difference to analysis. Translators regularly made significant changes in the meaning of words by, for example rendering *die Kunstfertigkeit* as "art" instead of "skillfulness" or "industrial art," and *die technische Gewandtheit* as "artistic versatility" instead of "technical versatility" (Schweinfurth 1918: 349, 352; 1874a, I: 111, 117). The Casati translation sometimes adds or omits important words and ideas while the Junker translation leaves out whole sections so that in some places it might even be considered a condensation. Overall, however, the attitude of the early explorers toward African art is preserved in the translations.

3 Even after the rediscovery of Mendel's studies many biologists believed that there might be single genes which controlled single traits. Thus in the early decades of the twentieth century eugenicists concluded that selective breeding could easily eliminate undesirable human traits (Gould 1981: 61–163). When the complex reality of genetics began to be understood in the 1920s and after, the simplistic and racist phenotypical classifications of everyday use began to erode.

4 Theories of race inequality have been best studied in the American case, where the race debate was one of the hottest issues of domestic politics and of the social and biological sciences. Even most white American defenders of Africans and African–Americans, however, assumed African racial inferiority. Some useful discussions of the race debate in America and Europe are Banton 1987, Gould 1981, Haller 1971, Mayr 1982, Stanton 1960, Stepan 1982.

5 Miani, an Italian explorer, visited the Mangbetu just after Schweinfurth, but died there in 1872 and left only cursory notes. Emin Pasha (Eduard Schnitzer), the German-born governor of Egypt's Equatoria Province, visited the region briefly in 1883, but stayed exclusively at Egyptian trading posts and was occupied by government affairs. His travel accounts deal more with

politics and economic development than with art and culture (Schweinfurth, Ratzel, *et al.* 1889). Emin Pasha collected a statue from "Monbuttu," the Egyptian designation for the whole of what is today known as northeastern Congo. Although it does not change the general point I am trying to make because he did not mention it in his writings, there is also the possibility that he could not have commented on it because he only collected it just before he was killed in 1892 on the Upper Bomokandi River, several hundred kilometers from the Mangbetu (Schildkrout and Keim 1990a: 236).

6 This view was displaced in the twentieth century by a better understanding of genetics. For further discussion of the problem see: Haller 1971: 153–54; Kuklick 1991: 75–118; Mayr 1982: 359–62, 526–27, Stanton 1960: 194–96.

7 Presumably objects from northeastern Congo were also making their way into private collections. There are, however, no published dates that would confirm such early collecting (see, for example, Burssens and Guisson 1992).

8 The journal reports are mostly found in issues of *Mouvement Géographique.* Since King Leopold destroyed the Free State archives when he lost the Congo in 1908 there are very few official records extant. A few of the personal records of those who served in the northeast during the conquest period have been preserved in archives such as those of the Musée Africain in Tervuren and the Ministry of Foreign Affairs in Brussels. A few other personal records most likely still exist in private hands. The two books of memoirs are those by Ferdinand Nys (1896) and Guy Burrows (1898). The ethnography is that by Van Overbergh and de Jonghe (1909).

9 Christiaens died in 1902. The mask came into the possession of Armand Hutereau, a state ethnographer who worked in the Uele region and he gave it to the Tervuren museum in *c.* 1911–13.

10 Presumably the reference to carved animals was to wood drums which sometimes had buffalo heads for handles and house posts which sometimes displayed crocodiles carved in bas relief.

11 An article by Nicholas Mirzoeff argues that Lang's photographic work, and by implication all of his work, is defined solely by his eugenic racism. Besides the factual errors and assumptions about Lang's career, beliefs, and even sex life, and about the situation in northeast Congo while Lang was there, this article seems one sided because it ignores Lang as an individual (Mirzoeff 1996).

SIX

Nineteenth-century images of the Mangbetu in explorers' accounts

CHRISTRAUD M. GEARY

Ⓖ

Until the late nineteenth century, wood engravings, etchings, and lithographs illustrated many well-known travel accounts, ethnographic treatises, and popular descriptions of foreign places and peoples (Degenhard 1987). The creators of these images were artists, who usually worked from verbal descriptions of the subject matter provided by the travelers, the firsthand observers and eye witnesses. In some instances the artists' renderings were based on actual sketches by travelers. Occasionally, illustrators also saw artifacts, which the travelers had brought back from distant places, and inserted them into their pictures. If left to their own devices, artists drew their inspiration from the works of their predecessors. They borrowed freely from the reservoir of earlier illustrations when composing their images of exotic peoples, landscapes, fauna, and flora.

Imagery accompanying the travelers' accounts played an important role, for, at the most obvious level, it confirmed in the reader's eye the descriptions given by the writers and seemingly added objectivity and realism. The illustrations functioned as a pictorial narrative based on the written narrative of the text. Yet as a result of the way in which these illustrations were created, it was a familiar pictorial narrative. Over the centuries of copying, prescribed iconographic conventions and standardized, narrow themes for the imagery developed. Several scholars have researched this image production and its history. Some studied particular *œuvres* and travel accounts, such as the art of Captain Cook's voyages (Joppien and Smith 1985), and the engravings of de Bry's *Great Voyages* (Bucher 1981). Bucher's structural analysis of the de Bry material is of particular interest, because she explores several recurring motifs and their iconological meaning. There are also some writings which begin to outline a broader history of this image making. Among them is Kramer's "The Influence of the Classical Tradition on Anthropology and Exoticism" (1989), which examines the influence of the classical canon of composition (such as contrapposto) in the art of the nude on the representation of the exotic nude. In this article Kramer takes up some themes of his earlier book, *Verkehrte Welten: Zur imaginären Ethnographie des 19. Jahrhunderts* (1977). In a brief 1985 essay, Theye explored the history of representation of the "savage," beginning with early woodcuts and etchings, and then devoting the major part of the article to photography (Theye 1985b). Following Bucher's model, Steiner traced one particular motif and its recurrence in illustrations over several centuries in his essay "Of Drums and Dancers" (1986). Finally, the most recent entry is Pieterse's book, *White on Black: Images of Africa and Blacks in Western Popular Culture* (1992), which first appeared in Dutch in 1990 and provides a broad overview of the history of visual representations of Africans and African-Americans.

In general, however, in comparison to the analysis of written texts, the critical and systematic examination of imagery has been neglected. Written texts have come under close scrutiny concerning the reproduction of discursive traditions deriving from the "tropology" of travel writing (Kohl 1981; Pratt 1992; Theye 1985a). We are only at the beginning of applying similar modes of examination to visual texts. The relationship between written and visual texts is another area of inquiry. Indeed, the complete history of the iconography of the Other and of pictorial tropology still needs to be written.

This essay is an effort to further our understanding of these processes of Western image making. In the form of a case study, it focuses on late-nineteenth-century depictions of the Mangbetu and Mangbetu-ized peoples in northeastern Congo. Looking at the way one particular region and its inhabitants have been visually represented in three books and an account in a popular journal, all intended for the general public and published between the years 1874 and 1892, provides an ideal arena to explore the establishment, continuation, and elaboration of visual traditions. In delineating the theoretical and methodological parameters for this study I rely, to some extent, on the critical analysis of travel writing, which deals with issues related to the ones encountered in the study of imagery.

In the second half of the nineteenth century, travel writing on Africa was situated within a particular historical arena – the expansion of European powers over the continent, and the beginning of colonial domination and exploitation. In *Imperial Eyes: Travel Writing and Transculturation* Pratt (1992) reveals and critiques the ideology from which these texts emanated. Besides examining ideology, she proposes to study genre by exploring the conventions of representation that constitute European travel writing (Pratt 1992: 11). Pieterse suggests that a similar interpretive strategy be applied to the examination of image making. He situates the creation of images in the historical process and in what he designates "the history of mentalities and ideas," as well as within the perimeters of iconographic conventions (Pieterse 1992: 13). Indeed, an interpretation of imagery along the three axes of history, ideology, and iconographic conventions (genre in Pratt's words) constitutes a most fruitful approach.

Thus, this study of imagery depicting the Mangbetu finds itself at the intersection of concerns regarding the influence of history, ideology and iconographic conventions on image making. While acknowledging the importance of history and ideology, this essay examines mainly the integration and formulation of iconographic conventions. What makes the Mangbetu case particularly interesting for such research are developments in the middle of the nineteenth century which ultimately affected Western ways of seeing and representing foreign peoples. One of the many factors which precipitated changes had to do with numbers: on the eve of colonial occupation and in the age of expanding economic interests, a multitude of explorers traveled through Africa and other parts of the world. Consequently, the number of accounts increased dramatically. In addition, their distribution was facilitated by improved printing techniques, which allowed larger print runs. Furthermore, translations of the works into other languages became more common.

The second half of the nineteenth century also marks a watershed in respect of modes and technical means of visual representation. A powerful new tool for image making had arrived on the scene: photography. With the advent of photography, the medium then hailed as the ultimate objective mode of documentation, illustrators were initially provided with new models from which to create more specific imagery, because photographic images could not yet be mass printed.[1] Therefore artists transformed photographs into wood engravings or lithographs, often taking liberties in their renditions (Jenkins 1993; Thomas 1960). With the advent of photomechanical reproduction techniques in the 1880s, allowing the cheap reproduction of photographs in books, photographic images slowly began to replace earlier forms of illustration. Even then, wood engravings, lithographs and photographs were still presented side by side until photography as the medium of illustration finally almost entirely took over after the First World War. The decades when some of the older practices of image making continued to live on side by side with photography are a fascinating era, allowing the exploration of image making practices and conventions. This is exactly the period during which the three books considered here were published, and two of them indeed also contain reproductions of photographs.

Texts and images relating to the Mangbetu were produced by Westerners of different national origins and backgrounds within what Pratt has called contact zones, "social spaces where disparate cultures meet, clash and grapple with each other, often in highly asymmetrical relations of domination and subordination – like colonialism, slavery, or their aftermaths as they are lived out across the globe today" (Pratt 1992: 4). The second half of the nineteenth century was a period of change and upheaval in northeastern Congo, home of the Mangbetu. In pursuit of ivory and slaves, Nubo–Arab traders had worked their way up the Nile River and finally arrived in Mangbetu country in the 1860s. They were followed by other foreigners: Egyptians in 1880 who in 1884 made the Nile traders official government agents and appropriated the region as their southernmost province;[2] Swahili from the Kenya coast in 1887; and Belgians, the future colonial power, in 1891 (Keim 1979: 230–31). The opportunity of gaining new knowledge and making profits attracted individual explorers and entrepreneurs from all over Europe. They traveled with the often ruthless traders up the Nile and thus came to northeastern Congo.

Among these travelers was the German botanist Georg Schweinfurth (1836–1925), a powerful writer and eloquent storyteller, who published a two-volume, lavishly illustrated, account of his voyages. His book, *The Heart of Africa*, appeared in 1874, and contains the first visual renderings and extensive descriptions of the Mangbetu and the area in which they lived. Other explorers later retraced Schweinfurth's steps. Gaetano Casati

(1838–1902), an Italian cartographer traveled and lived in the region from 1879 to 1889 and wrote the two-volume account *Ten Years in Equatoria and the Return with Emin Pasha* (1891). Wilhelm Junker (1840–92), a Russian-born physician turned explorer published three volumes in German on his experiences in Africa between 1875 and 1886, entitled *Reisen in Afrika 1875–1886* (1889). These volumes were subsequently translated separately into English as *Travels in Africa* (1891, 1892, 1893). Like Schweinfurth's classic, both works contain numerous illustrations.

In the case of the Mangbetu, the construction of a textual discursive tradition began with Schweinfurth's two-volume book *The Heart of Africa*. Originally published in German in 1874, the book was immediately translated into several major languages. Schweinfurth's brief encounter with the Mangbetu forever encoded the way in which his fellow travelers perceived the Mangbetu and their rulers. Curtis Keim, a historian, called this discursive tradition the "Mangbetu myth" and considered Schweinfurth to be "undoubtedly the most important perpetrator" of the myth (Schildkrout and Keim 1990a: 32). The Mangbetu myth consists of a set of stereotypical elements, first presented by Schweinfurth and then repeated and elaborated in other written texts describing the Mangbetu (Keim 1979: 308–09).[3] Among these tropes are, on the one hand, descriptions of the nobility of the Mangbetu royals and the splendor of the life at the courts, and on the other, references to their savagery and the repulsiveness of what was erroneously believed to be Mangbetu cannibalism. This construction of the Mangbetu recasts the nature of the nineteenth-century Western discourse on Africans and non-Western peoples in general, who were perceived in terms of the noble/civilized, ignoble/savage dichotomy (Miller 1985: 5).

Considering the brevity of Schweinfurth's visit with the Mangbetu from March 21 to April 12, 1870, the creation of the myth is an interesting process. He spent only thirteen days at Nangazizi, the capital of a Mangbetu kingdom ruled by a king named Mbunza (Munza in Schweinfurth's account). King Mbunza, whose reign over the Mangbetu heartland lasted from *c.* 1867 to 1873, was one of several rival rulers, all of either Mangbetu origin or Mangbetu-ized, who dominated the region. During much of his stay at Nangazizi, Schweinfurth barricaded himself into his tent in order to avoid being harassed and constantly observed by curious Mangbetu, in particular women (Schweinfurth 1874a, II: 59–60). Despite his obviously uncomfortable circumstances, he revels in his unique experiences, the culmination of his fantasies about the heart of the "dark continent."

As the following passage from Schweinfurth's writing indicates, he arrived with the heightened awareness and premonition that he was to find in the heart of Africa the epitome of a creative African people. Many of his expectations derived from rumors that he had heard about Mangbetu country from other Westerners and from African neighbors of the Mangbetu.

> A fresh world of novelty seemed to be awaiting us in this remote region, the very kernel of the continent, equally distant from the Indian Ocean and from the Atlantic. Everything was new. The bright and clear complexion of the natives, their singular garb, their artistic furniture, the convenience of their orderly houses, and finally, the savage etiquette of the pompous court, all struck me with fresh surprise and ever renewed the feeling of astonishment. There was, moreover, an exuberance of strange and unexpected vegetation; whilst plantations, sugarcanes, and oil-palms were everywhere to be seen in plentiful luxuriance. Truly, I now found myself in the heart of Africa, realising to the letter the fascinating dreams of my early youth. (Schweinfurth 1874a, I: 556–57)

Just as these premonitions and dreams now fulfilled set the stage for the beginning of the construction of the Mangbetu myth in written form, the lavish illustrations confirm and reinforce Schweinfurth's observations and give them reality in the readers' eyes. There is, throughout the volumes, a remarkably close resemblance between word and image. Written and pictorial narratives complement each other. This results from the fact that, with few exceptions, the wood engravings were prepared from Schweinfurth's own sketches, now preserved in the archives of the Frobenius-Institut in Frankfurt, Germany. Another of Schweinfurth's publications entitled *Artes Africanae: Illustrations and Descriptions of Productions of the Industrial Arts of Central African Tribes* (1875) is based entirely on his sketches of artifacts. Judging by his *oeuvre*, Schweinfurth was an accomplished artist (see also Thornton 1990: 46–48). Indeed, as will be seen below, he often refers in the text to the sessions when he produced his drawings, and in many instances his verbal descriptions reveal his keen sense of the visual.

The resemblance between Schweinfurth's written and pictorial narratives is obvious from the following quote and accompanying illustration. As if he were surveying a stage, a dreamlike panorama unfolded in front of him when he reached Mangbetu country. It is a classic discovery scene with the discoverer at an elevated viewpoint and in command.

> We enjoyed a view in front of a sloping area, void of grass, enlivened with an endless multiplicity of huts, of which the roofs of some were like ordinary sheds, and those of others of a conical form. And there, surmounting all, with extensive courts broad and imposing, unlike anything we had seen since we left the edifices of Cairo, upreared itself the spacious pile of King Munza's dwelling. (Schweinfurth 1874a, I: 558)

The wood engraving[4] of Mbunza's residence (Fig. 6.1) gives pictorial confirmation – a sweeping vista of an orderly landscape with oil-palms and banana groves. On the right, a house with an exaggerated conical roof serves as the clean and comfortable backdrop for the domestic scene of a woman and her child. Another such scene unfolds in front of a rectangular house to the left. At a distance, the viewer sees the large-scale royal residence. Similar to the written passages, the picture invokes the romantic vision – a calm and idyllic setting.

In September or October of 1881, eleven years after Schweinfurth's visit, Casati arrived in Mangbetu country. His arrival scene is clearly a derivative of Schweinfurth's passage, but shares little of its pathos. In fact, Casati defers to Schweinfurth's descriptions and presents by then common tropes about Mangbetu country when he writes:

> I was on the point of entering the Mambettu country which has been fully described by Schweinfurth; I had heard wonderful reports of the majesty of its scenery, of its rivers, with its celebrated galleries, the banquets of human flesh; the pigmies; the chimpanzee with semi-human form, the tragic death of King Munza and the iniquities perpetrated by the Arabs, all stirred up my curiosity. (Casati 1891a, I: 92)

However, there is no image showing the vista. Indeed, the halftone illustrations in Casati's books present mainly action scenes, depictions of Africans, and portraits of Europeans. There are only a few landscapes or views of towns/villages.[5] The emphasis on drama, such as fights with Africans, and on portraits reflects Casati's self-perception. He was a man of action, the hero who survived in darkest Africa, surrounded by (mostly

6.1 "Munza's Residence." Wood engraving.

hostile) "natives." It is noteworthy, that his books also contain halftone reproductions of photographs.

Like Casati, Wilhelm Junker saw himself as the hero who overcame adversity. His account, a terse recitation of his daily diaries, focuses on his own experiences and achievements and lacks the poetic quality of Schweinfurth's writings. He reached Mangbetu country in September of 1880. When he finally published his books in the years between 1890 and 1892, the illustrators helped themselves freely to Schweinfurth's imagery and composed fascinating lithographs, often by combining three or more motifs from Schweinfurth's wood engravings and inserting the hero into the picture (see for example Fig. 6.7). They also copied Schweinfurth engravings and worked from original sketches, attributing them to the source. Like Casati's, Junker's publishers also chose to include lithographic renderings of photographs.

Junker presents no arrival narrative in verbal form, while the illustrations in his book include finely honed idyllic landscapes, often with Junker and his party surveying the scene on a promontory, as in Figure 6.2 showing the Nepoko River. River crossings were critical moments in the explorers' voyages, for they had to depend on their ingenuity and often on the indigenous chiefs to provide them with boats to continue on. Indeed, such crossings take on metaphorical dimensions, for the hero moves deeper into the liminal, the place beyond, on his voyage into "the heart of darkness." The artist L. H. Fischer shows the explorer Junker during such a moment – standing on the banks of the Nepoko River, surveying a village on the other side. Next to him stands a Mangbetu, pointing into the distance. According to the text he could be the Mangbetu ruler Azanga Mombele who had followed Junker on his trip to the Nepoko River. A group of porters patiently waits behind the explorer. Like Schweinfurth's desire to reach Mangbetu country, the arrival at the river was a dream fulfilled for Junker.

> Anyhow, on May 6th, 1882, my wishes were at least gratified by the sight of the stream, whose name had haunted me throughout my southern wanderings ... When reached by me, the stream, though at low level, was about a hundred yards wide, but the banks, partly rocky and over thirty feet high, stood from fifty to sixty feet farther back, forming lower down flat margins, which are flooded at high water. The upper edge of the banks, and partly also the overhanging bluffs, were shaded by venerable

6.2 "View of the Nepoko." Lithograph by Ludwig Hans Fischer.

forest trees, underwood, and bush, while the flats were under grass. In many places the lianas and creepers twining round the undergrowth formed an impenetrable tangle of thickets. But the stream was visible only for a short distance, for towards the west it soon tended sharply round to the south. Its smooth surface showed no sign of reefs or ledges, and in mid-stream there was a strong current, while the water, which I tasted, was clear and pure, which doubtless is not the case during floods. It is said to abound in fish, some of them five or six feet long, though I saw nothing but some dried cat-fish. (Junker 1892: 92–93)

Once they arrived in Mangbetu country, all three explorers were fascinated by the Mangbetu kings. Again, Schweinfurth's verbal and visual narrative serves as a model for the other two travelers. Schweinfurth's portrait of King Mbunza (Fig. 6.4), the frontispiece in the second volume of his account, became one of the classic portraits of an "African ruler" and to this day has captured the imagination of Westerners.[6] Again, as in the case of other illustrations in Schweinfurth's book, there is congruence between the verbal and the visual. Schweinfurth writes:

I could now feast my eyes on the fantastic figure of the ruler. I was intensely interested in gazing at the strange weird-looking sovereign, of whom it was commonly reported that his daily food was human flesh. With arms and legs, neck and breast, all bedizened with copper rings, chains, and other strange devices, and with a great copper crescent at the top of his head, the potentate gleamed with a shimmer that was to our ideas unworthy of royalty, but savoured far too much of the magazines of civic opulence, reminding one almost unavoidably of a well-kept kitchen! His appearance, however, was decidedly marked with his nationality, for every adornment that he had about him belonged exclusively to Central Africa, as none but the fabrications of his native land are deemed worthy of adoring the person of a king of the Monbutto.

Agreeable to the national fashion a plumed hat rested on the top of his chignon, and soared a foot and a half above his head; this hat was a narrow cylinder of closely-plaited reeds; it was ornamented with three layers of red parrot's feathers, and crowned with a plume of the same; there was no brim, but the copper crescent projected from the front like the visor of a Norman helmet. The muscles of Munza's ears were pierced, and copper bars as thick as the finger inserted in the cavities. The entire body was smeared with the native unguent of powdered cam-wood, which converted the original bright brown tint of his skin into the color that is so conspicuous in ancient Pompeian halls. With the exception of being of an unusually fine texture, his single garment differed in no respect from what was worn throughout the country. It consisted of a large piece of fig bark impregnated with the same dye that served as his cosmetic, and this, falling into graceful folds about his body, formed breeches and waistcoat all in one. Round thongs of buffalo hide, with heavy copper bells attached to the ends, were fastened round the waist in a huge knot, and like a girdle held the coat, which was neatly-hemmed. The material of the coat was so carefully manipulated that it had quite the appearance of a rich *moiré antique*. Around the king's neck hung a huge copper ornament made in little points which radiated like beams all over his chest; on his bare arms were strange-looking pendants which in shape could only be compared to drumsticks with rings at the end. Halfway up the lower part of the arms and just below the knee were three bright, horny-looking circlets cut out of hippopotamus-hide, likewise tipped with copper. As a symbol of his dignity Munza wielded in his right hand the sickle-shaped Monbutto scimitar, in this case only an ornamental weapon, and made of pure copper. (Schweinfurth 1874a, II: 44–45)

In the passage, the king is rendered as the epitome of the noble exotic savage. Underneath, though, lurks the ignoble, uncivilized – the dangerous cannibal (see also Schweinfurth 1874, II: 46). Schweinfurth's own pencil drawing (Fig. 6.3) served as one of the models for the wood engraving in the second volume of his account (Fig. 6.4). Mbunza himself approved of the sketch, when Schweinfurth showed him his collection of pictures (Schweinfurth 1874a, II: 77–78). A comparison of sketch and engraving attests to the skill and accuracy of the engraver, in the case of the English edition J. D. Cooper. The sketch allowed him to create a profile portrait of the long-limbed ruler in an elegant seated pose. Other Schweinfurth sketches of Mangbetu objects helped the artist to recreate the setting, such as the bench on which the king is seated and the stools beside him (Fig. 6.4).

Besides the "splendor of Mangbetu royalty" and the "savagery lurking underneath that thin veneer" tropes, another stereotypical theme occurs in reference to Mbunza in Schweinfurth's writings. It derived from Western constructions of race and a classificatory racial hierarchy and referred to the place which the Mangbetu occupied in this hierarchy. In the second half of the nineteenth century, when scientists were busy

6.3 "König Munsa der Monbuttu." (King Munsa of the Mangbetu).
Pencil sketch by Georg Schweinfurth.

145

6.4 "King Munza in full dress." Wood engraving.

creating racial taxonomies and classifying mankind, theories of the relative development of African races were promulgated in German scholarly
circles. Skin color and physiognomic characteristics provided important
evidence. In popularized versions, these racial theories also emerged in
widely read books about the African continent, such as, for example,
Sievers' *Afrika. Eine allgemeine Landeskunde* (1891). In popular and
scholarly thought, variations in physiognomy and skin color were attributed to the mixture of negroes (Bantu) with Semitic and Hamitic races,
which occupied a higher position in the racial hierarchy (Sievers 1891:
226–27). This admixture resulted from sweeping migratory movements,
and elevated particular members of the "negro" race, such as the
Mangbetu, to higher intellectual levels.

Schweinfurth clearly perceived the Mangbetu as racially and thus
intellectually and culturally superior to other Africans. In fact, he
believed the Mangbetu had the "tokens of Semitic origin most thoroughly impressed upon their countenance" (Schweinfurth 1874a, II:
58). In another context, Schweinfurth draws parallels between the Fulbe
and the Mangbetu and suggests that they might probably be included
among Ptolemy's "Pyrrhi Aethiopes" (Schweinfurth 1874a, II:101).
Contemporary ideology, thus placed them above most other races in
Central Africa. This classification is also alluded to in the following
remark about Mbunza.

> Although belonging to a type by no means uncomely, his [Mbunza's] fea-
> tures were far from prepossessing, but had a Nero-like expression that
> told of ennui and satiety. He had small whiskers and a tolerable thick
> beard; his profile was almost orthognatic, but the perfectly Caucasian
> nose offered a remarkable contrast to the thick and protruding negro
> lips. (Schweinfurth 1874a, II: 46)

The passage perfectly matches the visual representation of Mbunza's
physiognomy which Schweinfurth captured in his portrait (Fig. 6.3).

Schweinfurth's pervasive first representation of a Mangbetu ruler
developed into an often repeated verbal and visual trope. In 1874, *Le Tour
du Monde*, a popular travel magazine for the French bourgeoisie, ran a
French chapter by chapter translation of Schweinfurth's account
(Schweinfurth 1874b). The magazine addressed a popular audience, and
much effort was spent on the illustrations. In many instances, French

artists copied the wood engravings of the English edition. The classic portrait of King Mbunza was presented in a full page version (Fig. 6.5). Emile Bayard, the illustrator, generally followed the wood engraving in the English edition, although he regularized some of the ornaments and rendered the feathers of the royal headdress in a more elaborate fashion. He also decided to move a supporting pole for the structure the king is sitting in closer towards the center of his composition.

Gaetano Casati encountered two rulers in Mangbetu country. Yangala was the son of a king of non-Mangbetu origin, who had been a rival of King Mbunza. Shortly after Mbunza was killed in 1873 by an alliance of Mangbetu dissidents, Yangala took over his realm. Casati was not as powerful a storyteller as Schweinfurth. Thus his description of Yangala is brief and less elaborate than Schweinfurth's passage. It also lacks the common reference to cannibalism.

> The king was glittering with arms and ornaments. Parrot feathers, leopard skins, lances embellished with brass, a brightly studded shield, boars' tails hanging on his back, armlets of iron wire to the elbow, gaiters of the same metal, and a tower-shaped hat fixed by large pins, adorned him. His women could not refrain from showing admiration and pleasure to their lord by clapping their hands and loud cries. (Casati 1891a, I: 150)

While there is no image of Yangala in the book, there is a portrait of Azanga Kpwokpwo, another Mangbetu ruler, whom Casati visited (Fig. 6.6). The illustrator for Casati used Schweinfurth's wood engraving as model for his rendering of a Mangbetu king. Like King Mbunza, Azanga Kpwokpwo sits on a finely made bench of raffia palm ribs and fiber, although the illustrator chose a slightly different angle. Pose and details of the royal dress resemble Mbunza's portrait. Like Mbunza, Azanga wears a headdress, copper head ornament, necklace and leg rings. Only the ceremonial knife is a different shape and the king holds it in a slightly different position. While Mbunza rests his feet on a mat, Azanga Kpwokpwo places his feet on a shield on top of a spear, an allusion to the perceived Mangbetu prowess in war. This flattering portrait of the ruler belies the fact that Casati was held against his will by Azanga Kpwokpwo and despised the king.

In Junker's account, this Mangbetu king image occurs again, this time

6.5 "Mounza, roi des Mombouttous. – Dessin de Emile Bayard, d'après l'édition
anglaise." (Mounza, King of the Mombouttos. – Drawing by Emile Bayard,
after the English edition.) Wood engraving. A copy of Figure 6.4, this image
shows numerous small variations.

6.6 "Sultan Azanga." Halftone.

as part of a tableau, showing the explorer at the royal court of Mangbetu
King Mambanga (Fig. 6.7). Junker shares the typical Mangbetu bench
with the king. In this image, the explorer becomes the central figure, while
the king is moved slightly to one side. Yet, as in Casati and to a certain
degree in Schweinfurth, the actual experience, the regal setting with the
explorer in full command, contradicts the actual circumstances of

Junker's stay. Junker was detained by an uncooperative Mambanga, and had to extend his stay against his will by several weeks (Junker 1891: 250).

Junker's verbal description of the king contains some of the elements found in Schweinfurth and Casati:

> Mambanga was of tall stature, and at once distinguished by his much lighter bronze complexion from his darker copper-coloured subjects. The careless bearing so often noticed in tall Negroes of the better classes was here betrayed, especially in a decided stoop, which caused him when seated to bend his head well forward. He was still a young man, with almost beardless face, which bore an expression of unbridled sensuousness, heightened by his large, prominent goggle-eyes. In other respects he scarcely differed outwardly from the rest of his tribe, and like them wore the national bark costume, though of better texture, and of light brown cigar colour. His hair was arranged in the form of a chignon, inclined backwards, and surmounted by a basket-shaped hat, which was secured by means of a long ivory pin. (Junker 1891: 225–26)

Most noteworthy is the reference to the lighter skin color of the king, once again alluding to his racial superiority. In addition, the theme of the "savagery lurking underneath that thin veneer" is recaptured in the reference to his unbridled sensuousness. Yet by comparison, this passage is less sympathetic than either Schweinfurth's or Casati's descriptions of Mangbetu royalty. This is in keeping with the often complaining and detached tone of Junker's writings.

Besides these recurring depictions of the kings, there are other renderings of Mangbetu nobility. An image of one of Mbunza's sons and another of a royal wife are of particular interest, for they show the process of transformation from initial sketches by Schweinfurth to wood engraving and composed illustration. Mbunza's son, depicted in one of the sketches, aroused Schweinfurth's interest (Fig. 6.8). He writes:

> The name of this distinguished personnage was Bunza, and he was about the lightest-skinned individual that I had here beheld. His complexion could not have been fairer if he had been a denizen of Central Egypt. His hair was equally pale and grizzly; his tall chignon being not unlike a bundle of hemp, and standing in marked contrast to the black tresses which stressed across the brow. As the hair above the temples does not grow sufficiently long for this purpose, the Monbutto are accustomed to use false hair; and as fair heads of hair are somewhat uncommon, false

6.7 "Meeting with Mambanga." Lithograph by Ludwig Hans Fischer.

hair to match the original is difficult to purchase. This young man, of whom I was successful in taking a deliberate sketch, exhibited all the characteristics of pronounced albinism, and in truth to a degree which can be often seen in a fair individual of the true Semitic stock, either Jew or Arabian. The eyes seem painfully affected by light, and had a constant objectless leer; the head, supported by a shrivelled neck, kept nodding with an involuntary movement, and whenever it rested it was sure to be in some extraordinary position. Bunza reminded me very vividly of some white twins that I once saw on the Red Sea. (Schweinfurth 1874a, II: 57–58)

In another instance, Schweinfurth describes his portrayal of two royal wives. In contrast to later writers and photographers, who were enchanted with the exotic air and elegant coiffure of Mangbetu women, Schweinfurth had ambivalent feelings about their beauty.

They all had comely, youthful, well-knit figures, and were for the most part tall, but much cannot be said in favour of their expression. They emulated each other in the extent of their head-gear and in the profusion with which they adorned their body. Two of them submitted to have their portraits taken; the whole party sat in a circle, taking up their position during the time that I was sketching the likenesses on the little single-stemmed stools which they had brought with them; when they took their seats they threw their bands across their laps. Some of the group stood out in marked contrast to the rest by their light complexion and fair hair, whilst others approximated very nearly the colour of *café-au-lait*. When I had finished my drawing, I was anxious to show my appreciation of the ladies' patience, and accordingly offered to present them with some beads, but they at once begged to refuse the proffered necklace, explaining that they were not at liberty to accept presents from any one but "Mbahly" (Aboo Sammat). (Schweinfurth 1874a, II: 58–59)

The sketch of Netolu, "one of the 100 wives of Munsa," may well have originated during this session (Fig. 6.9).

Although Schweinfurth gives the names of both sitters, Bunsa and Netolu, the main intent of the portraits is ethnographic/anthropological, as the execution of the sketches and several explanations next to the drawings demonstrate. There is an emphasis on the rendering of the facial features, i.e. race, and the coiffure, i.e. ethnographic detail. Both Mangbetu men and women sported long cylindrical chignons supported

6.8 "Bunsa, ein Sohn Munsa's." (Bunsa, a son of Munsa.) Pencil sketch by
Georg Schweinfurth.

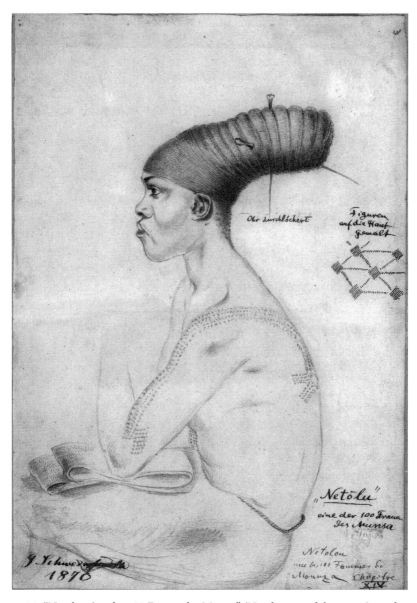

6.9 "Netolu, eine der 100 Frauen des Munsa." (Netolu, one of the 100 wives of
Munsa.) Pencil sketch by Georg Schweinfurth.

by reed structures. While both men and women wore ivory or bone hair-pins, men in addition fastened woven hats with feathers to the coiffure. Schweinfurth provides a long description of both coiffure and hats in a chapter devoted to the ethnography of the Mangbetu (Schweinfurth 1874a, II: 106).

In both portraits, the bodies of the sitters are not elaborated, except for neck and shoulders. However, the sketches indicate dress and, in the woman's depiction, body painting (Fig. 6.9). In Bunsa's likeness, there is a slight indication of bow and arrows which he holds in his left hand (Fig. 6.8). The comments on Bunsa's portrait are quite detailed and essentially repeat the information given about the sitter in the written text quoted earlier. They focus on the physical dimension and cultural attributes. In translation, the comments from top to bottom read as follows:

> Bunsa,
> a son of Munsa
>> eyebrows almost missing
>> constant fidgetiness
>> in the eyes
>> slight squinting
>> and constant shaking of the head.

> "Bunsa
> a young Monbuttu man"
> (16 years.)
> Color reddish brown like a
> *fellah* from the region around Cairo
> Eyes light brown, iris black-brown
> Hair dirty, light blond
> strongly frizzed
> stiff and thick.
> The cords of hair over the
> shaved part are, as usual, borrowed,
> and black.
> The cords of hair of the
> chignon, by contrast, are
> his own.

In the case of Netolu's portrait, there are two written comments. One makes reference to the fact that the woman's ear was pierced, "Ohr durch-löchert," another accompanies a line drawing of a design of her body

6.10 "Nétolu et Bounza – Dessin de O. Matthieu, d'après des croquis de l'auteur."
(Netolu and Bunsa. Drawing by O. Mathieu after sketches of the author.)
Wood engraving.

painting and indicates that these figures were applied to the skin,
"Figuren auf die Haut gemalt."

Apparently neither drawing was used in its entirety in the English
edition of Schweinfurth's book. However, in the *Le Tour du Monde* articles
both images were combined in a fine wood engraving, capturing Bunsa
and Netolu in what seems to be an intimate conversation (Fig. 6.10). This
technique, the collage of pictorial elements drawn from various sources
and presenting them in new arrangements was a typical device of illustrators. As it turns out, the French artist O. Mathieu worked from
Schweinfurth's original sketches, as indicated in the caption of the image.
Apparently, the images were sent to France, which explains the French
texts penciled in on the original drawings.

A general purpose idyllic landscape with several houses at a distance,
vaguely reminiscent of buildings in Figure 6. 1, serves as backdrop for the
two protagonists, who sit on what appears to be wooden logs. As in the
original sketch, Bunsa is bent slightly forward, seemingly listening
intently to Netolu. It should be noted here that both portraits have been

reversed from the original. There are numerous slight modifications of the original sketch. While Bunsa's facial features have been copied quite accurately, although distinctly more Caucasian in overall appearance, he now has nicely arching eyebrows. His somewhat scrawny upper torso has been filled out and he is no longer holding the bow and arrows. Netolu's depiction has undergone similar changes. Most obviously, her profile varies from the original sketch. The forehead and the rather fleshy nose have been straightened and the coiffure moved up so that the eyebrows are clearly visible. The lips protrude less and the very long chin has been shortened. By Western standards of beauty, Netolu's face has been rendered now in a more pleasing fashion. Her body is fully depicted. She raises her right hand, which Schweinfurth never completed in his sketch, and motions towards Bunsa. Perhaps the most remarkable transformation of the original images is the shift in emphasis. Schweinfurth's sketches conveyed above all ethnographic and anthropological information. Now the reader of *Le Tour du Monde* encounters a narrative scene and two individualized portraits of named Mangbetu royals carrying out a conversation.

In Junker's account, the portraits of Bunsa and Netolu are presented again. This time, however, they are separated and only their heads are depicted. Bunsa, referred to as "Son of the Mangbattu King, Munsa" in the caption illustrates Junker's discussion of the Mangbetu coiffure and the Mangbetu practice of shaping the head (Junker 1891: 241–42). Netolu according to the caption "Mangbattu woman" becomes a generic depiction of a Mangbetu female and accompanies two paragraphs about the demeanor of Mangbetu women in general and the female coiffure in particular (Junker 1891: 245). Both illustrations are accurate copies of the original drawings, which, according to the captions of the images were available to the illustrator. Finally it should be mentioned that Casati's publishers apparently either had no access to Schweinfurth's original sketches or no desire to use them, because they do not appear in his books.

All wood engravings depicting Mangbetu royals in Schweinfurth's book discussed thus far, were based on his sketches and thus are very specific in nature. They present physical appearance as well as ethnographic detail in the form of dress and objects associated with the royals. There is, however, a type of imagery which reverts back to older practices of representation. In the final part of this essay on Mangbetu depictions in the late nineteenth century, I would like to examine this type of imagery, which draws on established iconographic conventions, as already briefly hinted at in the discussion of the *Le Tour du Monde* wood engraving showing Bunsa and Netolu (Fig. 6.10). Both in Casati's and Junker's case, the artists relied on aesthetic conventions and illustration techniques established for centuries: the eclectic borrowing and variation of pictorial materials to be re-arranged for particular needs. Even Schweinfurth's books contain a few such composites. In the case of Mangbetu imagery, perhaps the most influential image of this nature in Schweinfurth is a wood engraving of two Mangbetu warriors (Fig. 6.11).

Quite obviously, the rendering of the two warriors alludes to the classical canon of the representation of the male body. The warrior on the left assumes a dramatic pose, highlighted by the contrapposto position. With his outstretched right arm, he plants a spear firmly on the ground. In his left hand he holds a shield and a bow with three arrows. The second warrior is presented in a profile pose, turning his back towards the viewer. If one follows these poses throughout the history of the depiction of non-Western peoples, one finds them in several classic illustrated accounts, such as de Bry's *Great Voyages* (1590–1634), in which he and later his sons represented inhabitants of the New World and other distant parts of the known world in classical poses.[7] Both Mangbetu men are clad in bark cloth attire, which is rendered as richly textured, flowing material, much like velvet and other precious fabrics lavishly represented in European paintings. Indeed, the illustration accompanies a description of the production of such cloth. In addition, the men wear typical Mangbetu hats with feathers.

Upon closer examination, this wood engraving appears to be an illustrator's collage of several elements in Schweinfurth's original drawings. Although the sketch of Bunsa, King Mbunza's son, does not occur in Schweinfurth's book, Bunsa's head apparently served as the model for that of the warrior on the left (see Fig. 6.8). Bunsa's features, his skinny face and his long thin nose, give the warrior figure's face a Caucasian appearance. In the wood engraving, a design – apparently painted – decorates the chest of the warrior. There is no design, however, in Schweinfurth's original drawing of Bunsa. It derives from Schweinfurth's profile portrait of King Mbunza (Fig. 6.3). The model for the head of the warrior on the

6.11 "Monbutto Warriors." Wood engraving.

right hand side, was adopted from the same image of King Mbunza. Other
details are also based on various Schweinfurth sources. The warrior on the
left holds a bow with three arrows, as does Bunsa in Schweinfurth's sketch.
Mangbetu spear heads, depicted in Schweinfurth's sketches and published on page 111 of the second volume of Schweinfurth's account, provided another model for the illustrator. The shields seem to be generic
renderings of a rectangular type described in Schweinfurth's text
(Schweinfurth 1874a, II: 115), not unlike the type of shields owned by the
Mangbetu.

6.12 "Guerriers mombouttous. Dessin de O. Matthieu, d'après l'édition anglaise."
(Mombouttou warriors. Drawing by O. Matthieu after the English edition.)
Wood engraving.

6.13 "Mangbattu war-game. (Drawn by L. H. Fischer.)" Lithograph.

This image of the Mangbetu warrior, which is rooted in the classical canon of representation, while presenting ethnographically correct information on Mangbetu dress and artifacts, became one of the most popular generic Mangbetu depictions among illustrators. The artist O. Mathieu adapted the wood engraving of the English version for *Le Tour du Monde* creating a full page illustration (Fig. 6.12). Once again – as in the composite image of Bunsa and Netolu – a lush generic landscape with rectangular houses and fields in the distance provides the romantic setting of the tableau. The protagonists in the picture are now reversed. The pose of the warrior with spear and shield has slightly shifted, for he holds the spear closer to his body, with the outstretched arm at a different angle. The design on his chest is more pronounced. His face still resembles that of Bunsa, although it is somewhat rounder and the eyes are no longer downcast. The second warrior, modeled on King Mbunza, remains essentially unchanged.

This Schweinfurth depiction of Mangbetu warriors influenced all other renderings of Mangbetu warriors and "commoners." Junker's illustrations are populated by variations of these Mangbetu warriors, such as, for example, an illustration showing Junker while receiving a "slave girl" as a "present" from Mangbetu-ized chief Nasima. Not only does the king's physical appearance, dress and adornment resemble the two warriors in Schweinfurth's wood engraving, two other figures in the background are also reminiscent of the original warrior figures.

Conventionalized Mangbetu warriors perform a war game in yet another Junker illustration (Fig. 6.13). Clad in identical dress and holding rectangular shields, the warriors simulate an attack in front of an audience, which comprises the king sitting on a bench at the far side of the square and another Mangbetu dignitary, judging by the coiffure a woman, on a similar bench closer by. This tableau is a fine example of the technique of collage employed by the illustrators. As in Figures 6.1 and 6.7, the arrangement and re-arrangement of borrowed pictorial elements allowed the artists to create a believable narrative scene.

Casati presents an illustration showing a similar event, a pantomime of warriors (Fig. 6.14). In this case, however, the artists did not borrow from Schweinfurth, but reverted to yet another ancient element of iconographic representation. The warriors with their feather headdresses here resemble the generic depictions of dancing "savages," common in

6.14 "Kriegerische Pantomimen." (Bellicose pantomimes.) Halftone.

illustrators' repertoires since the late sixteenth century (Steiner 1986: 110). The warriors dance around the seated explorer who watches the performance, the protagonist apparently being in control. Yet, the image must also have evoked deep fears of the foreign, the "savage," in the contemporary viewers.

To complicate matters further, reproductions of photographs add to the *bricolage* of illustrations in Junker's and Casati's books. Intermixed with lithographs and halftones, both Junker and Casati present photographs taken by Richard Buchta. Buchta (1845–94), was an Austrian artist and photographer who traveled to the Upper Nile regions in 1878–79 while living in Egypt (Killingray and Roberts 1989: 199–200). In fact, most of the depictions of Africans in Casati are renderings of photographs from two 1888 Buchta albums of Egypt and the Upper Nile, although Casati does not acknowledge the source. Casati's publisher employed what was then an advanced halftone printing technique for both artists' renderings and the photographs, developed by the Munich based company Dr. E. Albert and Co., whose name appears on every image. There are numerous albumen photographs of Richard Buchta proudly rendered as lithographs by Fr. Rheinfelder in Junker's text. In both books, only one photographic print relates to the Mangbetu. It portrays a Mangbetu woman (Fig. 6.15).

In this particular instance, Junker's lithograph of the photograph (Fig. 6.15) is an accurate, yet through the use of highlights, slightly dramatized translation of the original image. The artists took much more liberty in transforming other Buchta photographs (Thomas 1960). Since Richard Buchta never visited the Mangbetu region during his voyages in the Upper Nile areas, this particular portrait must have been taken outside Mangbetu country. In fact, the woman does not sport the much admired Mangbetu hairstyle. Rather, her hair is cropped short. She is wearing a bead necklace, a neck ring with an ornament, and armlets. Were it not for the identification in the caption, she would not be recognizable as Mangbetu. It is thus the caption that evokes and assigns meaning, relating the image to the written text and context into which it has been placed.

Both Junker's and Casati's visual accounts build on centuries of a pictorial discourse, which was based on *bricolage*, and iconographic conventions developed by artists and illustrators in collaboration with the

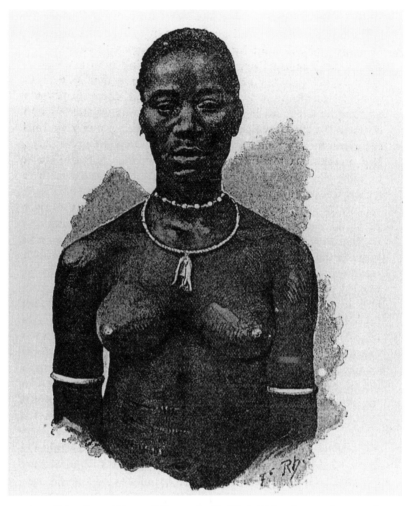

6.15 "Mangbattu Woman." (Drawn by Fr. Rheinfelder; from a photograph
by R. Buchta.)

travelers to foreign places. Schweinfurth's books contain very precise
wood engravings based on his sketches, yet at times older elements of the
pictorial discourse appear side by side with these visual documents. The
three accounts examined here provide a micro-cosmos of the world of
book illustration, ranging from accurate pictorial documents based on
the anthropological/ethnographic sketches of a traveler (Schweinfurth)
to highly conventionalized depictions springing from the reservoir of
iconographic models. At this particular moment in the history of

European expansion, the way foreign peoples were seen through the eyes of the artist was still based on established traditions of illustrating and long-established iconographic conventions.

The artists' and illustrators' engravings of the Mangbetu formed an important component of the Mangbetu myth, first created by Schweinfurth. They visualized this myth, and enacted its establishment and continuation as much as the written texts. When photography entered into the arena in full force at the end of the nineteenth century, the landscape of visual representation of the Mangbetu had been well laid out, the perimeters had been established. If the resilience of the iconographic conventions and earlier practices of representation with their established themes serve as a model, then it seems only logical to expect that photography continued to aid in the construction and invention of a people which, since its "discovery," has captured the Western imagination.

NOTES

1 The earliest photographic examples for Africa are daguerreotypes dating to the 1840s. A helmsman by the name of Vernet, who accompanied the French Naval Officer Charles Guillain on the voyage of the Ducouëdic to East Africa and Madagascar in 1846–48, took what we assume are the first daguerreotypes from Africa (Guillain 1856: XIX). These daguerreotypes were used to create lithographs for the illustrated account of the voyage, which were published in a splendid volume, accompanying the three part travel narrative (Guillain 1857). Such publications no doubt raised the level of expectation among the readership.

2 See Keim 1979: 240.

3 Enid Schildkrout and Curtis A. Keim present an excellent case study of what I would describe as a "regional discursive tradition," in their analysis of the European narrative about Self in Mangbetu country and the Mangbetu Other in the second chapter of their catalogue, entitled "Through Western Eyes: The Making of the Mangbetu Myth" (Schildkrout and Keim 1990a: 29–45). This myth making is not uncommon and occurred in reference to other African peoples as well (see, for example, Geary 1988).

4 For a description and analysis of printing processes see Ivins 1964.

5 A count of imagery in the first volume reveals the following breakdown: twenty-three action scenes, thirty-five depictions of Africans (mostly based on photographs), and thirteen portraits of Europeans.

6 It is noteworthy that Schildkrout and Keim decided to have the evocative portrait recreated with a mannequin – the first display one saw when entering their exhibition entitled "African Reflections: Art from Northeastern Zaire," which was shown at the National Museum of Africa Art in 1991. Their juxtaposition of the original sketch of Mbunza (Fig. 6.3) with the three-dimensional figure put the mannequin into its context. Schweinfurth's wood engraving of Mbunza has been published frequently.

7 See in particular Bucher 1981: Plates 7 and 15; and Steiner 1986: Fig. 9.

SEVEN

Personal styles and disciplinary paradigms: Frederick Starr and Herbert Lang

ENID SCHILDKROUT

🔕

In comparing the collecting styles of different individuals it is tempting to go beyond the quirkiness of personalities and try to explain historically documented events in terms of grander paradigms. In this chapter I compare two early twentieth-century ethnographic collections and collectors, Herbert Lang (1879–1957) and Frederick Starr (1858–1933), exploring in each case their relationship to prevailing notions of science, in particular biology and anthropology. I focus specifically on the Congo fieldwork experiences of these two collectors, for Starr this is from 1905–06, and for Lang 1908–15.

In the period in question, biology and anthropology were hardly distinct disciplines, both being closely linked to evolutionary paradigms. Anthropology, still in the early stages of legitimizing itself as an academic and museological discipline, was dependent on emerging Darwinian models (Coombes 1994; Stocking 1987). Not only were many of its practitioners, including Frederick Starr, trained in the natural sciences, but most ethnographers, embedded in the popular discourse of the day, were immersed in the ideas of biologically determined racial hierarchy, progress, and the superiority and civilizing mission of the West. Some anthropologists – and Starr was typical of this group – took seriously the task of collecting evidence to demonstrate these paradigms. Other collectors (and here I include Lang), were not immune to the Social Darwinism that pervaded popular discourse, but had different agendas that were more compulsively empirical; for such men collecting was an end in itself, and while it was circumscribed by categorical assumptions, this type of biological field scientist often assumed that others would study, reclassify and reinterpret the material.

The central African field experiences of Lang and Starr, both in the same period, both of whose collections are now in the American Museum of Natural History, were quite different and corresponded to these two types. I propose that, notwithstanding the pervasiveness of the Darwinian paradigm that affected all collectors operating in this era, at least two different approaches to collecting and interpreting material culture were already emerging. These two approaches correspond to different ways of thinking about African creativity and the meaning of authenticity and they are in a sense prototypes of different attitudes towards African art that are still evident today. Starr's ostensibly anthropological approach saw African material culture as evidence of Africa's essential primitiveness and otherness, of naturalized differences between populations; Lang's approach recognized a common biological humanity and ultimately rejected the equation of culture and race.[1]

Two challenges emerge from this: one is to explain differences in collecting styles – whether they were due to individual biographies including the collectors' class positions, education, financial status and institutional support; or rather to the imperatives of the scientific and collecting communities to which the collectors related – to what I would call disciplinary paradigms (nevertheless acknowledging that biology and, to a far greater degree, anthropology were – and are – still defining themselves as disciplines). The second problem concerns the effect these collecting styles and agendas may have had, and continue to have, on the production of African material culture. I maintain that the different modes of collecting that emerged in the early 1900s continue to this day to correspond to two paradigms of collecting, thinking about, and even producing African art. One paradigm celebrates a concept of authenticity and tradition that posits an "uncontaminated" (by the West) Africa. This has been described in some detail in terms of the invention of Africa (Mudimbe 1988), the invention of tradition (Ranger 1983), and the reification of tribal styles (as in Fagg 1965), a notion which became current several decades later, but whose prototype is found in the categorizing that methodologically guided collecting in these years.[2] The second paradigm celebrates objects and art from the "contact zone" –

"hybrid" art, "tourist" art and all the material culture that in one way or another evades the Western folk canon of African authenticity, including contemporary African art.[3] While many people often assume that these paradigms are sequential, I suggest that they both emerged in the early days of Western collecting in Africa and that they have less to do with modernism or post-modernism, colonialism and post-colonialism, than is commonly thought.

Herbert Lang and Frederick Starr both brought back large collections of over 4,000 objects, but the two men's collecting styles and methods were very different, as are the resulting collections. Both collections contain objects that observers today characterize as old and new, "real" and "fake," "authentic" and "tourist." Some of these categories make sense and some do not, but all can be understood in terms of the agendas, pre-conceptions, and collecting methods of the two early twentieth-century collectors.

FREDERICK STARR

The Starr family traced its lineage in America to settlers who came from Britain in 1635. The fourth son of a Presbyterian minister, Frederick went to the University of Rochester and received a Ph.D. in geology and biology in 1885 from Lafayette College in Pennsylvania. After teaching science for a few years, he worked at the American Museum of Natural History from 1889 to 1891 classifying ethnological specimens.[4] He left the Museum in 1892 to begin a thirty-one-year career teaching anthropology at the University of Chicago with a simultaneous appointment at the Walker Museum (McVicker 1986). Even though Starr was invited in 1892 to found a program in anthropology at the University of Chicago (Cash 1976: 1), no other anthropologist was hired during his tenure and he remained isolated from mainstream anthropology and from the emerging Boasian paradigm that came to define the discipline in America.[5] Antipathetic to Boas' rejection of the evolutionary approach to culture, Starr's thinking remained rooted in the biological paradigm and reflected the biases of popular Social Darwinism much more than the cultural relativism that came to dominate American ethnology and anthropology from the 1930s onwards.

Starr's passion for engaging in anthropology at the level of popular discourse may have been part of the reason he was never able to break out of the mold of a simplistic nineteenth-century approach,[6] for whatever Starr may have meant to say, the press reports and summaries of his provocative lectures inevitably highlighted the most sensational points, those that most caricatured non-Western peoples. As one dispatch noted:

> Prof. Frederick Starr, the man who brought the hairy Ainus from Yezzo, is to be the philosopher and guide of the expedition [through the 1904 Saint Louis Exposition]. Three hours every day he is going to steer the co-eds through the anthropological section, showing them the strange peoples in their strangest moods, after which all who can be kept in line will be taken to a lecture room where Prof. Starr will tell them why the strange peoples are strange and why they are not commonplace like civilized Americans. (*St. Louis Post Dispatch*, August 30, 1904)

Starr traveled and collected widely, from Japan to Korea, the Philippines, Mexico, and the Southwestern United States. He used his experiences to make titillating comparisons between exotic cultures and between Whites and Others. He was noted for outspoken opinions on controversial issues which he propounded in the popular press, on the lecture circuit, and in the classroom. Perhaps starting with his Chautauqua classes, or during his term as secretary to the World Colombian Exposition, Starr spent much of his career taking positions on "hot" issues such as the inferiority of women, the Japanese right to invade Manchuria, and the beneficence of the Congo Free State regime (Cash 1976: 21). While his Congo diaries include descriptions of incidents that confirmed the atrocities in the Congo, his published defense of the regime earned him a Belgian medal of honor.[7]

In 1904, Starr met Reverend Samuel P. Verner, the curious missionary/explorer/entrepreneur who had brought a group of Africans (including Ota Benga, the famous Pygmy) to the St. Louis Exposition. Intrigued by the idea of visiting Africa, Starr took the opportunity to join Verner (and Ota Benga) in the Kasai region in 1905. Accompanied by a Mexican photographer and companion, Manuel Gonzalez, Starr traveled without institutional support, planning to reimburse himself by selling artifacts.

In 1911, after much haggling, he concluded a sale of almost 4,000 artifacts to the American Museum of Natural History. Starr did some collecting himself, but much of what he acquired was actually collected by Verner who had been given a concession of land in the Congo Free State as a reward for his favorable propagandizing for the regime (Bradford and Blume 1992: 125). Working from his base camp at Mount Washington, Verner collected 9,000 objects (Bradford and Blume 1992: 144; Crawford 1982), while Starr managed the servants, interviewed Africans who were encouraged to come to borrow money and sell objects, and catalogued the collections.

The documentation that Starr provided to the American Museum with his collection was minimal – a simple list of objects with tribal or place identifications and a Western object name ("mask," "fetish," "basket"). But his field diaries, recently linked to the collection,[8] provide a running personal account of his African journey and contain dated lists of objects and the prices for those pieces Starr purchased himself. Verner's collections are barely documented.[9] Starr did have more serious and academic publication plans, most of which never materialized. In his *Ethnographic Notes from the Congo Free State: an African Miscellany* (1909: 13) – a compendium of folk tales, proverbs, children's games, tooth chipping patterns, and measurements of people, particularly Pygmies – he promised a "Handbook of the Peoples of the Congo Free State." In the end, he published only a photograph album in 1912, entitled *Congo Natives: An Ethnographic Album*, with sketchy descriptions of customs and scenery.

When Starr decided to follow Verner to Africa, the idea was that the two men would go on collecting expeditions together. Verner was the more knowledgeable field worker, while Starr was the trained scientist. Starr, often sick in bed, stayed at Verner's Mount Washington base camp from the end of December, 1905 until May 1906, while Verner went out and collected artifacts. Whenever Verner returned to camp, the two argued incessantly over the quality and value of the collections. Starr was relieved when Verner left for the United States at the end of May, 1906. It was soon after Verner's departure and the closing of the Mount Washington base camp, that Starr set out on a series of river journeys where he collected on his own.

When he returned to the United States, Verner made an awkward attempt to sell a collection to the American Museum, having previously sold some objects to the National Museum (Smithsonian) in Washington and to the Field Colombian Museum in Chicago. An unstable man who had a history of mental illness, Verner called on the Director of the American Museum, Dr. H. G. Bumpus early in August, 1906. Claiming that he was en route to St. Louis and would be back very shortly, he cajoled Bumpus into allowing him to leave his collection in the Museum along with two chimpanzees (one of whom had tuberculosis) and the unfortunate Pygmy, Ota Benga (AMNH Archives. Letter from H. G. Bumpus to Dr. C. Wissler, August 7, 1906). After almost a month, the chimpanzees were sent to the Zoo, Verner took Ota Benga to South Carolina, and the collections were seized by a sheriff subsequent to Verner's writing a bad check. Starr meanwhile carried on in Africa and eventually did manage to sell to the museum some of Verner's collection. In the end Starr's obituary depicted him in the mode of a long-lost explorer:

> He led an expedition into the African Congo. He was gone a year on that trip and was not heard from for six months, during which he visited twenty-eight tribes and traveled 22,000 miles. Before the expedition had gone far it dwindled to a Mexican boy and the professor. They continued their wanderings until Dr. Starr was satisfied that he could gain nothing more on that trip. (The *New York Times*, August 15, 1933)

After leaving Mount Washington Starr and Gonzalez began a steamer trip up the Congo River, making stops at the ivory and rubber "factories" along the way. At each station, Starr would collect as many objects as possible and interview whomever he could find on cannibalism, marijuana use, burial customs, scarification and tooth shaping. He documented children's games and collected stories and proverbs.

Despite the fact that the Africans who lived along this route had already been plundered for ivory, rubber, labor, and artifacts, Starr sought out examples of untouched, uncorrupted African life. He scorned Africans who had been tainted by contact with Europeans: "they have been degraded by contact with whites and white-influenced blacks" (Starr *African Diary* 6: 58, May 24, 1906). Once he described "men in excruciating European dress" who "insisted on occupying a prominent place, sitting on benches, which no one else did. We cut them out as far as we could but lost some interesting figures in the effort to do so" (*Diary* 6: 46, May 16, 1906). At best, the White man's influence could lead to curiosities, not collectibles: on May 6, 1906, not far from Leopoldville, he took a walk through adjacent White and African cemeteries and described what have become known as "bottle trees"[10]: "While the graves are clearly made under White man's direction, they are covered with the trunks, pans and basins, demijohns and bottles, some intact but many filled by being perforated or broken. Few have any distinguishing cross or other mark. The whole presents an interesting and curious mixture of old and new, whiteman and negro ideas, Christianity and paganism." (*Diary* 6: 33, May 6, 1906)

HERBERT LANG

In 1908 Herbert Lang was asked to lead a trip to the northeastern Belgian Congo by the President of the American Museum of Natural History, Henry Fairfield Osborn. He was charged with carrying out an exhaustive study of the fauna and flora of this forest–savanna border zone; to bring back exhibition specimens for the Museum's African mammal halls; and to bring back study collections for all departments of the museum. Trained as a taxidermist, but with previous experience as a field guide to a safari hunter in East Africa, Lang went to the northeastern Uele with one assistant – a young ornithology student named James Chapin who eventually became a Curator at the AMNH.

Lang focused on the mammals, Chapin on the birds, invertebrates, reptiles, and insects. Anthropology was something of an afterthought, although because of Lang's developing contact with, and interest in, the people of the region, it came to assume great importance as the expedition proceeded. There was no one on the museum staff at the time with any particular knowledge of, or interest in, Africa. Lang received only brief instructions from the department: Robert Lowie suggested that he bring back evidence of processes of manufacture as well as completed objects, and others urged him to bring back skeletons for the physical anthropology collections. At the same time, photography was high on his personal agenda and he invested his own funds in this endeavor (Schildkrout 1991b).

Lang seems to have done most of the anthropology collecting himself, as the anthropology field notebook is in his handwriting. The collection was made over a six-year period, starting in 1909, a year after the Belgians had taken over the Congo Free State. Because there was no anthropologist to serve as an amanuensis for Lang, as T. A. Joyce did for Emil Torday, for example, Lang was pretty much on his own. Even without explicit instructions from the Anthropology Department to study the Pygmies, they were of interest to Lang because of the notoriety they had assumed at the 1904 St. Louis Exposition; by then the question of their being a possible "missing link" had reached popular consciousness and after his return, Lang did write one article on this subject. But Lang became increasingly fascinated with the Mangbetu and the Azande, and as the months and years went on he began to see himself as someone who was making significant discoveries about African art. Like Torday, Lang envisioned exhibitions of African artifacts that would change the way people viewed Africa.

Lang and Chapin's field notebooks, divided into subjects corresponding to the museum's scientific departments,[11] list each specimen giving native name, date and place of collection, and in the case of artifacts, materials, native use and sometimes manufacturing technique and the price paid. In addition, Lang and Chapin sent back reports and letters to museum administrators and relatives and almost 10,000 photographs with captions keyed to the objects in the collection. Chapin was a watercolorist; in addition to painting birds, plants, and lizards, he copied the bold red, black and white geometric designs on Mangbetu house walls.

Unlike Starr with his Protestant pedigree and proper education, Lang did not have easy access into the scientific or social elite. A German immigrant who never became an American citizen, Lang remained an outsider. He went to grade school in Germany and worked as a taxidermist in Paris before coming to New York. He learned his trade in museums and in the field, ultimately gaining a reputation as a first class zoological field collector. After the discovery of the okapi in 1902, the American Museum decided to launch a two-year collecting and research expedition to the Uele region. Based on Lang and Chapin's reports and pleas from the field, funds were raised to continue the expedition for a further two years. But their pleas for more scientists were ignored, and when World War I broke out, they were still in the field. Lang's return trip on an Allied vessel became problematic; Chapin returned in 1914, and Lang traveled separately a few months later.

After his return to New York, Lang was made Assistant Curator of Mammalogy but his relationship with other curators was never easy. He was possessive about his field notes, particularly in mammalogy, and there were several curators who wanted to use his notes in describing the specimens. With mounting frustration, Lang disappeared during the course of his next expedition, this time to Angola. He moved to South Africa where he became a wildlife photographer. Chapin became an eminent ornithologist and Chair of the Department of Ornithology.

In the course of the Congo expedition, Lang collected almost 4,000 ethnographic artifacts from many groups living in the Uele region. The Anthropology Department had asked him to make collections in physical anthropology as well as ethnology, but he soon abandoned the idea of gathering skeletons, and documented physical types by making casts and measuring and photographing people. Lang wrote that he could not collect skeletons because it was "offensive to the natives." Starr, on the other hand, collected skeletons whenever and wherever he could (McVicker 1989: 221).

For the duration of the expedition, Lang and Chapin had a team of fifteen assistants, most of whom helped trap and hunt animals and prepare specimens. Because they remained in the same general area for over five years, working out of base camps at major villages, they got to know certain individuals well and often obtained items as gifts, through barter, or by commissioning them. Again in contrast to Starr, Lang wrote that during their entire stay in northeastern Congo neither he nor Chapin experienced a single day of illness.[12] Lang's first bout of fever came in Boma just as he was about to come home. Both men attributed their good health to exercise, especially to the fact that they walked thousands of miles and neither one was ever carried on a litter or on the back of a horse or donkey, and to a diet of mainly local food. While they employed many porters to carry collections and supplies back and forth to the west coast (38,000 men by the end of their stay making them perhaps the major employer in the region in the period), they prided themselves on the fact that no African was asked to carry the maximum load allowed by law, and no porter ever deserted or stole from them.

Starr and Gonzalez, on the other hand, were constantly quarreling and both were often sick. Starr reported illnesses at least once a week and was often laid up in bed with fevers, vomiting, weakness, or colds. When he traveled, he was carried on a litter. If his feet got wet, it was a matter of note. Starr spent much of his time persecuting and meting out physical punishments to employees who quarreled with him or with each other. He was often distressed about being robbed or cheated by Africans and he regularly dismissed and rehired servants. He was an overweight man who was fussy about the service he received, the food he ate, and the wine he drank. He took his meals (often described in the diaries) as often as possible in the company of Europeans – traders, missionaries, or Congo Free State functionaries.

MODES OF COLLECTING

Lang and Starr had very different attitudes towards the political situation in the Congo. Starr arrived in the midst of the Congo controversy, and wanted to investigate it. Lang arrived after the Belgian government had taken control and wanted to avoid political controversy as far as possible. Both men saw benefits in colonialism, but whereas Lang thought that some Africans would benefit from education and contact with Western civilization, Starr subscribed to the prevalent "degeneracy theory" (Coombes 1994: 39–42) and saw biological limits to African progress. Control, not education, was the right approach in Starr's view.

When informants' responses conflicted with Starr's theories about objects or customs he dismissed them as "mistakes." For example, on one occasion when he was collecting "fetishes," he dismissed the native explanation with the comment: "The explanation given was that the figures were male and female, which they were not" (*Diary* 2: 48, November 30, 1905). Lang, in contrast, frequently entered questions in his notes and acknowledged his ignorance. He attempted to get native explanations for much of what he collected, offering little interpretation, although once back in New York when he began writing popular articles, interpretations, embellishment, and conjecture flowed much more freely.[13] While Starr remained the skeptic and dismissed information that did not accord with theories derived from evolutionary paradigms, Lang had little in the way of theory to fall back on and was more gullible and prone to believe whatever his informants told him. The Africa that Lang thus portrayed in his popular articles was a mixture of commonplace late nineteenth-century evolutionary assumptions, empirical observation, and the myths and stories given to him by African informants.

Gossip was (and is) a major source of information for all traveler/explorer/collectors, and Starr's diaries illustrate how tips from fellow travelers shaped his itinerary and collecting. On the boat from Belgium, in the mission stations, and on the seven-month steamer trip, gossip was a source of information and misinformation. Starr thus began his field-work on the boat from Brussels, gathering a confabulation of lore about native life. Most important were clues about what, where and for how much "the best" artifacts could be found. Europeans regularly compared their collections, gave each other artifacts as gifts, and compared prices. According to Starr, the relative worth of artifacts was the most frequent topic of conversation among visitors to his house. Criticism of Frobenius was common since "the German" had recently been through the area paying what were considered to be outrageous prices for 10,000 artifacts. He alone raised the price of "bell hairpins" from ten centimes to one piece of cloth (*Diary* 6: 7–8, April 4, 1906). When Starr finally met Frobenius, to his surprise he liked him and admired his work (*Diary* 6: 43, April 15, 1906).

When Starr and Gonzalez first arrived at Verner's Mount Washington camp, an hour's walk from the village of the Kuba chief Ndombe and half an hour's walk from the Luba village of chief Chicoma, they found over a hundred people at the camp, either serving as staff or hoping for work. "About one hundred men are on the place, many of them rene-gades, vagrants etc. from all the surrounding country. The number will swell to any size if desirable and encouraged. A considerable number from villages are coming in and giving truly good labor" (*Diary* 3: 40, December 29, 1905). Starr complained about having to manage the per-sonnel, but he soon took over and began intimidating the staff to the point that there were frequent "runaways" and "mutinies." For three months, Starr and Gonzalez lived in Verner's house and occasionally visited local villages. More often, Africans would come to the house to trade, to listen to recordings, to look at the stereopticon, and even to sample European food. At these sessions Starr made impressions of their teeth, recorded them playing instruments or singing, watched them dance, and engaged in fierce bargaining for objects. Manuel Gonzalez took photographs.

Certain chiefs, especially Ndombe and the Baluba Chief Chicoma, returned again and again with objects. Starr soon had many of these chiefs indebted to him, leading them to collect and commission objects to repay the debts (*Diary* 5: January 26, 1906). Sometimes they paid for advances of cloth with cowries, sometimes with artifacts. All of these transactions involved lengthy negotiation but always followed a pattern, progressing from the exchange of "gifts," to the settlement of debts, to the purchase of artifacts.

While Starr stayed at Verner's headquarters, Verner was usually out collecting artifacts. Their relations quickly became strained and in the end Verner returned with fewer than the 9,000 commissioned pieces. Starr and Gonzalez then embarked on their river journey and began their own collecting. The steamer made regular wood stops to collect fuel at the European stations, some with mission stations, that dotted the river. The two men made short sojourns to nearby villages, where they would try to buy as many artifacts as possible, or, preferring the comforts of the boat, they would send out a call for artifacts. On the occasion of a visit to a Bateke village, for example, he notes, "I greeted them all, told them that I was perhaps going to be unable to come to each and every of their villages, but that I would be glad to have them come to see me and that I was buying all kinds of things" (*Diary* 2: 46, November 30, 1905). In many instances it was left to the villagers to decide what to offer for sale.

Because Starr planned to sell the collection, his diaries contain many references to what pieces might interest museums.[14] He was in the Congo before Belgian currency was used as a medium of exchange and he bartered with salt, cloth, iron bars, tobacco, cowries, and beads. As Nicholas Thomas notes, barter, especially on the colonial periphery, served as a means of defining ethnic difference and distance (Thomas 1991: 217). In his diaries Starr notes the "price" paid for almost every object and in many instances recorded the negotiations, but prices could be in goods, or European currency.[15] Starr became annoyed when pure market conditions didn't prevail, for example when he couldn't buy on Sundays because of agreements he had made with missionaries (*Diary* 2: 52, December 3, 1905).

Bargaining was an intense power struggle, and Starr would often pass up an artifact if the price was too high. At other times, he would go through a large inventory of his stock and barter until he found something that a reluctant seller would accept (*Diary* 5: 60, March 1, 1906; 7: 9, March 6, 1906; 7: 10, March 10, 1906). Sometimes he lost the finest pieces since he had no way of understanding the values that Africans put on their objects. On one occasion a Kuba chief came with a gift of ten fowls and a Luba *lukasa* board with a finely carved head. But Starr wouldn't pay the "piece" (of cloth) demanded and lost the board (*Diary* 5: 17, January 31, 1906).

While these transactions were a microcosm of power struggles taking place between Europeans and Africans, because the suppliers were Africans, this was one arena where the Africans had the possibility of partially defining the terms of trade. One day when a Dutchman named Adriaance, an employee of the Kasai Company was visiting, Starr noted:

> Chicoma came during the afternoon. He carefully picked out an inferior arrow which he presented me and then asked for tobacco. I gauged the tobacco to the arrow and he gave evident signs of dissatisfaction. Thereupon I returned his arrow and the tobacco and told Calama to tell him that I had a black heart over the transaction; that when he wished to *sell* [emphasis in original] me things he could bring them and I would haggle with him over prices. Adriance [sic] broke in "but this man is not telling him what you said! he says you are a bad white man and that he had better not come any more to see you." All of which is not particularly favorable to pleasant dealings with natives hereafter. (*Diary* 5: 3, January 19, 1906)

ART, COMMERCE, AND THE IDEA OF AUTHENTICITY

As time went on Starr's ethnographic observations became more detailed and toward the end of the trip he began to record vocabulary, proverbs, and folk tales. However, since he never spent a long time in any one place, he never got to know any person or society well. As we would expect, most of Starr's data were based on visual observation. His notes describe architecture, body adornment, the physical movements of people in dance or ritual. As McVicker (1989: 226) notes, Starr always remained a "museum person" in the sense that physical objects stood for groups of people or cultures. Ethnography was collecting and artifacts were the evidence which could be used to document stages of cultural evolution.

Starr had very definite notions about authenticity and this must have had some effect on the production of art. Collectors were able to communicate their preferences to suppliers, and these criteria were easily translated into exchange values. Starr had two main criteria by which he determined value: whether objects showed European influence (a negative value) and whether they represented African tradition as he defined it (a positive value). The latter related to the age of the object and to whether it looked used. Because Starr operated through middlemen who brought him objects from outlying villages – or from behind the next tree in the very same village – he was dependent on these people for obtaining and producing objects that met these criteria. But Starr distrusted what the middlemen told him and in some cases he seemed to know he was buying fakes, objects that were produced and finished specifically to meet his demands.

> Fetishes were too plenty and too fresh to be entirely satisfactory . . . Yesterday a well-carved wooden figure was offered. I refused it because it was rather new and empty [of medicine] in its stomach hole. Today it appeared again, this time with a fat round belly neatly sewed up and well smeared with cam and oil. I agreed to the price, getting it down to 1.50 francs. (*Diary* 2: 54–55, December 4, 1905)

Starr sometimes rejected objects that were "too old" because they were in poor condition. His criteria were similar to those of many modern-day collectors: the most valuable objects, particularly those associated with ritual life, needed to show signs of use, while even utilitarian objects should show signs of wear.[16] In Starr's view, it was all right to commission the manufacture of a musical bow that could be used to demonstrate a particular form of instrument, but not a fetish that had to have a history of ritual use (*Diary* 5: 36, February 15, 1906).

These nuances were not always clear to Verner who began to collect new examples of the same types of masks and figures that had passed muster as authentic. Africans understood Starr's criteria better than Verner did and in some cases deliberately added material confirmation of use and wear. As a result, Verner's collection includes totally new masks: honest objects but ones that become "fakes" according to Starr's criteria. Even though Starr himself sometimes turned items away because he believed them to be of poor quality, or because they were made for sale, the fact is that he encouraged faking in his determination to purchase vast quantities of "authentic" masks and fetishes. The commodification of artifacts in 1906 led to the commissioning of "fakes" exactly in the same way as occurs in 1996 (Steiner 1994). At a certain point, Starr realized that the process had possibly gone too far, defeating his own collecting agenda:

> I felt really badly when four little fellows came from Ndombe loaded down with beautiful new figures which they had prepared with much care, painting them fresh and bright and sticking feathers in them. We

had already begun to be worried with these new ones innocently made, as with little gourds carefully filled with fresh "medicine" and with cowries stuck on top of the mass. Now we had to draw the line and refused most of them . . . we were all day refusing nice new fetishes, . . . almost all they had were refused. (*Diary* 5: 249–50, February 11, 1906)

Starr then noted that they later "brought old figures, profiting by yesterday's lesson."

The requirement that an authentic object had to be made for African use and actually be used by Africans developed simultaneously in the first decade of this century with the great increase in demand for objects by foreigners. The demand was met by Africans who began forging authenticity and even by Europeans who made objects for sale to Africans, in African styles. These were then sold back to European collectors of ethnographic artifacts. On several occasions Starr was about to purchase well-made African-looking knives only to discover that these were being made in Europe for export to Africa!

Starr never questioned his own criteria of authenticity or his ability to discern the "real" object. But the objects he commissioned from Verner were more of a problem since he felt Verner did not have a discriminating eye and evaluated artifacts by count and cubic feet. "Verner writes he has 100 cubic feet of packed collections" (*Diary* 5: 18, February 2, 1906). However, "as for the stuff he is sending in, much is worthless. Thus, out of twenty bows less than eight were in condition for museum use; the three or four baskets have no recommendation except age, which in baskets (except of some California faddists) does not count" (*Diary* 5: 5, January 22, 1906). Later the two men quarreled because Verner had not collected enough: "While he had got some good things I was disappointed both in quantity and quality. After the Lukengu trip, when he ought to have known quite well how things were going, he told me he had 3000 articles in my collection and ought to get twice as many on the next trip" (*Diary* 7: 42, March 27, 1906). In fact, Starr complained, the objects Verner sent numbered "only 1000" (*Diary* 7: 42, March 27, 1906). Verner went without Starr to collect among the Pende and when he returned he claimed to have 406 Pende and Chokwe specimens. Starr added many of these pieces to the collection that ended up in the American Museum of Natural History even though he recognized some of them to be of inferior quality and made for sale.

Besides the written evidence contained in Starr's diaries, the Pende mask collection itself, now in the American Museum of Natural History, shows that by 1905 a European-dominated and defined commerce in "traditional" art was flourishing in southern Congo. By 1906, Pende masks were already a known quantity among Europeans. The day the Dutchman Adriaance visited Starr, Verner's first two shipments arrived (the first, on the backs of forty-two carriers). Starr wrote that Adriaance:

> at once urged my writing to M. Bertrand [a Congo Free State agent in the Pende area] to secure me things from the Bampende and Bachoko. He says the Bampende are famous for masks; the regular prices for which have been from one fathom of cloth for smaller ones to one piece for the larger and finer ones. Dr. Frobenius raised prices at least temporarily and took out seven cases of masks. As for the Bachoko he says they are noted for their fine chairs, cut from one block of good wood, and for baskets. (*Diary* 5: 2–3, January 19, 1906)

It is not surprising that Starr had great difficulty understanding the place of improvisation in African culture. If artifacts stood for tradition, with the "authentic" ones serving to both symbolize and stabilize it, music, performance and verbal art presented even greater problems because of their tendency to change continuously right before the observer's eyes. Starr would play records on his phonograph and then attempt to record African music. On one occasion he asked a man to recite the words of a song so he could write them down. The singer kept changing the words:

> We have had a dreadful time over Tumba's song. Ever since we made the record of it, I have intended to write the words. I found I could do nothing with him, tho I tried him repeatedly. He was eternally introducing new and before unknown lines or dislocating lines already written and to stop him in the middle of a line was pure suicide; he could not resume.

Finally Starr had one of his servants sing the song, "But in all this there was little of the original song except in tune – none of the choruses or side trimmings. I believe the whole thing was improvised. He could not have repeated it on order if his life had depended upon it." In his view the man simply "couldn't get it right." (*Diary* 9: 10, July 10, 1906).

The idea that there was a "right" version was based on Starr's assumption that there was a definitive and archetypal version of African culture and that authenticity represented cultural stasis. Improvisation and creativity in the African present was antithetical to the idea that progress occurred in civilized places.

LANG AS ETHNOGRAPHIC COLLECTOR

Although Lang had read Schweinfurth (1874, 1875), Junker (1890, 1891, 1892), and Casati (1891a, 1891b), the nineteenth-century visitors to the Mangbetu, and had been instructed by the American Museum to collect all kinds of artifacts, in all stages of manufacture, he had little idea of what to look for. Like Starr he went with preconceptions, not so much about the nature of African culture, but about African biological inferiority to Whites. It is in this context that one has to understand his expressions of astonishment and amazement at what he found. Like Starr, but in quite different ways, Lang influenced the production of artifacts by creating a certain kind of transactional context that valued some types of objects more than others. As Curtis Keim and I have shown (Schildkrout and Keim 1990a), the admiration that Lang and others in the area expressed for anthropomorphic art clearly influenced the production of certain forms, as well as the preference for certain materials, especially ivory.[17]

The forms and quantity of art produced in northeastern Congo had been changing since Schweinfurth's visit, and change escalated with the influx of more Europeans. Wood, ivory and ceramic objects adorned with naturalistic representations of the Mangbetu had not been described by nineteenth-century authors, but became increasingly common in the first two decades of the twentieth century. Whereas in recent years these carvings have been described as representations of ancestors, particularly deceased kings and queens, and bark boxes have been described as relic containers, there is no evidence that these objects had any spiritual significance. Lang had no problem accepting informants' statements that these were purely secular works. At the same time, he was fascinated by the medicinal and magical attributes of visually simple and unadorned charms, medicines, plants, divination sticks and whistles.

In his initial collecting, Lang simply acquired (usually in exchange for salt, beads and metal wire) whatever objects of daily use people were willing to offer. He later made a conscious effort to acquire objects in all stages of manufacture, tool kits, and photographic documentation of the production process. Lang's collecting agenda developed in the field. Unlike Starr, Lang did not censor the collections for "quality" although he sometimes noted when something seemed to be a fine example. He collected sculpture in much the same way as he collected specimens of fauna and flora.

Lang's field notes, which were meant to accompany the collection, consist of a consecutive list of objects with descriptions and "native terms." This was the same method he used for zoological specimens: recording the provenance, native name, and any other descriptive information he gathered from informants and assistants. Only on rare occasions do his notes include personal comments or anecdotes about his own adventures. He assumes the stance of the objective observer and attempts thereby to achieve a level of scientific objectivity. Personal comments can be found in the letters and reports Lang sent back from the field and in some of the articles Lang wrote for the popular press after his return (Lang 1918, 1919), but not in his field notebooks.

Lang recognized that he and Chapin were in many ways dependent on good relations with Africans. Their objective was to stay in one area and study it in detail and this required a welcoming community and dedicated staff. By the end of his stay he had formed relationships based on trust with many Africans, some of whom he came to admire greatly. This affected the collection in many ways: Queen Nenzima gave him a necklace made of her fingernail cuttings in exchange for a charm that incorporated his nail cuttings. Ivory carvers made him a set of forks and spoons to replace his crude pewter ware. There is no evidence in any of Lang's notes that objects were coerced from people, nor that he put people into debt to him to get them to produce quantities of artifacts.

It was not that Lang was immune from notions of European superiority, but rather that he was drawn into the community and dependent upon Africans in a way that contrasted with the behavior of most Europeans at the time. With little in the way of anthropological theory to guide his ethnographic research, he was truly surprised by the way in which the reality he encountered conflicted with his preconceptions. He did not expect to find the kind of metal working or ivory carving that he found, and his letters to the museum comment at length on the abilities and talents of the African smiths, carvers, trappers, and hunters. He believed that his "discovery" of this artwork would show people in America that at least some African societies were on a par with Western and Asian civilizations. Lang saw art and artistry as a sign of Civilization, and when he encountered this in Africa, he began to re-examine his ideas about the relationship between Africa and the West:

> The real jewels among this ethnographic material are doubtless the several hundred most beautiful objects of carved ivory. Many of them are so delicate and of such high artistic composition that neither the scientist nor the public would define them at once as products from a Central African Negro country, especially so, as other Museums possess in this line relatively few and unimportant examples. They will prove a revelation with regard to estimating at their fair value the capacities of the perfectly uneducated negro. They show the great care their authors have bestowed upon them, and conclusively prove that the negro artist is able to vary his really handsome conceptions within an unusually wide range. They also demonstrate a certain concentration of their faculties, happily assisted by an ambition of accomplishing the very best. (Congo Expedition Report 21, December 7, 1914:20)

INNOVATION AND IDEAS OF PRIMITIVISM

Unlike Starr, Lang celebrated innovation and saw it as evidence of Africans' ability to learn, adapt, and acquire the trappings of civilization. The most obvious examples were the intricately carved open-work ivory forks, spoons, knives, and models that were made for him. But more significant is the entire genre of anthropomorphic art which flourished around and after the period of the American Museum of Natural History Congo Expedition.[18] Even though Mangbetu-style anthropomorphic art was subsequently seen by many collectors and museums as examples of "traditional" art, there is no evidence that the collectors of the time saw it that way. Lang, for one, was quite clear that certain forms of "art pottery" were new developments, and he also noted the innovations that were taking place in ivory carving and painting. Incised drawings on gourd and ivory, bark cloth paintings, representational banana leaf appliqués on women's aprons, and house paintings, were increasingly incorporating images of Europeans. Some of the wood sculpture Lang collected incorporates Western dress and Western objects like guns and cartridge belts. Lang collected these pieces as "art" and remarked on the originality of the artists' conceptions. Perhaps because he did not see himself as an anthropologist, he never thought about this work as a violation of tradition.

Elsewhere Curtis Keim and I (Schildkrout and Keim 1990a, 1990b; Schildkrout, Hellman and Keim 1989) have described the emergence of anthropomorphic art among the Mangbetu in the first quarter of the twentieth century. While boxes, pots, knives, musical instruments, and furniture adorned with sculpted heads existed in northeastern Congo before Westerners collected them, the new demand in the colonial period gave the artists of the region new opportunities. Certain genres, for example figurative pottery with representations of Mangbetu women, were based on earlier regional forms, but they were produced in greater numbers once the market began. These objects, whether elaborations of older forms, as in the case of pots or musical instruments, or totally new forms like steamer chairs, napkin rings, and letter-openers, contained formulaic representations of Mangbetu men and women with their elongated heads and carefully dressed hair.[19] In his determination to collect every example of artistry and material culture, Lang collected these new objects along with perfectly mundane and unadorned objects that were in daily use. He considered the innovative objects "art" whereas the rest was ethnography, and unlike Starr he was not bothered by the idea of European contamination. He celebrated the craftsmanship and skill of the artists and saw it as evidence of an innate African intelligence. While I would not argue that Lang came to Africa without prejudice, I would argue that his outlook was affected by his experience.

Even though Lang himself celebrated innovation, this did not prevent the artists and the art purchasers from reifying tradition in a visual trope. The elongated Mangbetu woman's head, often with bare-breasted torso, became a symbol of Mangbetu ethnicity and of the exotic and erotic African (woman).[20] While Starr rejected innovation and saw it as evidence of the corruption of (primitive) African culture by Europeans, he gave a variation of the same message to local artists – that their most saleable commodity was a representation of Africa coinciding with Western ideas of the primitive. In both instances tradition was constructed and art, whether innovative or derivative, was affected by the Western perception of Africa. The question that remains is whether these different messages had similar or different effects on the local art.

FAKES AND TOURIST ART

Lang's visit and collecting agenda encouraged a certain type of new art that could awkwardly be described as a form of "proto-tourist art," art produced in the "contact zone" of the early colonial period.[21] Starr, on the other hand, with his very different agenda, encouraged the production of what would today be seen as "fakes" – objects made to simulate artifacts that were used in contexts "uncontaminated" by foreign influence.

In northeastern Congo the anthropomorphic art that flourished in the early colonial period ceased to be produced by the 1930s with the passing of the generation of artists that responded to the new demands.[22] The Mangbetu-style objects that one finds in African art collections today were mostly made in the early colonial period and explicitly express, in their forms and iconography, a moment in the changing development of the arts of this region. Some of the masks that Starr and Verner collected, on the other hand, present a different set of issues. Because many of these were made expressly for collectors, but were not given the look of age and use, Starr regarded them as inferior examples. He nonetheless included them in the collection he sold to the American Museum of Natural History. In museum storage, these masks still look today as if they were made yesterday, despite the fact that they are some of the oldest documented examples of art from the Congo. They are masks in the process of manufacture – neither aged by use nor given a false finish. But to scholars, they are nonetheless important because in the details of their iconography they show how Africans chose to represent themselves to Westerners in 1905–06. In southern Congo, collecting continued and demand never ceased, partly because the area produced a wide variety of masks and sculptures for indigenous use. How much influence the kind of collecting Starr and others like him had on the region is an open question, far beyond the scope of this essay.

Whereas Lang thought about art, and acknowledged African pieces as art, Starr did not. To him, the "good" African pieces were good because they conformed to his idea of authenticity and represented the African primitive. Always an evolutionist, Starr saw these pieces as crude evidence of African backwardness. Starr literally had an intellectual and financial investment in collecting examples of culture which accorded with this view. For Lang, one purpose of collecting ethnographic artifacts was to enable the Museum to address the "negro question" in its exhibitions. By this he meant that the collections would show "scientists and the public" that Africans, even without formal [Western] education and the trappings of European social class, were human beings who could become as civilized as White men. Such a notion would have been anathema to Starr who never seemed to conceive of Africans as anything other than examples of the primitive.

In the end, is there anything to be said about the question posed at the beginning of this essay: the differing methodologies and paradigms of Lang, the biologist/zoologist, and Starr, the anthropologist? Clearly the anthropologist comes out the worse in this case, with misconceived notions of authenticity leading to the production of fakes. The zoologist, more naive about African culture, induces local artists to produce a genre of innovative art that, had there been a market in northeastern Congo, might have burgeoned into tourist art. In the end, there may still be something left to the question of disciplinary influences, but with a major *caveat* – Starr represented a brand of Victorian anthropology soon to be left behind as the discipline moved further and further from evolutionary biology. Starr cannot be taken as a representative of modern anthropological thinking, but rather, as a Social Darwinist who freely used biological metaphors to describe cultural evolution. Lang was a biologist but above all a field collector, not a theorist. At least while he was in the field – the period from which his collection and related documentation come – he shied away from metaphor and did not accept, nor perhaps even think about, the grand theories of cultural evolution. As an empirical field collector, with few theories about cultural evolution and about the relationship between race and culture, he was more open to accepting African explanations of the meaning of objects. In both instances, however, African informants, artists, and suppliers seemed to understand the collecting agendas of the Europeans and furnished objects and information that fed into their paradigms. In this instance, however, perhaps because Lang was an empiricist and Starr an unreconstructed social evolutionist, the enterprise of ethnographic collecting was less tainted by association with biological field collecting than it was by the anthropologist's need to reify the primitive.

NOTES

1 Despite pressure on Lang to adopt the paradigm of eugenics that pervaded anthropology at that time, I would argue that his approach to African creativity and the production of material culture implicitly rejected the arguments of the eugenics movements. In this I take issue with Nicholas Mirzoeff who, in my view, misreads Lang's photographs and writings by looking only at selective publications and not the entire corpus of his work. Lang was not a "eugenic anthropologist" (Mirzoeff 1996: 42); in fact he was not trained and did not claim to be either an ethnologist or a [biological] anthropologist.

2 There have been many critiques and discussions of these notions including those by Clifford 1988; Kasfir 1984, 1992; Schildkrout and Keim 1990a; Steiner 1994; Vansina 1984. Nevertheless, in galleries and exhibitions where knowledge about the African context is secondary to the experience and commodification of art, this ethnic style typology is still invoked: see for example the literature referring to the exhibition mounted in 1995–96 at the Royal Academy of Art in London (Phillips1996, and the critique by Beidelman 1997).

3 See, among other relevant works: Barber 1987; Graburn 1976; Phillips and Steiner forthcoming; Pratt 1992; Vogel 1991.

4 His obituary in the *New York Times*, August 15, 1933, erroneously referred to him as "curator of ethnological subjects." He never held that title.

5 For a discussion of the rivalry and intellectual rivalry between Starr and Boas see McVicker 1989.

6 Coombes (1994) argues, with regard to Britain in the same period, that it was in its attempt to use popular presentations like museums and expositions that anthropology most retarded its own development.

7 The newspaper articles were published in book form as *The Truth About the Congo: The Chicago Tribune Articles* (Starr 1907).

8 These notes, with other Starr papers, are in the Regenstern Library, University of Chicago.

9 Gordon Gibson, Curator Emeritus at the National Museum of Natural History, has noted that the documentation provided with Verner's collection in the Smithsonian is also minimal. Gibson, unpublished paper (1990).

10 See R. F. Thompson 1993.

11 At that time he collected for the departments of mammalogy, herpetology, entomology, ornithology, and ichthyology in addition to anthropology.

12 The normal tour of duty for a European in the Congo at the time was a maximum of two years, and many people were afraid of staying longer.

13 As in Lang 1918, 1919.

14 McVicker (1986: 9) describes how Starr collected Mexican artifacts in the years before going to Africa. It was the sale of these problematic antiquities to the Field Museum in Chicago that financed Starr's African trip.

15 Guyer (1993) uses Starr's diaries to suggest that the manipulation of different kinds of currencies were being used to stabilize value in this period.

16 Consideration has been given to modern manifestations of these issues by among others Clifford 1988, Price 1989, and Steiner 1994, but little attention has been paid to early instances of such practices, partly because of the confabulation of age and authenticity.

17 Not all of the objects that were produced to fulfill Western commissions were collectible: the most noteworthy example of a non-portable object is the monumental building that was constructed on the model of King Mbunza's hall that Schweinfurth had described four decades earlier (see Schildkrout and Keim 1990a: especially 104, 143).

18 Lang and Chapin were not the only collectors in the region at the time. The Belgian Armand Hutereau, from the Musée royal de l'Afrique centrale, collected approximately 12,000 objects, and administrators and traders collected even more. See Schildkrout and Keim 1990a for further discussion of this.

19 In the Musée royal de l'Afrique centrale in Tervuren, for example, there is a folding steamer chair modeled on a European chair, adorned with heads and feet wearing shoes. Ivory hairpins that usually had simple discs and geometric finials were produced with multiple heads. Objects made expressly for Westerners, like ivory letter-openers, forks and spoons, often had heads on them.

20 See Schildkrout (forthcoming in Phillips and Steiner) for further discussion of eroticism in Mangbetu art.

21 From this perspective, Portuguese ivories of the fifteenth century are tourist art. Neither the Portuguese ivories nor the Mangbetu art discussed here were marketed to a mass and anonymous audience, but both were produced in the context of the interaction between Africans and foreigners.

22 One reason for this is that there never was a significant settler population in the area, the demise of local chiefs who acted as middlemen between artists and consumers, and the worldwide depression followed by World War I that affected the economy of the region.

EIGHT

Where art and ethnology met
The Ward African Collection at the Smithsonian

MARY JO ARNOLDI

⑥

The Herbert Ward collection is atypical when compared with other African collections housed at the Smithsonian in the opening decades of this century. The Ward collection would have been noteworthy for the fact alone that it was the largest single African collection to have been donated to the Smithsonian, numbering 2,714 objects. Perhaps more importantly the ethnographic objects and zoological specimens were all collected from a single geographical region in the Congo. What is singular, however, about Ward's collection is that it also included seventeen bronze sculptures, most depicting Congolese peoples, that Ward had sculpted between 1901 and 1911.[1] In accepting this collection, the Smithsonian agreed to keep it – Congo objects, zoological specimens, and the bronzes – intact and to put the collection on public display in its entirety and in perpetuity. The Ward exhibit opened in 1922 and remained on public view with only minor modifications until it was dismantled in the early 1960s.[2]

The Ward exhibit was clearly an anomaly when compared to the other ethnographic exhibits extant at the Smithsonian. After the founding of public museums in the eighteenth century a new public display style began to emerge which differed significantly from fashionable installations of private collections. Private displays were dominated by sensory values and their many assorted and sundry objects were generally installed together primarily to create a pleasing decorative effect. Museums by contrast were more concerned with organizing the materials according to systems and rules governing the taxonomies of objects, although they did not wholly abandon an interest in the aesthetics of display. Curators clearly intended their exhibits to be pedagogical and to teach important lessons in the natural sciences, the history of art or – beginning in the late nineteenth century – in anthropology (Fisher 1975: 590). By at least the 1880s an overwhelming bias towards taxonomic classification dominated the ethnographic displays at the Smithsonian.

The Ward collection and its exhibition broke with the conventional wisdom. Art and ethnology and private and public exhibit styles came together in a novel way. Thousands of Congo objects, classified and studied as ethnological specimens, were installed with bronze sculptures, which the curators defined as fine art objects. The first forty years of the Ward collection's institutional history involved it being continually on view and this public gaze shaped in significant ways collecting and interpreting the Congo at the Smithsonian. The juxtaposition of the collection's ethnographic specimens and its fine art sculptures in a single gallery and the drama that the curators achieved through lighting effects, color choices, and the decorative arrangement of objects on the gallery walls did not go unnoticed by the public. The collection created a powerful narrative about Africa where the impressionistic and intimate voice of the artist/collector existed if somewhat uneasily alongside the dispassionate voice of the museum scientist.

HERBERT WARD AND THE MAKING OF THE CONGO COLLECTION

Herbert Ward amassed a large number of Congo objects between 1884–89 when he worked in the Congo Free State. Ward, who was born in London in 1863, left home at the age of fifteen and traveled first to New Zealand and Australia, later to Borneo, and finally to the Congo. In his first years in the Congo he was employed in the transport division of the Association Africaine Internationale; later he worked for the Sanford Exploring Company, an American trading concession; and in his final year he joined the ill-fated Rear Guard of Henry Morton Stanley's Emin Pasha Relief Expedition.

An element of trophy collecting certainly motivated the making of his collection. Sixty-four percent of the collection (1,733 objects) consists of weaponry of various types. Throughout the eighteenth and nineteenth centuries, collections of African and other non-Western weapons were regularly made by Europeans and they constituted a logical and desirable category for collecting because they were such potent symbols of conquest and domination. Yet, I suspect that Ward's interest in Congo weapons was also shaped by principles which had guided collectors of natural history specimens throughout the nineteenth century.

Ward's great-grandfather was a leading London taxidermist and his grandfather, Henry Ward, also a taxidermist, traveled on collecting expeditions with James Audubon to the United States in 1828 and 1831 (Adams 1966: 385; Ford 1964: 246). Edwin Ward, Herbert's father, was described in family accounts as a distinguished naturalist (S. Ward 1927: 4). Considering his family's long and keen interest in natural history and the size and nature of his own collection, Herbert Ward probably shared their passion and must have developed a fairly good working knowledge of the principles of natural history taxonomy.

The sheer numbers and groupings of Congolese weapons in the collection strongly suggest that his collecting impulses went far beyond acquiring weapons only as highly charged symbols of European domination, and was at least loosely intended to be a scientific exercise. His collection includes thirty-two examples of shield types and hundreds of spears, bows and arrows, and knives. Ward collected multiple examples and variations on the major types of Congolese weapons and in some cases carefully labeled pieces as to place of origin or point of collection.

The availability of weapons, their durability, as well as the ease with which they could be acquired must also have influenced Ward's collecting program. In the 1880s in the Congo knives, spears, bows, and arrows were plentiful. They were standard tools, the primary hunting implements, and weapons of warfare and defense. Some types were used as currency, while others were important objects of status and prestige. For the Congolese weapons had monetary, practical, and social value and were important items within regional exchange systems among various groups. Ward's collecting ambitions and his particular interest in collecting weapons of all varieties would have merely inserted him into an already existing trade network.

Besides satisfying his typological interests Ward was also strongly drawn to these weapons for purely aesthetic reasons. The diversity of their forms and the variety of decoration incised, engraved, and embossed on these weapons clearly appealed to his artistic sensibilities.

Reflecting on the Congo and on his collection in 1910, he wrote: "They [the Congolese] all appeared to possess the sense of form, a fact that is proved by their truly artistic productions both in their weapons and in the carving of their wooden idols" (Ward 1910: 218). As a practicing artist, his attention to the formal and decorative qualities of these Congo materials could also have been aroused by the many popular theories about the evolution of art.

In addition to weapons Ward also assembled more than 800 other Congolese objects. There are well over thirty carved wooden figures, satisfying Ward's curio, typological, and artistic desires and interests. He also assembled hundreds of objects from other well-established ethnographic categories. He acquired costumes and textiles, jewelry and ornamentation, musical instruments, basketry, pottery, and other domestic wares. He seems to have consciously selected these objects in order to document different techniques of manufacture, and sought out examples made from the full range of local materials including metal, ivory, stone, wood, clay, leather, gourd, tree bark, grasses, and cotton.

In the catalogue which he prepared of his collection, Ward numbered the pieces individually or by lots and organized them according to geographical or ethnic groupings (Gordon Gibson Papers, National Anthropological Archives, Smithsonian Institution). Geographical groupings, organized under the rubric of trading and mission station locations, by administrative districts or by rivers, predominate in his catalogue. For Ward and other Europeans in the Congo in the 1880s, the river systems and the trade and mission stations along these systems constituted the primary European cognitive map of the area. While ethnicity played a role it was a far less important role in the 1880s for classifying peoples and their material culture than it would shortly become at the turn of the century when the power of the Belgian colonial administration increased. Twenty-six objects in the catalogue are identified as Mongalla, which is a tributary of the Congo river and ninety-five objects are identified as Kasai, also a major river and region. Ward did use a few ethnic designations and these ethnic names were those commonly used by Europeans in the Congo at the time. They included Bakongo, Bangala, Baluba, and Mongbettu (Mangbetu).

The actual size of his field collection is yet to be determined. In 1887 just prior to taking his last post with Stanley's expedition, he prepared eight loads to be shipped back to England including three boxes of curios and papers, natural history trophies packed in canvas, and a bundle of spears and a bundle of shields (S. Ward 1927: 67). Ward's travels extended from the coast up to Stanley Falls (above present-day Kisangani), yet many of the objects in his collection came from outside his direct experience. Diary entries indicate he did exchange objects with local peoples, but he also traded items with other Europeans that he had met along the river. The trading and mission stations along the Congo river and its tributaries were certainly termini for objects coming from extensive internal networks and he would probably have acquired at least some of these objects at the various river stations.

Once he returned to Europe, Ward continued to collect. He probably bought items from fellow Congo travelers or exchanged objects with them. He might have also acquired objects from ethnographic dealers in London and Paris. According to his widow, Sarita Ward, he added appreciably to this core collection while in Europe (Ward 1927: 165). It is particularly noteworthy that the focus of his collecting remained the Congo even when large numbers of ethnographic items from British and French West African colonies were making their way into Europe (Coombes 1994; Paudrat 1984). His interest in acquiring only Central African objects strongly suggests that he intended to enlarge and refine his object typologies, and that his collecting program was still intimately tied to his personal experience in the Congo.

THE WARD BRONZES: VIGNETTES OF CONGO LIFE

Following his return from Africa, Ward began a career first as a writer and lecturer about his Congo experiences, only later did he choose fine arts as his vocation. In 1893 he began formal art training and in 1900 he turned his hand to sculpture. Throughout his artistic career Ward used the Congolese as his primary subject matter.

Exotic subjects enjoyed a certain popularity in artistic circles in Europe in the nineteenth and early twentieth centuries and Ward was one of a number of painters and sculptors who achieved success working with African subjects (Roquebert 1994: 5–32; Thornton 1990). His handling of materials and form and the naturalism of his sculptures met the academic standards of his day (Fig. 8.1). The regular acceptance of his works in the annual Paris Salon, whose judges awarded him several prizes, and the

8.1 Herbert Ward in his Paris studio *c.* 1911. In the foreground is the model for "The Fire Maker" (1911) and in the background is the "The Charm Doctor" (1902).

acquisition of his sculptures by both fine art and natural history museums attest to the general regard that his work enjoyed.

Although his formal style is wholly academic, his treatment of the Congolese subject matter vacillates between two extremes: allegory and scientific illustration. "Sleeping Africa," an early work, and "Distress," his

8.2 "Sleeping Africa" (1902) by Herbert Ward.

last sculpture, are both clearly allegorical. "Sleeping Africa" represents a reclining female with her arm thrown over her face. She is semi-nude and lying on top of the map of the African continent (Fig. 8.2). This work draws its inspiration from two well-known and long-standing European artistic conceits: the long-standing representation of the continents as female, and the slumbering "primitive," an image with a certain popular currency that served to represent the supposed backwardness and ignorance of the continent (Connelly 1995: 16–18).

"Distress" (Fig. 8.3) is a representation of a nude African man which was described as the Incarnation of the Tragedy of the Congo (Ward 1927: 169). The figure's attitude is acutely expressive. The head is bowed and the back and shoulders hunched forward. The arms are pulled forward, elbows bent and forearms crossed in front of the chest with hands clasping the body. Here, Ward chose the common European dramaturgical gesture for grief, which has its roots in the classical period, was revived in the Renaissance, and had been used regularly since that period in theater and art.

At the other end of this spectrum are two bronze busts, "The Bakongo Girl" and "The Aruimi Type" (Fig. 8.4). These works at first seem to be portrait busts, but their titles belie such a simple definition. They closely resemble a whole group of sculptures commissioned by anthropology museums during this period to serve as scientific illustrations of "racial types" (Roquebert 1994: 5–25). Ward based his busts on sketches he had made while in the Congo. Many of these sketches were full face or in profile and when he published examples of them in his various books he always gave them the title of "type." He apparently intended the sketches and later the busts to be read, not simply as portraits of individuals, but at

8.3 "Distress" (1912) by Herbert Ward.

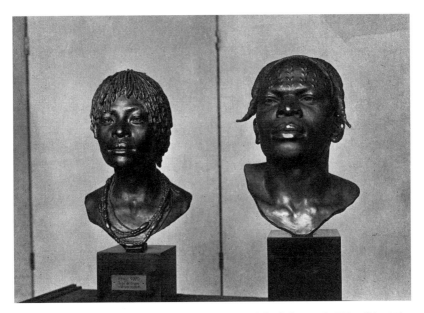

8.4 Bronze busts, "The Bakongo Girl" (1901) and the "The Aruimi Type" (1900)
by Herbert Ward.

least in part, as an empirical record of "racial types" in line with the
anthropological interests of his day.

The majority of Ward's sculptures fall between these two representational poles and might best be described as exotic narrative or genre subjects, a category of academic art "that employed the trappings of
particular cultures . . . as stage settings for traditional narrative or genre
subjects" (Connelly 1995: 120 ftnt 58). A good example of this type is
"The Charm Doctor," which depicts a moment in a Bakongo ritual. The
figure represents a ritual specialist, the *ngang'a nkisi*, shown dancing with
a small sculpture, a Bakongo power figure, in his upraised hand (Fig. 8.1).
The small power figure is modeled after one that Ward had collected in
the area. The scene is based on a firsthand description of the ritual which
he published in his 1890 book:

> Dead silence ranged as the *nganga* leapt into their midst, rattling in his
> hands images, leopard claws and calabash-tops, and chanted a weird
> song . . . he executed a dance, the like of which I had never seen before.
> The wild, leaping figure, with its dress of leopard skins and charms, pre-
> sented a weird picture. (Ward 1890: 43–44)[3]

Like "The Charm Doctor," other works such as "The Forest Lovers,"
"The Tribal Chief," "The Idol Maker," and "The Fugitives" read as exotic
narrative or genre subjects. "The Fugitives," for example, is a sculptural
group – mother and her two small children – which Ward depicts as
fleeing in terror from slave traders. An anti-slavery passage in Ward's
1890 book sets the interpretive frame for this sculpture,

> As civilization spreads, and the ways of the white men become known to
> the dwellers of the far interior, a desire to imitate the more agreeable
> modes of living then presented to their gaze will spring in the breasts
> of these poor African savages liberated by that time, let us hope, from
> the devastating scourge of Arab slave-raiding in their midst. (Ward
> 1890: 163)

Ward employed both Africans and West Indians living in Paris as the
models for his sculptures, but for the details of physiognomy,
scarification, and coiffures he mined his field drawings in order to
"Congoize" all of his figures. He also regularly used objects from his own
collection including textiles, clothing, jewelry, figurative sculptures,
weapons, ceremonial staffs, and furniture as models for the exotic trappings of these sculptures whether they were intended to be allegorical,
"race types," or narrative and genre representations. The authenticity of
his representations must have been at least partially based on the public
perception that his images were drawn from the artist's firsthand
observations in the Congo. His use of actual objects from his collection in
these works must have also contributed to their aura of veracity.

Despite his careful attention in creating the impression of ethnographic accuracy, Ward insisted that these works were first and foremost
Art and not merely scientific illustration. Of his artistic intentions he
wrote that he did not want to make "an absolute realistic thing like wax
works in an anatomical museum," and that he was more concerned that
his sculptures "have the spirit of Africa in its broad sense" (*Evening Star*,
March 15, 1913: 2–3).

Hugh Marles has recently argued that in the process of creating his
Congolese images, Ward filtered his firsthand experiences of Congo societies through the lens of popular anthropology, especially the theory of
arrested development. According to this theory the development of certain non-Western cultures had been physically and culturally retarded

and Ward's Congolese certainly came within this category. This theory granted superiority to Western cultures, naturalized the distinctions among cultures, and legitimized European economic and cultural imperialism in Africa (Marles 1996). In Ward's own words:

> In the foregoing pages I have endeavored to convey the spirit of something that is deep within me – a fellow feeling for the Central African natives. They are not altogether the degraded race that one might infer by reading instances of their brutality and cannibalism. They are a people whose development has been temporarily arrested by adversity. They are very human; they are often cruel, but they are often kind. (Ward 1910: 319)

THE SMITHSONIAN'S AFRICAN COLLECTIONS C. 1880–1920

When Ward first announced his promised gift to the Smithsonian in 1913, the museum was eager to acquire his collection.[4] There were about 197 African collections of various sizes in the Ethnology Division, made by military officers, commercial agents, diplomats and missionaries, who had worked or traveled in Africa. Other African collections were acquired from anthropology exhibits at world fairs including the World Columbian Exposition and the Panama–Pacific Exposition. A few were acquired as the result of museum exchanges such as those pieces acquired from the Leipzig Museum in Germany and the Trocadero Museum in Paris.

Around twenty-two of the African collections were from Central Africa totaling about 1,347 objects. The Smithsonian's Congo collections included over 400 weapons, 361 examples of costume and jewelry, seventy-one musical instruments, sixty figurative sculptures, and over 500 other objects classified under the general rubric of arts and industries.

The museum had contracted for several Congo collections including those made by Dorsey Mohun, a commercial agent, and by Reverend Samuel Verner, a missionary, but these collections were small when compared to the Ward collection. In lieu of mounting a collecting expedition to the Congo itself, the department's acquisition of the Ward collection of over 2,700 objects represented the possibility of more than doubling the size of its Central African holdings and must have been seen as a boon for its scientific and educational mission.

In 1912 most Smithsonian ethnology curators were Americanists and the possibility of acquiring Ward's African collection was seen as an opportunity not to be squandered precisely because of the donor's ability to provide a catalogue of his pieces. In 1912 when Ward first proposed leaving his collection to the Smithsonian Institution, Walter Hough, a curator, wrote in a memo to William Henry Holmes, the Head of the Anthropology Department:

> Since I have read Mr. Ward's letter, I have become a hundred fold more interested in his specimens for the reason that he is competent to classify and give them their origin of locality, thus making the way of the museum man smooth and adding enormously to the scientific value of the material. (Walter Hough Papers, National Anthropological Archives, Smithsonian Institution)

The museum's enthusiasm for Ward's Congo collection paralleled an expanding American public interest in the Congo. In 1890 the American journalist and adventurer, Henry Morton Stanley, published his book on the Emin Pasha Expedition, *In Darkest Africa* (1890), and it became a popular bestseller. America had commercial agents stationed in the Congo and there was a growing national interest in investment and trade in this region. American mission societies were active in the area and they regularly kept their stateside congregations informed of their work through lectures and publications. At the turn of the century reports of labor atrocities in the Congo written by missionaries, diplomats, and others were published in Europe and America. These reports led to heated debates, calls for action, and the establishment of Congo Reform Associations in Europe with branches in the United States (Cookey 1968).[5]

No doubt the name recognition and popular appeal of Herbert Ward himself also played a part in both the Smithsonian's and the public's interest in the acquisition of his collection. In 1893 Ward had lectured in a number of American cities about his Congo experiences and the accounts of his lectures were widely syndicated in newspapers throughout the United States. By 1913 he had also published three books about the Congo. When the Smithsonian announced Ward's intended gift, Washington newspapers gave the announcement ample and enthusiastic coverage. The newspaper headlines read: "Dark Continent Trophies

Given to the Smithsonian–Herbert Ward, Famous Sculptor will Send
Valuable Collection to Capital" (*Washington Herald*, March 15, 1913);
"African Stone Age Relics Given to Smithsonian–Herbert Ward, Sculptor,
Donates Complete and Valuable Collection" (*Evening Star*, March 15,
1913); "Unique Gift for the Smithsonian" (*Sunday Star*, March 16, 1913).
An article in the *Sunday Star* also included an extended interview with
Ward and a photograph of his Paris display.

The "Congo" which Ward created in the installation of his collection in
Paris is graphically revealed in a photograph taken in about 1911. His was
a carefully and painstakingly designed installation intended to maximize
an overall decorative effect (Fig. 8.5). Three of the room's walls are literally filled with weapons, assorted other objects, and an elephant head and
antelope heads arranged in a series of symmetrical patterns. Decorative
wall arrangements of objects were certainly not unique to Ward and were
popular throughout this period in domestic displays, temporary exhibitions and some museum displays. Yet, Ward's massing of these materials
to fill almost every available surface with elaborate, decorative arrangements extended this fashionable aesthetic to its absolute limits. Even the
ceiling lamp was encircled with a fan of spears and decorated with grass
aprons. Turkish kilims, African animal skins, and Congo raffia textiles
were used as furniture upholstery, as coverings for pedestals for the
bronzes, and on the floor. He created a somber atmosphere by his choice
of a grey-green wall color and further enhanced the atmospheric effect by
placing an elaborately carved North African *mashrubeya* screen in front
of the windows to filter out the daylight. A stuffed python, an elephant
skull, and several gorilla skeletons reinforced Ward's invention of an
exotic Africa and his Congo collection served as the foil for his bronze
vignettes of Congolese life. Ward's wife later wrote that he arranged,

> each trophy carefully and symmetrically, with an infinite amount of
> patience, carrying out his idea with such arresting effect that no one who
> had ever seen this studio, a veritable museum in itself, could forget the
> impression of its mystery, its subtle suggestion of the darkness of Central
> Africa. The sinister poison arrows, the barbaric knives and spears, glint-
> ing in a cunningly subdued light against the gray-green walls, were an

8.5 Herbert Ward's installation in Paris c. 1911. The Congo collection is installed with Ward's bronze statues.

appropriately descriptive background to the huge bronze figures grouped in the various phases of savage life, so fierce, so brooding, so startlingly life like, they seemed to have just emerged from the Congo swamps and forests. (S. Ward 1927: 165)

A description of the exhibition plan for ethnology exhibits was published in the National Museum's 1914 annual report and it carefully outlines the taxonomic and pedagogical philosophy of the Institution. This curatorial orientation stands in sharp contrast to Ward's vision.

The arrangement of the ethnological exhibits is geographical, the material belonging to each area being displayed as an assemblage or by classes of objects. The exhibits find their key in family lay-figure groups placed centrally in the halls, which typify the physical characteristics, the social organization, the manners and customs, and the arts and industries of selected human types. The design of the exhibit is to illustrate systematically the comparative differences in material culture and advancement of modern groups of mankind, thus giving an impression of the effects of environment and racial tendencies on the arts and industries of peoples. (Annual Report, United States National Museum, 1914: 15)

The style of the Smithsonian installations closely resembled those in other public museums in Europe and America during this period. A photograph taken sometime after 1922 shows the arrangement of the Oceanic collections in the museum (Fig. 8.6). Wooden and glass cases were installed in rows the entire length of the hall. On one side of the aisle there were small cases containing models showing village layouts with the appropriate dwellings and figures engaged in various activities. Installed directly across the aisle was the related "life-group" case. These dioramas had originally been developed by the museum for use in anthropology exhibits at various world fairs and later they were reinstalled in the permanent ethnology exhibits. Unlike most contemporary dioramas with painted backdrops where the visitor stands directly in front of the display, these early life-group dioramas were installed in glass cases without backdrops. The visitor could walk completely around the installation to study

8.6 Photograph of Oceanic Collections at the National Museum, after 1922.

the scene from every angle. Next to and behind the large life-group dioramas and the model villages were other cases which held groups of
objects from a specific region installed generally according to taxonomic
principles. The overwhelming sensation of precision and orderliness
which visitors must have experienced as they traversed these halls would
have certainly intensified the authoritative voice of museum science.

By 1922, the African exhibit included only one complete cultural
display as outlined in the exhibiting program. It featured the Zulu in a
life-group diorama which had originally been created by the museum for
the Panama Pacific Exposition of 1915 in San Francisco. It included six
full-size figures – two standing and two seated women, a seated man, and
a young boy – in a domestic scene taking place in front of a partial
reconstruction of a Zulu house. The seated women were cooking and the
man was playing a xylophone with a drum lying on its side behind him.
The two standing women appear to have just arrived at the household. All
of the mannequins are dressed in clothing and beaded jewelry which were
part of the accessioned African objects.

Near the life-group case was a case containing a model Zulu village
with houses and a cattle kraal and figures engaged in a variety of domestic

activities. Installed in yet another case there was a startlingly life-like plaster mannequin of a Zulu man wearing a head ring, a skin cape, and carrying a spear (Fig. 8.7). Other cases in the African section included additional mannequins representing "racial types" from north, west, and east Africa.[6] Because the size and scope of the African collections did not include a sufficient number of objects from the ethnic group represented by the six different mannequins, each figure was installed in a case with an assemblage of objects from different regions in Africa. By comparison, curators more closely achieved their ideal in the Hopi exhibit, from the same period, where a single large case, for example, was devoted to over a hundred examples of kachina dolls.

THE RECONCILIATION OF STYLES IN THE SMITHSONIAN'S WARD EXHIBIT

The correspondence between the anthropologists' invention of African peoples and Ward's personal vision of the Congo is complex and subtle. Ward and the Smithsonian anthropologists did share a fundamental belief in the intellectual, moral, technological and artistic superiority of their early twentieth-century Western society. They also ascribed to the same social evolutionary theories about "primitives." Yet, their invention of Africa, though parallel, was not identical.

Ward's "savage" as invented in his writings, his sculptures, and his Paris studio museum, was more overtly romantic than the museum's scientific "primitive man." His approach to Africa was impressionistic, deeply personal, and intimate. In contrast, the "primitive" created in the Smithsonian's exhibits were consistently naturalized, de-personalized, typed, ordered, and classified in both the life-group dioramas, the single mannequins, and in the object displays. This representation was given the imprimatur of science and the implied standard of comparison was always modern Western society. The "primitive" was carefully defined as developmentally inferior in every category.

When the Ward collection was installed in the newly reopened National Museum building in 1922, the style of this exhibit was a clear departure from the museum standard (Fig. 8.8). The exhibit mirrored Ward's Paris studio museum in several important ways. Archival photographs taken soon after the exhibit opened show that the curators of the

8.7 Mannequin representing a Zulu man, one of the mannequins featured in the
Smithsonian's African exhibits in the 1920s.

8.8 Installation of the Ward collection at the National Museum (currently the Museum of Natural History and the Museum of Man) *c.* 1922.

Smithsonian exhibit consciously intended to capture some of the drama that Ward had achieved in his Paris installation. To this end they hung curtains over the windows to recreate a somber atmosphere evocative of the "jungle." They mounted antelope and elephant heads on the walls, surrounded by African weapons arranged in decorative patterns, although the museum's decorative installations were noticeably more restrained than the one Ward had created in Paris.

The Smithsonian curators also chose to create a separate gallery for the exhibit and to distinguish the Ward collection from the museum's other ethnology exhibits. Museum carpenters made a series of low, wooden dividers and these dividers created a segregated space for the collection, made even more distinct by personalizing the exhibit discourse. A brief biography of Ward was mandated by the deed of gift, it was prominently displayed on a stand and it presented an interesting departure from the single line legend crediting the donor in most exhibits even up to the present. In the label, biographical information about Ward acknowledged his role as both the collector of the artifacts, and the artist–interpreter of Africa through his bronze sculptures. While the Smithsonian consciously tried to recapture some of the drama of the original Paris installation, the curators did assert the museum's voice in this display. In the Paris installation Ward had organized his display primarily for aesthetic effect. At the Smithsonian the curators separated the Congo objects from the zoological specimens and both from the bronze sculptures. In line with conventional ethnographic displays, the objects and zoological specimens were organized by type or function in cases around the perimeter of the exhibition space. In each of these cases text labels were included which reinforced the museum's interpretation. For example, one label, "Native Fetiches and Wood Carvings," read:

> The African native displays much skill in carving wood. He does not hesitate to boldly attempt the fashioning of the human form in his fetiches and this barbaric sculpture achieves what to him are satisfying works of art and which convey their interest to civilized man. Stools, headrests, and domestic utensils are worked with a view to pleasing forms and decoration. (Records of the Anthropology Department, National Anthropological Archives, Smithsonian Institution)

The bronze sculptures, rather than being fully integrated with the African objects as they had been in Paris, were all positioned in the open space within the gallery. They now formed a secondary exhibition within the larger, ethnographic display. Gone was the domesticity and intimacy of the Paris installation. Ward's aesthetic style had been compromised and the museum's scientific voice advanced both through the physical rearrangement of the collection and through the addition of explanatory text labels. Ward's "Congo" was now partially institutionalized and was incorporated into the official scientific discourse on the "primitives."

The inclusion of the Ward sculptures with the African material as mandated by the deed of gift seems not to have been overly difficult for the staff to reconcile with their exhibition philosophy. Initially there was some debate over where in the museum to install the collection. In an internal memo to the administration, Walter Hough suggested that "If Ward Sculptures are to be included place them in West end of East Hall to connect with art gallery" (Walter Hough Papers, National Anthropological Archives, Smithsonian Institution).

During the 1920s the National Museum building (now the Museum of Natural History) housed not only natural history and ethnology collections, but history and fine arts collections. Hough's suggestion to shift the order of the East Hall of ethnology and to install the Ward collection directly adjacent to the Fine Arts collection was rejected by the administration because of budgetary and space constraints. The Ward collection was eventually installed in the east end of the East Hall which necessitated removing some of the other African exhibits.

Despite the fact that the anthropologists considered the Ward bronzes to be works of Western fine art, the hyper-realism of these bronzes do share an affinity with the mannequins in the ethnology exhibits. Without a tremendous leap of the imagination the bronzes could be comfortably read as illustrations of "racial types" as were the other mannequins already on display throughout the halls. The narrative and genre qualities of the Ward bronzes also shared a certain kinship with the popular dioramas that anchored the ethnology exhibits. "The Tribal Chief" and "The Idol Maker," like the "The Charm Doctor," included representations of actual objects that were displayed in cases in the gallery. It gave the sculptures a certain authentic air which echoed the effect that the museum had hoped to achieve in the dioramas.

Since the Smithsonian's dioramas always presented scenes that depicted the "primitive" before contact with "civilization," many of the Ward bronzes including "Defiance," "The Tribal Chief," "The Fire Maker," "The Charm Doctor," "The Congo Artist," and "The Idol Maker" would have been interpreted in much the same way. Romantic ideas about lost innocence after contact would have been alluded to and reinforced in bronzes like "The Fugitives" and "Distress."

For William Henry Holmes and Walter Hough, the Ward bronzes installed in the same gallery as the Congolese objects read as a powerful developmental sequence in the evolution of art. Holmes, who had devoted much of his research to the study of "primitive" art, held strong views about the evolution of art. He believed art proceeded "from geometric, non-ideographic to delineative forms; from motives of religious superstition to refined sense of beauty, from imitation to spontaneity" (Hinsley 1981: 105). To Holmes, no admirer of early twentieth-century abstract art, the Ward sculptures must have represented examples of the highest artistic achievement of Western culture. By placing the bronzes alongside the geometrically decorated African weapons and the more abstract African "idols," the museum public would surely be able to see for themselves the stages in the evolution of art. Walter Hough confirmed the anthropologists' intention to highlight this evolutionary theme when he wrote, "The maker of an African sword and Praxiteles were one in the effort to express themselves in terms of art. The steps from the aboriginal craftsman to the sculptures of Mr. Ward are plain to those who study the development of art" (Hough 1924: 41).

The spatial organization of the 1922 Ward gallery strictly maintained the distinction between fine art and artifact. The Smithsonian anthropologists had no intention of rethinking their categories or embracing the new definitions of African sculpture as fine art which were emerging in European and American avant garde art circles. While the decorative qualities of the Congolese artifacts were openly acknowledged, there was never any intention of elevating any African objects to the status of fine art at the Smithsonian. As Gertrude Brigham, a critic, perceptively wrote:

> African ethnology in a leading art exhibition is a novelty, not merely in Washington, but the world ... Guests were received in the apartment specially designed to accommodate the immense collection . . . the walls were bedecked with the fantastic array of knives and other weapons . . . Below them, in cases were exhibited other trophies – a huge elephant's head, a giant python, ivory carvings, a variety of textiles and garments, musical instruments, drums – the whole forming a setting for the magnificent sculptural compositions in bronze. (*Christian Science Monitor*, March 15, 1922: 8)

Despite the Smithsonian's departure from its standard for ethnographic display, or perhaps because of it, the museum ended up creating a powerful interpretation of Africa which never questioned the accepted "verities" of late nineteenth-century theories of race and social evolution. Rather, through objects and texts, the curators intentionally and powerfully reconfirmed them.

That the style of the Ward exhibit continued to have an impact on the public is borne out in Herbert Krieger's Annual Report of 1931–32. Krieger, a curator in anthropology, strongly urged the museum to undertake a new American Indian exhibit. He suggested that it take its stylistic cue from the popular Ward gallery. He wrote that such a large exhibit is "the type arousing most interest and is the type bound to characterize future exhibits, departing radically from the fragmentary exhibit of isolated specimens from one area" (Herbert Krieger Papers, National Anthropological Archives, Smithsonian Institution).

The Smithsonian began to modernize its ethnology halls in the 1950s and the Africa section and the Ward gallery were finally dismantled in 1961. This was the heady period of African independence from colonial rule, and the Ward exhibit was by then seen as an anachronism both in its style and in its representation of Africa. In the reconfigured Africa Hall, all of the zoological specimens were removed and the African objects were integrated with other African collections to create new narratives. The Ward bronzes had no place in this new hall of African cultures; most were removed to storage or relocated to museum stairwells and alcoves. The dismantling of the Ward gallery, the integration of Ward's African collection with the other Smithsonian African collections, and the removal of the bronzes effectively eradicated the once intimate association between the collector and his collection. Ward's voice was stilled, art and ethnology went their separate ways, and the final transformation and institutionalization of Ward's collection was complete.

NOTES

1 In 1960, with the full agreement of the surviving Ward heirs, the Smithsonian filed a petition with the United States District Court for the District of Columbia to grant the museum relief from the conditions of Sarita Ward's bequest. It was granted in May 1961.

2 Some of the Ward biographical materials and certain descriptions of Smithsonian anthropological exhibitions prior to 1921 have appeared in Karp, Kreamer and Lavine 1992: 428–57. These materials are published here with the kind permission of Smithsonian Institution Press.

3 For an informed discussion of the complex role which these ritual specialists play in Kongo culture see MacGaffey and Harris 1993: 20–103.

4 Although Herbert Ward first publicly announced his intention to donate his collection to the Smithsonian in 1913, it was not until 1921, two years after his death in 1919, that the museum received his bequest.

5 While King Leopold had his ardent supporters in the American press and lobbying the United States Congress, other prominent Americans, including George Washington Williams and Mark Twain, who published letters and essays, agitated for reform (Franklin Jr. 1985; Twain 1905).

6 Photographs of the Zulu diorama, the model village and the seven
mannequins representing "race types" were featured in a 1922 article, "Racial
Groups" by Walter Hough in the Smithsonian's Annual Report. The case label
for the Zulu man read:

> Zulu man. The Zulus live in southeastern Africa and belong to the Bantu
> division of the Negroid peoples, who occupy nearly the whole of the Dark
> Continent south of the Equator. Their superb physical development has
> often been remarked by travelers, while their strong political and military
> organization and prowess in war have brought them prominently before the
> world. They are tall, black, with woolly hair of elliptical section, and long
> skull. They are unclothed except the apron or *isenene* and their weapons are
> the spear, shield, and club. Southeastern Africa 175.257. Modeled by Henry J.
> Ellicott.

NINE

"Magic, or as we usually say, Art"
A framework for comparing European
and African art

WYATT MACGAFFEY

&

The purpose of this paper is to explore the relationship between words and images in the three categories "art," "African art," and *minkisi*. The last of these is a class of objects produced by the Bakongo of western Congo and usually referred to as "fetishes;" the preferred term in recent catalogues is "power objects." I will pay particular attention to a class of *minkisi* called *minkondi* which includes wooden figures, full of nails and other hardware, commonly called "nail fetishes." I intend to begin with art, make my way to African art, and end with *minkisi*.

My overriding theoretical concern, as an anthropologist, is to compare institutions interculturally, using a consistent perspective. The anthropology of art has generally failed to do this.

THE OBJECT OF THE ANTHROPOLOGY OF ART

The anthropology of art is paradoxical in that it restricts itself to the art of "primitive" societies, from which, however, it can be argued that art is in fact generally absent (Mudimbe 1986). On the other hand, both "our" art – that is, the art of "modern" society – and that which is usually called "oriental art" are excluded. In *The Anthropology of Art* (1991), Layton explicitly limits himself to primitive art but prefers to say that he is dealing with the art of "small-scale societies." He does not explain or examine this category, which apparently includes dynastic Egypt. His usage is not exceptional, however.

Related to this paradoxical restriction is the problem of defining the material to be studied. None of the currently proposed definitions is satisfactory. Layton says that the subject matter of the anthropology of art is usually defined in one of two contrasting ways: "One deals in terms of aesthetics, the other treats art as communication distinguished by a particularly apt use of images" (Layton 1991: 4). Neither approach, he says, is universally "applicable"; by this expression he apparently means that each kind of definition excludes some objects which on other grounds we feel bound to include. For example, Kalabari sculptures are not evaluated aesthetically by the Kalabari, but they are based on images. In the end Layton seeks to combine the two definitions, arguing that art shares general principles of communication with language, but also enhances both visual and verbal communication through the aesthetics of form (Layton 1991: 148).

All of the criteria deployed in anthropological definitions of art, including Layton's, are contradicted by the example of objects to be found in any museum of modern art. All the definitions also suffer from being ahistorical; they fail to allow for the fact that whole classes of objects that were once neither "art" nor "aesthetic" have become both. Neither "art" nor "primitive art" is a class of objects existing in the world, to be identified and circumscribed. Both are categories of our thought and practice; they are related as subcategories of a broader institutional set, and have evolved continuously as part of the history of the west (Danto 1981: 44).

"ART" AND "SYMBOLISM": THEORETICAL QUESTIONS

The two criteria that Layton identifies as having served anthropologists to identify art correspond closely to those that have been used to delimit the field of symbolism. The symbolic in anthropology, according to Sperber (1975: 1), has been defined negatively as either the mental minus the rational or the semiotic minus language. In either case, it is what remains after we have set aside something we feel we know and understand; the criteria are ethnocentric (Layton 1991: 132).

According to the criterion of aesthetic value, art is the fabricated minus the useful. It consists of useless products, or of aspects of products which are redundant to utility. What makes a Chinese bicycle seat art, or potentially art, is the fact that it includes design elements some other, equally useful bicycle seat does not. Agricultural implements and other tools of bygone days become "antiques" whose aesthetic merit is roughly proportional to their present uselessness. A thirteenth-century Madonna only becomes a work of art when, for a particular public, it loses its efficacy as an object of devotion.[1]

The alternative criterion is that of communication, that is, of an idea, a transforming metaphor, which the maker intended to have some effect on a recipient. Layton correctly emphasizes that we have to be sure there was an intention, and that the message we see is what was intended. By this criterion, our Chinese bicycle seat is not art. That is not a problem, but once again our definition is residual – the semiotic minus language – and raises the problem, why images and not words? What exactly is communicated by a work of art? Is art an efficient means of communication – that is, does the degree of elaboration of the work correspond to the simplicity or complexity of the message? Is there any regularity in the meanings assigned to given artworks?

These questions can perhaps be answered, but there is a yet more serious problem. A semiotic view of art implies a distinction between the signifier and the thing signified, in fact a distance between the two. Freedberg (1989) challenges this understanding of images with respect not only to exotic arts but to our own. In a wide range of instances, including a Nupe mask, medieval reliquaries, sculptured figures of saints, and paintings of the nude, he shows that images do have power and that this power is the result of perceived identity between the signifier and the signified. The mask as danced is terrifying because it is the spirit it represents. The statue of the Virgin that answers your prayer is not equivalent to another statue of the same Mother of God in the next parish, and it will punish you for giving thanks at the wrong shrine. The nude in the painting in your bedroom may no longer cause you to conceive beautiful children, as she did in centuries past, but she still arouses the same sort of physical reactions as does the nude of real life. In all these instances, the "artistic" features of the painting or sculpture are intrinsic to its usefulness.

Freedberg's most radical argument is that most of art theory is a response to fear of the power of images; it is a set of ideological devices for denying and neutralizing their power, a form of iconoclasm. The idea of the virtual space of the art object, isolated from real space by its frame or its base, is one of these devices, whose antecedents Freedberg finds in the iconoclastic arguments of the church fathers.

For the same reason, according to Freedberg, modern art theory attempts to strip the image of all narrative reference, saying that it does not signify anything, it is only itself. Fear of the power of the image explains Gombrich's insistence that representation depends on a context of convention; Jackson Pollock's belief that he could paint a picture devoid of reference to nature; Nelson Goodman's insistence that likeness is wholly symbolic; and Clement Greenberg's idea that flat is all (Freedberg 1989: 425). Formalism ("high critical talk") distracts attention from the possibility that a nude might be a pin-up by insisting, after Maurice Denis, that before being a nude it was an arrangement of form and color; historicism, the other prominent trend in art criticism, similarly evades recognition of the emotional impact of images by confining it in the past, among the painter's contemporaries (Freedberg 1989: 431).

Freedberg thus suggests that the theory of art, presupposing a discontinuity between the reality of the world and the reality of art, is, as Sperber says of the semiotic theory of symbol, a "native notion," a feature of the ideology of one particular society during a certain period of its history.

AN INSTITUTIONAL APPROACH

Art is identified by a particular, institutionalized pattern of behavior. It is possible for something to be a work of art because we treat it in a particular way that contrasts with the behaviors appropriate to non-art. Art in this sense is, at least as a first approximation, a peculiarity of modern society and comes into existence, together with the other institutional features of modern society, in the seventeenth century.

For something to become a work of art, a labeling process must take place that requires three participants: an artist who produces an apt object, a client or public, and a critic or connoisseur who mediates between the artist and the public to assure them of the artness of the thing. If I make a painting, it is not sufficient for the painting to be "art" that I consider it so, nor even that you, my friend and neighbor, admire it and hang it on your wall; it must be certified as art by competent authority and exhibited in the institutionally appropriate place, a gallery or museum.[2] A pile of tires in front of a museum (Alan Kaprow's "Yard,"

1961) is to be viewed as art, indeed becomes art, whereas the same pile in a service station is not (Danto *et al.* 1988: 11).

Similar processes are required to identify a poet, a witch, or a murderer, none of whom is evidently so to the eye. The concept must exist and must be applied as a label to an apt individual by a standardized process. Application does not mean that the public unanimously endorses the identification; on the contrary, the natives may well dispute the result. The important point, anthropologically, is the content of the debate, which reveals the culturally defined categories that it presupposes. Among the Bakongo of western Congo it is possible to disagree whether a given individual is a chief or a witch; it has not been possible until recently to argue whether he is a poet or an artist, since these categories did not exist.

The prerequisite configuration for the existence of art – an apt object, a connoisseur, and a client – can be said to have come into existence in 1610, when the first book of connoisseurship was published, intended to advise a developing class of purchasers of art how to tell the difference between real art and fakes (Ginzburg 1980).[3] Connoisseurship was first formulated and rationalized by Giovanni Morelli in the nineteenth century. Although his method, focusing on boilerplate elements in portraits, such as fingers and ears, was widely hailed as scientific, he himself insisted that ultimately no technique could substitute for what he called the diviner's gift, *Divinationsgabe*. It is characteristic of the ethnocentrism of anthropology that whereas the rationality of claims by African and other primitive diviners to be able to see what is not visible to the ordinary eye has long seemed to be a proper subject of investigation, the occult powers of our own diviners have been taken for granted. Magic has been regarded as a bizarre phenomenon, the artness of art has not. Yet the plain fact is that though the natives themselves are unable to identify a work of art with any certainty, they generally believe that artness is a real and consequential attribute of some objects which, once correctly identified, become quasi-sacred and absurdly expensive.

By art, in European context, I mean painting and sculpture, although a fuller account would have to take notice of architecture, ceramics, furniture, and other categories. Since Socrates, if not before, art has been contrasted with literature, not merely descriptively but normatively; that is, the two have been assigned contrasting functions and moral values. The partisans of poetry, philosophy, and other authoritative forms of words have simultaneously deprecated art as able to show only surface realities, and deplored its seductive ability to lead the public astray.

The contradictions in this effort to contrast word and image, and to downgrade images, have been explored in a genuinely anthropological spirit by W. J. T. Mitchell (1986). Why is it, he asks, that the most knowledgeable and authoritative of native experts insist on the essential difference between word and image when no such contrast appears in practice? The contradiction suggests that we are dealing with an ideology whose real focus is elsewhere than art. Mitchell concludes that the real issue is that of defending authority (usually white and male) against the indiscipline of Others: images are denounced on the assumption that others (women, children, Catholics, natives) are in their power. "The rhetoric of iconoclasm is thus a rhetoric of exclusion and domination, a caricature of the other as one who is involved in irrational, obscene behavior from which (fortunately) we are exempt" (Mitchell 1986: 113).

Domestic debates about the nature of art thus implicitly serve to define our civilization in contrast to others. Art itself has an ambiguous position in this play of judgments: although as image it is inferior to, and subversive of, the authoritative word, it participates in the superiority of our civilization over those which by definition are incapable of art. Or perhaps we should say, are incapable of art criticism. William Rubin explains what he says is the generally low quality level of African tribal art partly by the absence of "a concept of Fine Arts supported by an ongoing critical tradition which, in turn, requires a written language" (Rubin 1984, I: 21). For good art to exist, according to Rubin, there must be present not only the artist and the public, but the critic, the word-smith.

The supposed contrast between words and images is salient in four fields of interest here. The first is the obvious one, the pejorative devaluation of African idols, fetishes, fertility figures, and the like from the sixteenth century through the heyday of imperialism to the present. The second is the progressive dissociation effected between word and image in the main trends of European art since about 1860. Third, the well-known tension between the art–curatorial approach to exotic artifacts, now regarded as art, and the ethnographic approach. Lastly, the inseparability of word and image in *minkisi*. In short, I am going to use the question of the relation between words and images as a common perspective in which to consider European art, African art, and the relation between the two.

Layton specifically excludes fetishes from the visual representations that are art (1991: 6), although both the journal *African Arts* and major museums and auction houses think differently. Fetishes were certainly not art at the turn of the century; they have become so only in the last decade or two. In the introductory essays to a volume commemorating the 300th anniversary of the death of Olfert Dapper, it is argued that the force emanating from some African objects is so disturbing that in the sixteenth century it was thought necessary to burn them because they were too uncomfortably suggestive of the Devil; graven images subverted the authority of the Word of God. Only in the nineteenth century, after the founding of the Ethnological Society of Paris in 1832, did such forbidden objects attract the attention of the new science of ethnography, whose mission was to measure the progress of civilization from the primitive to the modern. Works formerly rejected as of the Devil began to be collected not as art but as evidence of Otherness. When some of them began to be thought of as art, they could only be included in private and museum collections after being stripped of some of their elements (Husson 1989).

Paul Gauguin interested himself in primitive objects and drew inspiration from them as early as 1889, when he visited a show of "native villages" at the Universal Exposition in Paris. There he acquired two typical Loango *minkisi,* which he proceeded to modify, cleaning them up and adding paint and other materials to suit his taste. On these "readymades aided," as Marcel Duchamp would have called them, he then inscribed his initials, "P.Go." (Fondation Dapper 1989: 10).

The archetype of such disturbing figures is the Kongo *nkisi* called *nkondi,* known in catalogues as nail fetish; to this day, *minkondi* (the plural) retain their power simultaneously to fascinate and to repel. In the 1960s, when I began to study Kongo culture, *minkondi* were rarely shown in coffee-table books of African art; nowadays they sometimes appear on the cover.[4]

The process by which an African object becomes art includes removing it from its context of origin to the accompaniment of varying sorts and degrees of violence. Besides the literal violence of theft, confiscation, and the like, we must include violence done to the object itself, which is often stripped of its accoutrements, varnished or even remodeled. In the past it has also usually been stripped of its name, identity, local significance, and function.

Such violence alone does not make the object art. In exchange for what it has lost, the African object is given a new context and a new identity. Its first lodging in Europe would have been an ethnographic museum, itself an invention of the middle of the nineteenth century, where its function was precisely to exemplify not art but the contrast between primitive cultures and those capable of producing art. It was renamed and re-identified as a fetish, fertility figure, or ancestor figure, and presented as a characteristic cultural product of a "tribe." Primitive art began life as failed art, and to a considerable extent continues to be so regarded.

The ethnographic museum invites us to look at objects in a particular way, and confers a certain character on them. In a thought-provoking exhibition, Susan Vogel explored the effect of the context and manner of display on the way we see objects (Danto *et al.*1988). An African object, once labeled as, for example, "Kongo fetish," is likely to be displayed along with other examples of "Kongo culture," such as baskets, fish-traps, and raffia cloth, or else grouped with other "fetishes" from around the world. In each case, an implicit message is conveyed that has nothing intrinsically to do with the object itself but recalls and confirms elements of the museum-goer's world view. "Fetish" is an entirely European category, with its own history and cultural functions; a Kongo *nkisi* has in fact less in common with a Zuni fetish, for example, than with the relic of a saint in medieval Europe (Clifford 1988; Cushing 1883; Geary 1986; MacGaffey 1977; Pietz 1985, 1987).

The shaping of the viewer's experience continues with the manner in which the objects are displayed; traditionally, ethnographic materials were displayed in horizontal specimen cases, in clusters on the wall, or in a mock-up of a native habitat. The primary theme in such a display is the density of presentation and the relatedness of the objects, which are associated with an implicit anthropological narrative.

For an artifact to become art, a further stripping and re-identification is necessary, abandoning not only the indigenous context but also the anthropological narrative.

How we behave towards an object, thus how we see it, is conditioned by the context. In a gallery we put on our gallery eyes; to look at, and in other ways behave toward an object as though it were art does much to make it so. The American designer of the winning pavilion at the Venice Biennale, 1990, whose art consists of truisms displayed in electronic illuminations, said of them that if they were shown in a public place they would be simply pronouncements.[5] Much counter-cultural art in the 1970s invited us to look at natural objects with the same gallery eyes so that they too could be recognized as art even though they were located outside the gallery, often in a wilderness. This aesthetic program to enhance ordinary experience, which might be described as the "monosodium glutamate approach," has a precedent in the eighteenth-century notion of the "picturesque."

The archetype of all such objects that become art by the context of seeing is Duchamp's "Fountain," which is of course a urinal. The point of Duchamp's irony is that whereas a fountain, like a traditional work of art, projects something toward you, a urinal only achieves its function when you project something into it. The artness of an object is at least as much a matter of how we behave toward it as of the aptness of the object itself.

Our behavior is governed by the space in which we find ourselves. The art museum is a display space intended to favor a particular kind of seeing. The portico is impressive, the lighting is even, the wall-space bland, the floor uncluttered. As far as possible, each work has a space to itself, a kind of aesthetic privacy; one of the scandalous features of the Barnes Foundation's display of Impressionist paintings in Philadelphia is that they are densely clustered. So strong is the contribution of the space that more than one artist has put on a "show" consisting of an entirely blank, unfurnished, white-painted apartment. A critic confers art status on the experience, describing such a show as "articulating interior and exterior spaces, light and shadow," but admitting that "to a general public there is, indeed, nothing there."[6] A performance by the artist Andrea

Fraser consisted of a parody of a museum tour; Fraser has also created a museum catalogue as an art work. Simon Linke's "October 1985" consists of fifteen paintings reproducing pages of the magazine *Artforum* that advertised art exhibitions.[7]

In spite of such raucous critiques from the fringe, the dominant theory of art in the twentieth century, particularly in America and particularly in New York, denies the importance of context altogether, insisting on the unmediated confrontation of the eye with the object. Viewers, we are told, must face the challenge of coming to terms with the work on their own. The object itself is supposed to make no reference to any other context of experience. Art ceases to be representational, and artists struggle to free themselves, as they put it, from tradition. The most obvious mark of such denial of context is the word "untitled" on the label of a work.

The pure vision of unmediated confrontation with the object is as much of an illusion, in fact, as the idea that a Quaker meeting, having done away with ritual, makes possible the spontaneous movement of the spirit. Non-ritual is itself a ritual. The word remains indispensable to the image, though now it is no longer found in the narrative reference of the work itself, the descriptive title, or the informative label; garrulous as ever, it is heard from the pages of reviews and magazines, and in the voice of the museum guide. "The emphasis on vision as the primary activity in the museum setting is evident from the reluctance many curators have to provide extended labels. Museum educators," writes Danielle Rice, herself curator of education at the Philadelphia Museum of Art, "are often accused of trying to trivialize aesthetic experience by attempting to explain objects with words. The irony of people who devote their entire lives to studying art proposing that all one has to do to is look at art in order to understand it is not lost on museum critics" (Rice 1987: 2).

The best guide to the metapragmatic aspects of art, that is, the features of the gallery situation that make the experience of art possible, is the series of movements, from Duchamp to Minimalism, that make up anti-art. Anti-art has variously, but never simultaneously, denied the importance of permanence and noble materials, grand themes, the uniqueness of the object, technical skill, the distinction between people and objects, the museum as a display space, display at eye level, behavioral rules (don't touch, don't make noise, etc.), the individual artist, the art object itself, and more besides. It has become a cliché, that the artist "seeks to provoke a dialogue about what is art,"[8] "challenges the viewer to examine his or her expectations and perceptions,"[9] "challenges the assumption that only precious materials and privileged surroundings are suitable for serious art,"[10] or "questions the function of the gallery and the market in relation to the making, understanding and evaluation of art."[11] None of these questions, no matter how often repeated, evokes an answer.

None of this has made anti-art any less art, because the definitive institutional features remain untouched; though the work be a "happening" in the street, it is still art when it is reported as such in the appropriate magazine.[12] The sculptor Richard Wentworth says: "I was glad to stop worrying about whether things looked like art, but I guess if you make things in studios and show them in a gallery they will tend to look like art, so you've lost anyway. You're not going to find it anywhere else."[13]

The paradox of the effort to separate narrative from visual experience is that the less a work refers in itself to some context of representation, the more the public depends on the gallery situation and the authority of the critic to tell them how art objects differ from physically identical non-art objects. As a minimum, we need a label, identifying the uniqueness of the work by giving the artist's name, the date of the work, and the title, such as, "Untitled, No. 23."

THE CURATOR AND THE ETHNOGRAPHER

Curators are, by definition, image people. Their business is to assemble and display objects in such a way that we see art, and see it to the full extent of its artness. The museum is the spatial context in which the seeing of what we might not otherwise see is to be encouraged. Ethnographers, on the other hand, add words to images. The intent of their words is to refer us to another context, that of the original production and use of the object, so that we might see something of what, say, the Bakongo saw, but which is in any case not empirically visible.

Though there need be no contradiction between these two programs, in practice the tension is considerable (Mitchell 1986: 156). To the extent that the curator cedes space to the ethnographer, his own authority is diminished, but there is more to the conflict than professional rivalry. To transpose African objects into the category "African art" means fitting them into the gallery context I have just described. This context is not just a standardized space but a set of institutional expectations of that which is art.

Africans began to acquire art in the 1950s, at the same time as they acquired national independence and history. The new breed of specialists in African art, part art historian and part ethnographer, worked hard to confer artness upon African objects not only by commenting upon their aesthetic qualities and their significance to indigenous users but by identifying in them at least some of the attributes of art. Sculpture in bronze, later in wood, qualified as art at an early stage and remains the preferred form; ancestors and fertility were recognized, however abusively, as suitably noble themes.

Since art is produced by an artist and should be individualized as a unique work identified by time and place, the critics strove to individuate the African artist and his product. Unlike ethnographic artifacts, art works were to be the product of an autonomous, creative individual, not of an anonymous, collective, and timeless culture. Biebuyck's *Tradition and Creativity in Tribal Art* (1969) announced the theme of spontaneity, in opposition to mere convention, as the guiding force of African art; the contributors to this volume proceeded to liberate the figure of the African artist from the block of tradition in which he had been imprisoned. The tribe as matrix of artistic production was abandoned in favor of the *atelier*, producing for a transcultural market. Indigenous aesthetic canons were elicited and efforts made, albeit unsuccessfully, to establish criteria that would distinguish real art from fakes (Ben-Amos 1989; Cornet 1975; Willett 1976). In sculptures, expressions of broad and noble human virtues were discerned, but indications of relatively sordid concerns and motives were overlooked (Siroto 1979). In galleries and glossy magazines, African objects received the art treatment. In short, if Africans were to have art, its institutional matrix and creative motivation had to be much like ours.

Reappropriation of artifact as art includes replacing old words with newer ones that reclassify the object in the viewer's cognitive and moral universe. An example is the recent preference for the term "power object" to replace the traditional "fetish." The aim is laudable, but how much text do we need? How much reorientation can be accomplished on a label? What does "power object" mean, anyway?

"Power" is vague enough and it correctly implies that a *nkisi* is supposed to do something. "Object," however, is misleading, if our aim is to convey something of what the Bakongo saw in a *nkisi. Nkisi* is one of four categories that structure the religious practice of Kongo and much of Central Africa. The other three are ghost, ancestor and nature spirit. All four are personalities from the land of the dead. A *nkisi*, in its wooden figurine, cloth bundle or clay pot, is as much a personality as is an ancestor in his grave. The initiation of an expert (*nganga*) in the operation of a *nkisi* is very much like the inauguration of a chief dedicated to the ancestors of his clan; in fact, in the seventeenth century, chiefs were called *minkisi*. Once composed, the *nkisi* obliges people to behave toward it in a manner appropriate to chiefs; the great Loango *nkondi*, Mangaaka, was carried in a litter like a chief. On the other hand, chiefs were treated in some ways as though they were objects. The expression *koma nloko*, "to nail a curse," describes invocations made either to a nail-fetish or to a chief. All persons, including both *minkisi* and ordinary people, consist of a body of some kind and an animating spirit, which can be transferred into another body by appropriate procedures (MacGaffey 1986). Nsemi Isaki wrote this account of *minkisi* in Kikongo in about 1915:

> The *nkisi* has life; if it had not, how could it help and heal people? But the life of a *nkisi* is different from the life of people; it is such that one can damage its flesh, burn it, break it or throw it away, but it will not bleed or cry out. Yet the magicians think that a *nkisi* possesses life because when it heals a person it sucks illness out. In this sense they think a *nkisi* has inextinguishable life coming from a source. When a *nkisi* wishes to exert its strength it strikes people until some high priest supplicates it, his *nkisi*; then it will leave off. (Janzen and MacGaffey 1974: 35)

This way of thinking is very primitive, no doubt; surely, one of the basic assumptions of rational thinking is that people and objects must not be confused? A cross-culturally fair view of power objects requires us to recognize that in fact this assumption is not unambiguously evident in our own approach to art (MacGaffey 1990). Art objects are more than just objects. Critics have noted the quasi-religious status of art works as embodiments of spiritual value, and the place of the museum as successor to the municipal temple. Gallery behavior includes a sort of reverence that would not be appropriate in a hardware store, for example.

In order to allow art works their full artness, we believe we should behave towards them in a particular way – should enter, in fact, into a sort of social relationship with them. We speak of encountering art, of being in its presence, of allowing it to speak to us. A study of the views of art curators and other "people who ought to know, because of long training and professional involvement, what the aesthetic experience . . . was all about," evoked such comments about the art object as that it was "telling you about itself," "communicating," or "giving you something." Even when respondents did not explicitly refer to the process of communication as dialogue, most of them used expressions referring to speech; according to the authors of the report, the prevalence of this metaphorical language indicates that the process of communication was an important part of the aesthetic experience (Cziksentmihalyi and Robinson 1986). Communication, and especially speech, are capacities of people, not objects.

I am asking here what kind and quantity of words are suitable to add to an object displayed in a museum so that the viewer can begin to understand what the Bakongo saw in it. I suggest that the task calls not just for a description of the Kongo cultural context but, to be fair, for a similar description of the museum experience. I would like to explain that, anthropologically speaking, what the natives think about *minkisi* is no more and no less remarkable than what other natives think about art. In both instances, however, the native's subjective experience, guided by cultural expectations and practices, is real and powerful. Doubting that I can fit all this on a label, I reluctantly side with the traditional curator: once an object has been appropriated as art, preferably by honest means, its original context and visual effect cannot be recovered and may be irrelevant.

WORDS AND VISUAL EFFECT IN *MINKISI*

I hold that culture is untranslatable, but I am not advocating simple relativism. To compare cultural elements, in their similarities and differences, is to demonstrate why translation is impossible but also furthers our understanding of them. So far I have suggested that the culturally guided encounter with art, like the encounter of Bakongo with *minkisi*, includes the conviction that the viewer has experienced an invisible spiritual presence, that he has seen something that is not there.[14] In both instances, cultural guidance consists partly of words, which are provided, in the case of art, by the label, the catalogue, and the critic. The more aesthetic theory insists on the disjunction between word and image, the more verbiage is necessary to make art of a given object.

In the case of *minkisi*, the relation between word and image is intrinsic, thus much more intimate than that between picture and label. Mitchell (1986) summarizes Nelson Goodman's comparison of pictures and texts in a way that illuminates *minkisi* (1976). Writing, according to Goodman, is a "disjunct" system, depending on a set of discrete symbols, such as the letters of the alphabet, which contrast in precise ways. A painting, on the other hand, is semantically "dense," meaning that no mark may be isolated as a unique, distinctive sign; the meaning of a mark (a spot of paint) depends on its relations with all other marks in a dense, continuous field.

In these terms, a *nkisi* is like a text rather than like a painting, a sculpture, or even a collage. As I have said, a *nkisi*, like a person, consists of a body of some kind, that is, a container, which is animated and endowed with forces by the medicines (*bilongo*) that are put in it. Some of these ingredients, such as grave-dirt, represent the incorporation of a personality from the land of the dead. Most of the rest serve to express metaphorically the powers of this particular *nkisi* and the uses to which these powers can be put. Many of the medicines are reduced by scraping (*teba*) to a powder which is incorporated with others in a sealed medicine-pack. In this condition they can no longer be seen, but their presence is announced, and their significance specified, by formulaic phrases recited as each one is prepared. A large proportion of the medicines in any *nkisi* are selected for purely linguistic reasons: the name of the plant, or whatever it is, recalls by a kind of pun the name of some desired quality. For example, *kazu* (kola nut), that the *nkisi* may "bite off" (*kazuwa*) witchcraft; *ngongo* (Calabar bean), that the witch may "become anxious" (*budika ngongo*) and desist; *nkiduku* (a fruit kernel), that one may be "protected" (*kidukwa*, from *kila*, "to paint lines," hence "to be magically protected").

Other medicines remain visible on or in the completed *nkisi*. Among them we should often include the container itself; if that container is an anthropomorphic figure it may show a series of metaphorically intended features describing either the characteristics of the *nkisi* or the effects it is supposed to have on those whom it attacks. *Nkisi* Lunkanka takes the form

9.1 Lunkanka.

of a monkey-faced, female anthropomorphic figure hung about with many things that I do not have space to discuss.[15] The figure itself holds its hands to its head in the gesture *sa ntaala*, to resemble those who will display their grief over Lunkanka's victims. The figure is in a kneeling position to recall one of its taboos: "If the one carrying the *nkisi* should fall, he had to kneel down there on the ground and salute and say, 'I kneel in apology, I kneel like a goat [as though to a chief]. Relax your neck, do not stiffen it.'" Among Lunkanka's appendages is a fragment of the poison bark *nkasa*, meaning that someone who survived the poison ordeal and was found innocent of witchcraft, but whose accusers refused to pay compensation, fixed this in Lunkanka "so that the *nkisi* might seize them in their village where they plotted this against him" (Matunta, in MacGaffey 1991).

These snippets are only a sample of what one might write to explain what Bakongo saw in only one *nkisi*; too much already for a label, or even a catalogue. On the other hand, when I have shown pictures of a number of very different *minkondi* to groups of students, it has been interesting to hear how often their comments unwittingly recognize the metaphors intended by the makers of these *minkisi*. Noting the mass of hardware and other items attached to the figures, some said that they seemed to be weighted down or burdened – which is exactly right: *minkondi* are believed to inflict diseases of the chest such as pneumonia, which make you feel as though you were carrying a great load of firewood.[16] It may therefore be sufficient to follow the curator's preferred approach and let the image speak for itself.

CONCLUSION

The intimacy of the relationship between word and image in the case of *minkisi* precludes any normative assertion about the superiority of one to the other, let alone a covert association between words and men, images and women, such as has been constitutive of the idea of art. This contrast with art illuminates the curator's problem and the source of our difficulties in cultural translation better than does any dubious distinction between primitive and modern, religious and secular, or context-bound and context-free. The existence of difficulties of this order does not mean that we should not struggle with them; nor is there any implication in what I have said that the process of making their artifacts into our art is intrinsically improper. On the contrary: if Bakongo, in 1905, could appropriate a green glass wine bottle to make into a work of magic, *nkisi* Nkondi a Mungundu, it is only fitting that we should reciprocate by recognizing the result as art.[17]

A final *caveat*: I have oversimplified the contrast between European and Kongo art objects, implying that all Kongo objects which we regard as art were produced in ritual contexts, although that is not the case, and I have neglected the historical dimension. From about 1860 onward, the Bakongo of the coastal regions produced for sale to other Bakongo (including traders from inland) as well as to Europeans, a number of types of representational object that were simply remarkable, or intended to record noteworthy developments. Such objects thus implied a narrative context, but they did not incorporate words in the way that *minkisi* did. Obvious examples include the soapstone figures called *mintadi*, which were expensive objects acquired as things to marvel at. They often ended their Kongo careers as mementoes on graves, along with other remarkable belongings of the deceased, such as umbrellas, flintlock guns, and old gin bottles. If we need a comparison, such Kongo products may best be likened to American folk arts. Through no accident at all, the "discovery" of folk arts in Europe and America is contemporary with the discovery of African art in France.[18] Like folk arts, these African objects have been transferred in recent decades to new careers as museum material; to maintain the distance between our folk and their folk, however, the African objects have been endowed, willy-nilly, with ritual contexts.[19] So *mintadi* have been described as guardians of the village on behalf of the chief, although their lack of medicines renders them incapable of this function. Not all art is magic, nor is all magic art.

My title borrows a phrase from Edmund Leach's *Social Anthropology*, London: Oxford University Press, 1982: 29.
1 "A Romanesque crucifix was not regarded by its contemporaries as a work of sculpture; nor Cimabue's Madonna as a picture" (Malraux 1974: 13). The tension between the values of the religious devotee and those of the art-lover is patent, for example, when one visits the side-chapel in the cathedral at Ghent to see Van Eyck's "Adoration of the Lamb."
2 My criteria are also those of the United States government: sculpture is the

work of one who is "a graduate of a course in sculpture at a recognized school of art (free fine art, not industrial art), or [is] recognized by name in art circles as a professional sculptor by the acceptance of his/her works in public exhibitions limited to the free fine arts." Cited in *African Arts* 11, 3 (1978: 5).

3 For the purposes of this paper, connoisseur, critic, and other experts are not distinguished. I also use "museum" and "gallery" interchangeably.

4 A distinguished example of the *nkondi* called Mangaaka is reproduced as the frontispiece to Rubin 1984, I.

5 Quoted in *Newsweek*, June 11, 1990.

6 Yves Klein, "Le vide," Paris, 1958; M. Asher, New York City, 1967 (Lippard 1984: 73).

7 Lisson Gallery, London, April 1987. In fact only thirteen of the fifteen paintings were on display. The director of the gallery said the artist regards them as a set but there wasn't room to hang them all, and that I was the first person to notice the deficiency.

8 R. Artschwager, Whitney Museum, February 1988. Reviewed in *Philadelphia Inquirer*, February 18. He used to make furniture and now makes art that verges on furniture.

9 W. Anastasi, "Displacement of plaster from wall to floor," 1966. Philadelphia Museum of Art, placard.

10 A. McCollum, Lisson Gallery, London, 1987. Review in *Time Out* (London), May 13, 1987.

11 *Newsweek*, August 6, 1990, on Tyree Guyton, who piles abandoned houses with colorful junk.

12 Richard Long's "Windstones" (1985) consists of an announcement, set in attractive type in a Royal Academy catalogue (1987), that during a fifteen–day walk in Lappland he had turned 207 stones to point into the wind. The catalogue described this as "discreet yet decisive marking."

13 R. Wentworth, exhibition catalogue, Riverside Studios, London, April 1987.

14 A real Rembrandt is an object of pilgrimage, a fake or imitation is no more than a curiosity, but experts are still arguing which is which.

15 Folkens Museum, Stockholm; accession number 1954.1.2338; MacGaffey and Harris 1993: 77, Fig. 54.

16 A *nkondi* in Folkens Museum (accession number 1919.1.538), consisted of a figure carrying a miniature load of wood, but the wood itself is now lost.

17 Folkens Museum, accession number 1907.26.166. MacGaffey and Harris 1993: Fig. 54.

18 Societies of Arts and Crafts were founded in Boston and Chicago in 1897.

19 "The famous carved human figures of the Mangbetu have been described as ancestral effigies and as memorial figures for deceased rulers, and their bark boxes surmounted by carved heads have been assumed to hold sacred relics" (Schildkrout and Keim 1990a: 15–16).

Adams, Alexander 1966, *John James Audubon. A Biography*, New York: G. P. Putnam's Sons.

Ames, Michael 1991, "Biculturalism in Exhibitions," *Museum Anthropology* 15(2): 7–15.

Anstey, Roger 1962, *Britain and the Congo in the 19th Century*, Oxford: Clarendon Press.

1966, *King Leopold's Legacy*, London: Oxford University Press.

Appadurai, Arjun (ed.) 1986, *The Social Life of Things*, Cambridge: Cambridge University Press.

Arnoldi, Mary Jo 1992, "A Distorted Mirror: The Exhibition of the Herbert Ward Collection of Africana," in I. Karp, C. M. Kreamer and S. D. Lavine (eds.): 428–57.

1995, *Playing with Time: Art and Performance in Central Mali*, Bloomington: Indiana University Press.

Ascherson, Neal 1964, *The King Incorporated: Leopold II in the Age of Trusts*, Garden City, New York: Doubleday.

Bal, Mieke 1992, "Telling, Showing, Showing Off," *Critical Inquiry* 18(Spring): 556–94.

Baldwin, James, Romare Bearden, *et al.* 1987, *Perspectives: Angles On African Art*, New York: The Center for African Art.

Balfour, Henry 1893, *The Evolution of Decorative Art*, London: Rivington Percival.

1912, Review of E. Torday and T. A. Joyce, "Les Bushongo," *Man* 25: 45–48.

Banton, Michael 1987, *Racial Theories*, Cambridge: Cambridge University Press.

Barber, Karen 1987, "Popular Arts in Africa," *African Studies Review* 30(3) September: 1–79.

Bassani, Ezio 1977, *Scultura africana nei musei italiani*, Bologna: Edizioni Calderini.

Bassani, Ezio and William Fagg 1988, *African and the Renaissance: Art in Ivory*, New York: The Center for African Art.

Baudrillard, Jean 1994, "The System of Collecting," in J. Elsner and R. Cardinal: 7–24.

1968, *Le Systeme des Objets*, Paris: Gallimard.

Beidelman, Thomas O. 1997, "Promoting African Art," *Anthropos* 92(1): 3–21.

Belepe Bope Mabintch 1981, "Les oeuvres plastiques africaines comme documents d'histoire: Le cas des statues royales ndop des Kuba au Zaire," *Africa–Tervuren* 27: 9–17.

Belgian Congo, 1916, *Rapport. L'Administration de la Colonie, Congo Belge*, Brussels: A. Lesigne.

1931, *Rapport. Commission de la Main-d'oeuvre Indigène, 1930–31*, Brussels: A. Lesigne.

Ben-Amos, Paula 1989, "African Visual Arts from a Social Perspective," *African Studies Review* 32(2): 1–53.

Benedetto, Robert 1990, "The Presbyterian Mission Press in Central Africa, 1890–1922," *American Presbyterians* 68(1): 55–69.

Bettelheim, Bruno 1976, *The Uses of Enchantment: The Meaning and Importance of Fairy Tales*, New York: Vintage Books.

Biebuyck, Daniel P. 1969, *Tradition and Creativity in Tribal Art*, Berkeley: University of California Press.

Binkley, David A. 1987, "Avatar of Power: Southern Kuba Masquerade Figures in a Funerary Context," *Africa* 57(1): 75–97.

1993, "The Teeth of the Nyim: The Elephant and Ivory in Kuba Art," in Doran H. Ross (ed.), *Elephant, The Animal and its Ivory in African Culture*, Los Angeles: Fowler Museum of Cultural History, UCLA: 277–91.

Birmingham, David and Phyllis M. Martin 1983, *History of Central Africa*, 2 vols., London: Longman.

Blier, Suzanne 1996, "Enduring Myths of African Art," in *Africa: The Art of a Continent. 100 Works of Power and Beauty*, New York: The Solomon R. Guggenheim Foundation: 26–34.

Bourdieu, Pierre 1984, *Distinction: A Social Critique of the Judgement of Taste*, London: Routledge.

Bradford, Phillips Verner and Harvey Blume 1992, *Ota Benga: The Pygmy in the Zoo*, New York: St. Martin's Press.

Braekman, E. M. 1961, *Histoire du protestantism au Congo*, Brussels: Librairie des Eclaireurs Unionistes.

Brantlinger, Patrick 1986, "Victorians and Africans: The Genealogy of the Myth of the Dark Continent," in Henry Louis Gates Jr. (ed.), *Race, Writing and Difference*, Chicago: University of Chicago Press: 185–222.

Brett-Smith, Sarah C. 1994, *The Making of Bamana Sculpture: Creativity and Gender*, Cambridge and New York: Cambridge University Press.

British Museum 1910, *Handbook to the Ethnographical Collections* [London]: Trustees of the British Museum.

Bucher, Bernadette 1981, *Icon and Conquest. A Structural Analysis of the Illustrations of de Bry's Great Voyages*, Chicago: University of Chicago Press.

Burrows, Guy 1898, *The Land of the Pigmies*, New York: Thomas Y. Crowell and Co.

1903, *The Curse of Central Africa*, London: R. A. Everett and Co.

Burssens, Herman and Alain Guisson (eds.) 1992, *Mangbetu. Art de cour africain de collections privées belges*, Brussels: Kredietbank.

Cannizzo, Jeanne 1990, *Into the Heart of Africa*, Toronto: The Royal Ontario Museum.

1991, "Exhibiting Cultures: 'Into the Heart of Africa,'" *Visual Anthropology Review* 7(1): 150–60.

Casati, Gaetano 1891a, *Ten Years in Equatoria and the Return with Emin Pasha*, 2 vols., translated by Mrs. Randolph Clay, London and New York: Frederick Warne and Co.

1891b, *Zehn Jahre in Äquatoria und die Rückkehr mit Emin Pascha*, 2 vols., Bamberg: C. C. Buchnersche Verlagsbuchhandlung.

Cash, John M. 1976, "Guide to the Frederick Starr Papers," Joseph Regenstein Library, The University of Chicago, MS.

Chalux (pseud.) 1925, *Un an au Congo belge*, Brussels: Albert Dewit.

Choprix, Guy 1961, *La naissance d'une ville. Etude géographique de Paulis (1934–1957)*, Brussels: Edition Cemubac.

Christiaens, Emile 1896, "Le pays des Mangbettus," *Causerie du cercle africain*, 23 November, 1–31.

Christian Science Monitor Brigham, Gertrude 1922, "Smithsonian Institution Receives Herbert Ward Statues of African Jungle People," March 15: 8–9.

Clifford, James P. 1988, *The Predicament of Culture: Twentieth Century Ethnography, Literature and Art*, Cambridge: Harvard University Press.

1990, "On Collecting Art and Culture," in Russell Ferguson *et al.* (eds.), *Out there: Marginalization and Contemporary Cultures*, Cambridge: The MIT Press: 141–90.

Collins, Robert O. 1968, *King Leopold, England and the Upper Nile*, New Haven: Yale University Press.

Connah, Graham 1987, *African Civilizations*, Cambridge: Cambridge University Press.

Connelly, Frances Susan 1995, *The Sleep of Reason: Primitivism in Modern European Art and Aesthetics 1725–1907*, University Park, PA: Pennsylvania State University Press.

Conrad, Joseph 1902, *Heart of Darkness*, London: J. M. Dent and Sons.

Cookey, Sylvanus John Sodienye 1968, *Britain and the Congo Question, 1885–1913*, Ibadan History Series. London: Longmans, Green and Co., Ltd.

Coombes, Annie E. 1994, *Reinventing Africa: Museums, Material Culture and Popular Imagination*, New Haven: Yale University Press.

Coquery-Vidrovitch, Catherine 1972, *Le Congo au temps des grandes compagnies concessionnaires, 1898–1930*, Paris: Mouton.

Cornet, Joseph-Aurélien 1975, "African Art and Authenticity," *African Arts* 9(1): 52–55.

1982, *Art Royal Kuba*, Milan: Edizioni Sipiel Milano.

Crawford, John R. 1982, "Pioneer African Missionary: Samuel Phillips Verner," *Journal of Presbyterian History* 60(1, Spring): 42–57.

Cunard, Nancy (ed.) 1934, *Negro Anthology*, London: Wishart and Co.

Cushing, Frank H. 1883, *Zuñi Fetiches*, Washington, D.C.: U. S. Government Printing Office.

Czekanowski, Jan 1924, *Forschungen im Nil-Kongo-Zwischengebiet*, VI(2), *Ethnographie Uele, Ituri, Nillander*, Leipzig: Klinkhardt and Biermann.

Cziksentmihalyi, M. and R. E. Robinson 1986, "The Art of Seeing: Towards an Interpretive Psychology of the Aesthetic Experience," Research report submitted to the J. Paul Getty Foundation, University of Chicago.

Danto, Arthur 1981, *The Transfiguration of the Commonplace*, Cambridge, MA: Harvard University Press.

Danto, Arthur, *et al.* 1988, *Art/Artifact. African Art in Anthropology Collections*, New York: The Center for African Art.

Darish, Patricia J. 1989, "Dressing for the Next Life: Raffia Textile Fabrication and Display Among the Kuba," in Annette Weiner and Jane Schneider (eds.), *Cloth and Human Experience*, Washington, D. C.: Smithsonian Institution Press.

1990, "Dressing for Success: Ritual Occasions for Ceremonial Raffia Dress Among the Kuba of South-Central Zaire," *Iowa Studies in African Art*, II.

de Bry, Theodor, Johan Israel and Johan Theodor de Bry (eds.) 1590–1634, *Great Voyages* 13 vols. Frankfurt, Germany: Matthias Becker.

de Dampierre, Eric 1991, *Harpes Zandé*, Paris: Klincksieck.

Dearborn Independent Culver, D. Jay 1922, "Herbert Ward – An Artist and Adventurer," May 27: 2, 11.

Degenhard, Ursula 1987, *Entdeckungs- und Forschungsreisen im Spiegel alter Bücher*, Stuttgart-Bad Cannstatt: Edition Canz.

DeYampert, Lucious 1904, Letter from Luebo dated February 28, American Presbyterian Congo Mission Papers, Department of History, Montreat-Anderson College, Montreat, North Carolina.

Duncan, Carol and Alan Wallach 1980, "The Universal Survey Museum," *Art History* 3(4): 148–69.

Ede, Harold Stanley 1987 [1931], *Savage Messiah, a Biography of the Sculptor Henri Gaudier-Brzeska*, London: Gordon Frazer.

Elliot Smith, G. 1924, *Elephants and Anthropologists*, London: Kegan Paul.

Elsner, John and Roger Cardinal (eds.) 1994, *The Cultures of Collecting*, Cambridge, Massachusetts: Harvard University Press.

Epstein, Jacob 1963, *Epstein: An Autobiography*, (An extended version of Epstein's *Let There be Sculpture*), London: Vista Books.

Evening Standard (London), September 28, 1889–4.

Evening Star "African Stone Age Relics Given to the Smithsonian. Herbert Ward, Sculptor, Donates Complete and Valuable Collection" 1913, (Washington, D.C.) March 15.

Exposition internationale Bruxelles–Tervueren 1897, *Guide de la section de l'Etat Indépendant du Congo à l'Exposition de Bruxelles–Tervueren en 1897*, Brussels: Imprimerie Veuve Monnom.

Fabian, Johannes 1983, *Time and the Other: How Anthropology Makes its Object*, New York: Columbia University Press.

1987, "Hindsight: Thoughts on Anthropology Upon Reading Francis Galton's *Narrative of an Explorer in Tropical South Africa* (1853)," *Critique of Anthropology* 7: 37–49.

1992, "White Humor," *Transition* 55: 56–61.

Fagg, William 1965, *Tribes and Forms in African Art*, New York: Tudor Publishing Co.

Fisher, Philip 1975, "The Future's Past," *New Literary History* 11(3): 587–606.

Fondation Dapper 1989, *Objets Interdits* Paris: Fondation Dapper.

Forbath, Peter 1977, *The River Congo*, New York: Harper and Row.

Ford, Alice 1964, *John James Audubon*, Norman, Oklahoma: University of Oklahoma Press.

Four Presbyterian Pioneers in Congo: Samuel Norvell Lapsley, William H. Sheppard, Maria Fearing, Lucy Gantt Sheppard 1965, Anniston, Alabama: First Presbyterian Church.

Franklin, John Hope Jr 1985, *George Washington Williams, A Biography*, Chicago: University of Chicago Press.

Fraser, Douglas and Herbert M. Cole (eds.) 1972, *African Art & Leadership*, Madison: The University of Wisconsin Press.

Frazer, James G. 1890, *The Golden Bough. A Study in Comparative Religion*, London: MacMillan and Co.

Freedberg, David 1989, *The Power of Images: Studies in the History and Theory of Response*, Chicago: Chicago University Press.

Frobenius, Leo 1907, *Im Schatten des Kongostaates. Bericht über den Verlauf der ersten Reisen der D. I. A. F. E. von 1904–1906, über deren Forschungen und Beobachtungen auf geographischem und kolonialwirtschaftlichem Gebiet*, Berlin: Georg Reimer.

 1985, 1987, 1988, 1990, *Ethnographische Notizen aus den Jahren 1905 und 1906*, 4 vols., edited by Hildegard Klein, Wiesbaden and Stuttgart: Franz Steiner.

Further Correspondence Respecting the Taxation of Natives, and Other Questions in the Congo State. Africa 1909 [Cd. 4466], Great Britain (Thesiger Report). Presented to both Houses of Parliament by Command of His Majesty January 1909, copy in American Presbyterian Congo Mission Papers, Department of History, Montreat–Anderson College, Montreat, North Carolina.

Galton, Francis 1972 [1855, 1872], *The Art of Travel; or Shifts and Contrivances Available in Wild Countries*, Newton Abbot, Devon: David and Charles Reprints.

Gann, Louis and Peter Duignan 1979, *The Rulers of Belgian Africa, 1884–1914*, Princeton, New Jersey: Princeton University Press.

Geary, Christraud M. 1988, *Images from Bamum: German Colonial Photography at the Court of King Njoya, Cameroon, West Africa, 1902–1915*, Washington, D.C.: Smithsonian Institution Press.

Geary, Patrick 1986, "Sacred Commodities: The Circulation of Medieval Relics," in Arjun Appadurai (ed.): 169–91.

Gibbins, Rosa 1939, "Historical Research on Rev. William H. Sheppard, D.D., F.R.G.S." material gathered by Rosa Gibbins, American Presbyterian Congo Mission Papers, Department of History, Montreat–Anderson College, Montreat, North Carolina.

Gibson, Gordon D. n.d., "Samuel Phillips Verner in the Kasai," MS. National Museum of Natural History, Smithsonian Institution, Washington D.C.

 1990, "Samuel Phillips Verner, Amateur Anthropologist," paper given at American Museum of Natural History symposium on collecting in the Congo.

Ginzburg, Carlo 1980, "Morelli, Freud and Sherlock Holmes: Clues and Scientific Method," *History Workshop* 9: 7–36.

Goldwater, Robert 1969, "Judgements of Primitive Art, 1905–1965," in Daniel Biebuyck (ed.): 24–41.

Goodman, Nelson 1976, *Languages of Art,* 2nd ed., Indianapolis: Hackett.

Goody, Jack R. 1991, "Icones et iconoclasme en Afrique," *Annales ESC* 6(November–December): 1235–51.

Gould, Stephen Jay 1981, *The Mismeasure of Man,* New York: W. W. Norton.

Graburn, Nelson H. H. (ed.) 1976, *Ethnic and Tourist Arts. Cultural Expressions from the Fourth World,* Berkeley: University of California Press.

Guillain, Charles 1856, *Documents sur l'histoire, la géographie et le commerce de l'Afrique orientale,* I, Paris: A. Bertrand.

1857, *Voyage à la côte orientale d'Afrique: exécuté pendant les années 1846 et 1848,* Paris: A. Bertrand.

Guggenheim Museum of Art 1995, *Africa The Art of a Continent, 100 Works of Beauty and Power.* New York: Guggenheim Museum.

Guyer, Jane I. 1993, "Wealth in People and Self-realization in Equatorial Africa," *Man* 28(2): 243–65.

Haddon, Alfred C. 1895, *Evolution in Art As Illustrated by the Life-histories of Designs,* London: W. Scott Ltd.

1910, "Comment on E. Torday's 'Land and Peoples of the Kasai Basin,'" *The Geographical Journal* 35: 55–56.

Haller, John S., Jr. 1971, *Outcasts from Evolution. Scientific Attitudes of Racial Inferiority, 1859–1900,* Urbana: University of Illinois Press.

Haraway, Donna 1985, "Teddy Bear Patriarchy: Taxidermy in the Garden of Eden, New York City, 1908–1938," *Social Text,* 11: 20–64.

Harms, Robert W. 1981, *River of Wealth, River of Sorrow. The Central Zaire Basin in the Era of the Slave and Ivory Trade, 1500–1891,* New Haven: Yale University Press.

Hilton, Anne 1985, *The Kingdom of Kongo,* Oxford: Clarendon Press.

Hilton-Simpson, Melville W. 1911, *Land and Peoples of the Kasai,* London: Constable and Co.

Hinsley, Curtis M., Jr. 1981 *Savages and Scientists: The Smithsonian Institution and the Development of American Anthropology 1846–1910 ,* Washington, D.C.: Smithsonian Institution Press, 1981.

Hocart, Arthur M. 1954, *Social Origins,* London: Watts.

Hodder, Ian (ed.) 1978, *The Spatial Organization of Culture,* London: Duckworth.

Holmes, William H. 1924, "Herbert Ward's Achievements in the Field of Art," *Art and Archeology* 18 (3) September: 113–25.

Honour, Hugh 1989, *Image of Blacks in Western Civilization,* IV: *From the American Revolution to World War I,* (2) *Black Models and White Myths,* Houston: Menil Foundation, Inc.

Hooper-Greenhill, Eilean 1992, *Museums and the Shaping of Knowledge,* London and New York: Routledge.

Hough, Walter 1922, "Racial Groups," *National Museum Annual Report,* Washington, D.C.: Government Printing Office, 1922: 612–47.

1924, "An Appreciation of the Scientific Value of the Herbert Ward African Collection," in *The Herbert Ward African Collection*, Washington, D.C.: United States National Museum: 37–49.

Husson, Laurence 1989, "De la curiosité à l'art," in Fondation Dapper, *Objets Interdits*, Paris: Fondation Dapper: 12–31.

Impey, Oliver R. and Arthur G. MacGregor (eds.) 1985, *The Origins of Museums: The Cabinet of Curiosities in Sixteenth and Seventeenth Century Europe*, Oxford and New York: Clarendon Press, Oxford University Press 1985.

Ivins, William M., Jr. 1964, *How Prints Look: Photographs with a Commentary*, 3rd edition, Boston: Beacon Press.

Janzen, John M. and Wyatt MacGaffey (eds.) 1974, *An Anthology of Kongo Religion. Primary Texts from Lower Zaire*, Lawrence, Kansas: University of Kansas Press.

Jenkins, Paul 1993, "The Earliest Generation of Missionary Photographers in West Africa and the Portrayal of Indigenous People and Culture," *History in Africa* 20: 89–118.

Jewsiewicki, Bogumil 1983, "Rural Society and the Belgian Colonial Economy," in D. Birmingham and P. Martin, II: 95–125.

1991a, "Painting in Zaire: From the Invention of the West to the Representation of the Social Self," in S. Vogel (ed.), *Africa Explores*: 130–51.

1991b, "Peintre de case, imagiers et savants populaires du Congo, 1900–1960," *Cahiers d'études africaines* 123, 31–33: 307–326.

Johnston, Harry H. 1908, *George Grenfell and the Congo*, 2 vols., London: Hutchinson and Co.

Joppien, Rüdiger and Bernard Smith 1985, *The Art of Captain Cook's Voyages*, I: *The Voyage of the Endeavor 1768–1771*, New Haven: Yale University Press.

Joyce, Thomas Athol 1910a, "On a Carved Wooden Cup from the Bakuba," *Man* 9: 1–3.

1910b, "On a Wooden Portrait-Statue from the Bushongo People of the Kasai District, Congo State," *Man* 10: 81–82.

1925, "The Portrait-Statue of Mikope Mbula, 110th Paramount Chief of the Bushongo," *Man* 25: 185–86.

1932, "Emil Torday. Obituary," *Man* (n.s.) 53–55: 48–49.

Jung, Hwa Yol 1995, "The *Tao* of Transversality as a Global Approach to Truth: A Metacommentary on Calvin O. Schrag," *Man and World* 28: 11–31.

Junker, Wilhelm 1889, *Reisen in Afrika 1875–1886*, 3 vols., Wien: Eduard Hölzel.

1890, *Travels in Africa during the Years 1875–1878*, translated by A. H. Keane, London: Chapman and Hall.

1891, *Travels in Africa during the Years 1879–1883*, translated by A. H. Keane, London: Chapman and Hall.

1892, *Travels in Africa during the Years 1882–1885*, translated by A. H. Keane, London: Chapman and Hall.

Karp, Ivan and Steven D. Lavine (eds.) 1991, *Exhibiting Cultures: The Poetics and Politics of Museum Display*, Washington: Smithsonian Institution Press.

Karp, Ivan, Christine Mullen Kreamer and Steven D. Lavine (eds.) 1992, *Museums and Communities: The Politics of Public Culture*, Washington: Smithsonian Institution Press.

Kasfir, Sidney Littlefield 1984, "One Tribe, One Style: Paradigms in the Historiography of African Art," *History in Africa* 11: 163–193.

— 1992, "African Art and Authenticity: A Text with a Shadow," *African Arts* 25 (3): 40–53, 96–97.

Keim, Curtis 1979, "Precolonial Mangbetu Rule: Political and Economic Factors in Nineteenth-Century Mangbetu History (Northeast Zaire)," Ph.D. dissertation, Indiana University, Bloomington.

— 1983, "Long-distance Trade and the Mangbetu, c.1865–1885," *Journal of African History*, 14(1): 1–22.

Kellersberger, Julia Lake 1947, *A Life for the Congo. The Story of Althea Brown Edmiston*, New York: Fleming H. Revell Co.

— 1965, *Lucy Gantt Sheppard, Shepherdess of His Sheep on Two Continents*, in *Four Presbyterian Pioneers in Congo*.

Kevles, Daniel J. 1986, *In the Name of Eugenics: Genetics and the Uses of Human Heredity*, Berkeley: University of California Press.

Killingray, David and Andrew Roberts 1989, "An Outline of Photography in Africa to ca. 1940," *History in Africa* 16: 197–208.

Kjersmeier, Carl 1935, *Centres de Style de la Sculpture Negre Africaine*, Copenhagen: Illums bogafdeling (reprint – New York: Hacker Art Books, 1967).

Kohl, Karl-Heinz 1981, *Entzauberter Blick: Das Bild vom Guten Wilden*, Berlin: Medusa Verlag.

Kramer, Fritz 1977, *Verkehrte Welten. Zur imaginären Ethnographie des 19. Jahrhunderts*, Frankfurt: Syndikat.

— 1989, "The Influence of the Classical Tradition on Anthropology and Exoticism," in Michael Harbsmeier and Morgens Trolle Larsen (eds.), *The Humanities Between Art and Science. Intellectual Developments 1880–1914*, Copenhagen: Akademisk Forlag: 203–23.

Kuklick, Henrika 1991, *The Savage Within: The Social History of British Anthropology, 1885–1945*, Cambridge: Cambridge University Press.

Lang, Herbert 1915, "An Explorer's View of the Congo," *The American Museum Journal* 15(8), December: 379–88.

— 1918, "Famous Ivory Treasures of a Negro King," *American Museum Journal* 18(7): 527–52.

— 1919, "Nomad Dwarfs and Civilization," *Natural History* 19(6): 696–713.

Lapsley, Samuel N. 1891, Letter in *The Missionary* June: 203–04 in R. Gibbins.

— 1893, *Life and Letters of Samuel Norvell Lapsley. Missionary to the Congo Valley, West Africa, 1866–1892*, J. W. Lapsley (ed.), Richmond, Virginia: Whittet and Shepperson.

Lavachery, Henry 1934, "Essays on Styles in the Statuary of the Congo," in Nancy Cunard (ed.), *Negro Anthology*, London: Wishart and Co.: 687–93.

Layton, Robert 1991, *The Anthropology of Art*, 2nd edition, New York: Columbia University Press.

Lelong, Maurice-Hyacinthe 1946. *Mes frères du Congo*. 2 vols. Algiers: Editions Baconnier.

Lewis, Wyndham 1969 [1919], "The Caliph's Design," in W. Michel and C. J. Fox: 129–83.

1969 [1913], "A Review of Contemporary Art," in W. Michel and C. J. Fox: 58–77.

Lippard, Lucy 1984, *Get the Message?*, New York: Dutton.

MacGaffey, Wyatt 1977, "Fetishism Revisited," *Africa* 47: 172–84.

　1986, *Religion and Society in Central Africa*, Chicago: Chicago University Press.

　1988, "Complexity, Astonishment and Power: The Visual Vocabulary of Kongo Minkisi," *Journal of Southern African Studies* 14(2), January: 188–203.

　1990, "The Personhood of Ritual Objects," *Etnofoor* (Leiden) 3(1): 45–62.

　1991, *Art and Healing of the BaKongo Commented by Themselves*, Folkens Museum, monograph series. Stockholm: Almqvist and Wiksells.

　1993, "The Eyes of Understanding: Kongo *Minkisi*," in W. MacGaffey and M. D. Harris: 20–103.

　and Michael D. Harris 1993, *Astonishment and Power*, Washington, D.C.: Smithsonian Institution Press.

Mack, John 1990 *Emil Torday and the Art of the Congo, 1900–1909*, London: British Museum; Seattle: University of Washington Press.

　1991, "Documenting the Cultures of Southern Zaire: The Photographs of the Torday Expeditions, 1900–1909," *African Arts* 24(4): 60–9.

McVicker, Donald 1986, "Frederick Starr and the Walker Museum," *Council for Museum Anthropology Newsletter* 10: 1.

　1989, "Parallels and Rivalries: Encounters Between Boas and Starr," *Curator* 32(3):212–28.

Maes, Joseph 1936, "Les statues des rois Bakuba", *Les Beaux-Arts* 7: 18–21.

Maitland, Frederic William 1911, *Collected Papers*, 3 vols., Cambridge: Cambridge University Press.

Malraux, André 1974, *The Voices of Silence*, translated by C. A. Foulkes, London: Paladin.

Marles, Hugh, 1996, "Arrested Development: Race and Evolution in the Sculpture of Herbert Ward," *Oxford Art Journal* 19(1): 16–28.

Martin, Motte 1910, "A Visit into the Bakuba Country," *Kassai Herald* March: 3–4, American Presbyterian Congo Mission Papers, Department of History, Montreat–Anderson College, Montreat, North Carolina.

Martin, Phyllis M. 1972, *The External Trade of the Loango Coast, 1576–1870*, Oxford: Clarendon Press.

Mayr, Ernst 1982, *The Growth of Biological Thought: Diversity, Evolution, and Inheritance*, Cambridge, MA: Belknap Press.

Meurant, Georges 1986, *Shoowa Design, African Textiles from the Kingdom of the Kuba*, New York: Thames and Hudson.

Michel, Walter and Cyril J. Fox (eds.) 1969, *Wyndham Lewis on Art; Collected Writings, 1913–1956*, London: Thames and Hudson.

Miller, Christopher 1985, *Blank Darkness: Africanist Discourse in French*, Chicago: University of Chicago Press.

Miller, Joseph C. 1983, "The Paradoxes of Impoverishment in the Atlantic Zone," in D. Birmingham and P. Martin, I: 118–59.

　1988, *Way of Death*, Madison: University of Wisconsin Press.

Mirzoeff, Nicholas 1996, "Photography at the Heart of Darkness," *Elvehjem Museum of Art Bulletin, 1993–95*: 29–44.

Missionary "The People on the Congo," September 1891.

Mitchell, W. J. Thomas 1986, *Iconology: Image, Text, Ideology*, Chicago: University of Chicago Press.

Morel, Edmund D. 1968, E. D. Morel's *History of the Congo Reform Movement*, Roger Louis and Jean Stengers (eds.), Oxford: Clarendon Press.

Mudimbe, Valentin Y. 1986, "African Art as a Question Mark," *African Studies Review* 29(1): 3–4.

1988, *The Invention of Africa. Gnosis, Philosophy, and the Order of Knowledge*, Bloomington: Indiana University Press.

New York Times, Obituary, "Frederick Starr," August 15, 1933.

Norden, Hermann 1925, *Fresh Tracks in the Belgian Congo*, Boston: Small, Maynard & Co.

Nys, Ferdinand 1896, *Chez les Abarambos, ce que devient l'Afrique mystérieuse*, Antwerp: R. Huybrechts.

Nys, K.B. 1954, "In Memoriam Broeder Marcolinus Meylemans," *Band. Tijdschrift voor Vlaams Kultuurleven* (Leopoldville) 13(2): 71–76.

Olbrechts, Frans M. 1946, *Plastiek van Kongo*, Antwerp: W. V. Standaard (In French translation as *Les arts plastiques du Congo belge*, Brussels: Grasme, 1959; and in English translation as *Congolese Sculpture*, New Haven: Human Relations Area Files, 1982.)

Paudrat, J.L., 1984, "The arrival of tribal objects in the west from Africa," In *Primitivism in 20th century Art*. W. Rubin(ed). New York: Museum of Modern Art, I: 125–75.

Pearce, Susan M. 1988, *Objects of Knowledge*, London: Athlone Press.

1992, *Museums, Objects and Collections: A Cultural Study*, Leicester: Leicester University Press.

(ed.) 1994, *Interpreting Objects and Collections*, London: Routledge.

Phillips, Tom (ed.) 1996, *Africa: The Art of a Continent*, London: Royal Academy of Arts; Munich and New York: Prestel.

Phillips, Ruth and Christopher Steiner (eds.) forthcoming, *Unpacking Culture: Art and Commodity in Colonial and Post Colonial Worlds*, Berkeley: The University of California Press.

Phillipson, D. W. 1985, *African Archaeology*, Cambridge: Cambridge University Press.

Pieterse, Jan Nederveen 1992, *White on Black. Images of Africa and Blacks in Western Popular Culture*, New Haven: Yale University Press.

Pietz, William 1985, "The Problem of the Fetish, I," *Res* 9: 5–17.

1987, "The Problem of the Fetish, II: The Origin of the Fetish," *Res* 13: 23–45.

Pomian, Krzysztof 1990, *Collectors and Curiosities: Paris and Venice 1500–1800*, translated by Elizabeth Wiles-Portier, Cambridge, U.K.: Polity Press.

Pound, Ezra 1916, *Gaudier-Brzeska, A Memoir*, London: Laidlaw and Laidlaw.

1934, "Leo Frobenius," in Nancy Cunard (ed.), *Negro Anthology*, London: Wishart and Co.: 623.

Pratt, Mary Louise 1992, *Imperial Eyes. Travel Writing and Transculturation*, London and New York: Routledge.

Price, Sally 1989, *Primitive Art in Civilized Places*, Chicago: University of Chicago Press.

Ranger, Terence 1983, "The Invention of Tradition in Colonial Africa," in Eric
Hobsbawm and Terence Ranger (eds.), *The Invention of Tradition*, Cambridge:
Cambridge University Press: 211–62.

Reefe, Thomas Q. 1983, "The Societies of the Eastern Savanna," in David
Birmingham and Phyllis Martin, I: 160–204.

Rice, Danielle 1987, "On the ethics of museum education," *Museum News* 65(5):
16–17.

Richter, Dolores 1980, *Art, Economics and Change*, La Jolla, California:
Psych/Graphic Publishers.

Rivers, William H. R. 1914, *The History of Melanesian Society*, 2 vols., Cambridge:
Cambridge University Press.

Roquebert, Anne, 1994, "La sculpture ethnographique au XIX siècle, objet de
mission ou œuvre de musée," *La sculpture ethnographique de la Vénus
hottentote à la Tehura de Gauguin*, Paris: La Réunion des Musées Nationaux.

Rosenwald, Jean B. 1974, "Kuba King Figures," *African Arts* 7(3): 26–31.

Royal Anthropological Institute of Great Britain and Ireland 1980, *Observers of
Man: Photographs from the Royal Anthropological Institute*, London: The
Institute.

Rubin, William (ed.) 1984, *Primitivism in 20th Century Art: Affinity of the Tribal
and the Modern*, 2 vols., New York: Museum of Modern Art.

Rydell, Robert W. 1984, *All the World's a Fair: Visions of Empire at
American International Expositions, 1876–1916*, Chicago: University of
Chicago Press.

Salmon, Pierre 1992, "Réflexions à propos du goût des arts zaïrois en Belgique
durant la période coloniale (1885–1960)," in Emile VanBalberghe (ed.), *Papier
blanc, encre noire. Cent ans de culture francophone en Afrique centrale (Zaïre,
Rwanda, et Burundi)*, I, Brussels: Editions Labor: 179–201.

Schildkrout, Enid forthcoming, "Gender and Sexuality in Mangbetu Art," in R.
Phillips and C. Steiner (eds.), n. p.

   1991a, "Ambiguous Messages and Ironic Twists: 'Into the Heart of Africa' and
   'The Other Museum,'" *Museum Anthropology* 15(2): 16–23.

   1991b, "The Spectacle of Africa Through the Lens of Herbert Lang," *African Arts*
   24(4): 70–85, 100.

   and Curtis A. Keim 1990a, *African Reflections: Art from Northeastern Zaire*, New
   York: The American Museum of Natural History; Seattle: The University of
   Washington Press.

   1990b, "Mangbetu Ivories: Innovations Between 1910 and 1914," Boston
   University, African Studies Center, Humanities Program, *Discussion Papers in
   the African Humanities*, AH Number 5.

   and Jill Hellman and Curtis A. Keim 1989, "Mangbetu Pottery: Tradition and
   Innovation in Northeast Zaire," *African Arts* 22(2): 38–47.

Schrag, Calvin O. 1992, *The Resources of Rationality: A Response to the Postmodern
Challenge*, Bloomington, Indiana: Indiana University Press, 1992.

Schubotz, Hermann 1913, "The Mangbetu Country," in Adolf Friedrich, *From the
Congo to the Niger and the Nile*, II London: Duckworth and Co.

Schweinfurth, Georg A. 1874a, *The Heart of Africa: Three Years' Travels and Adventures in the Unexplored Regions of Central Africa from 1868 to 1871*, 2 vols., translated by Ellen E. Frewer, New York: Harper and Bros.

1874b, "Au cœur de l'Afrique. Trois ans de voyages et d'aventures dans les régions inexplorées de l'Afrique centrale," *Le Tour du Monde* 2: 193–273.

1875, *Artes Africanae: Illustrations and Descriptions of Productions of the Industrial Arts of Central African Tribes*, Leipzig: F. A. Brockhaus.

1918, *Im Herzen von Afrika. Reisen und Entdeckungen im zentralen Äquatorial-Afrika während der Jahre 1868–1871*, Leipzig: F. A. Brockhaus.

and Friedrich Ratzel, Gustav Hartlaub, and Robert William Felkin (eds.) 1889, *Emin Pasha in Central Africa, Being a Collection of His Letters and Journals*, translated by R. W. Felkin, New York: Dodd, Mead.

Shaloff, Stanley 1970, *Reform in Leopold's Congo*, Richmond, Virginia: John Knox Press.

Sheppard, Lucy Gantt 1895, Letter from Luebo dated October 19, American Presbyterian Congo Mission Papers, Department of History, Montreat–Anderson College, Montreat, North Carolina.

Sheppard, William H. 1893, "Into the Heart of Africa," *Southern Workman* 22: 182–87.

1917, *Presbyterian Pioneers in Congo*, Richmond, Virginia: Presbyterian Committee of Publication.

Sieg, J. Mc. C. 1905, "The Outlook Among the Bakuba," *Kassai Herald* (July): 28–29, American Presbyterian Congo Mission Papers, Department of History, Montreat-Anderson College, Montreat, North Carolina.

Sievers, Wilhelm 1891, *Afrika. Eine allgemeine Landeskunde*, Leipzig and Wien: Bibliographisches Institut.

Siroto, Leon 1979, "Witchcraft Belief in the Explanation of Traditional African Iconography," in Justine M. Cordwell (ed.), *The Visual Arts: Plastic and Graphic*, The Hague: Mouton: 241–91.

Slade, Ruth 1959, *English-Speaking Missions in the Congo Independent State (1878–1908)*, Brussels: Académie royale des sciences coloniales.

1962, *King Leopold's Congo*, New York and London: Oxford University Press.

Smith, Robert E. 1987, "Leo Frobenius et Emil(e) Torday, Les premiers ethnographes du Kwilu," *Annales Aequatoria* 8: 76–98.

Smithsonian Institution 1914, *United States National Museum, Annual Report for the Year Ending June 30, 1913*, Washington, D.C.: Government Printing Office.

Sperber, Dan 1975, *Rethinking Symbolism*, New York and Cambridge: Cambridge University Press.

St. Louis Post Dispatch, August 30, 1904.

Stanley, Henry Morton 1878, *Through the Dark Continent*, 2 vols., London: Sampson, Low, Marston, Searle, and Rivington.

1885, *The Congo and the Founding of its Free State. A Story of Work and Exploration*, 2 vols., London: Sampson, Low, Marston, Searle, and Rivington.

1890, *In Darkest Africa: or, The quest, rescue and retreat of Emin, governor of Equatoria*, 2 vols., London: Sampson, Low, Marston, Searle, and Rivington.

Stanton, William 1960, *The Leopard's Spots. Scientific Attitudes toward Race in America, 1815–1859*, Chicago: The University of Chicago Press.

Starr, Frederick 1907, *The Truth About the Congo: The Chicago Tribune Articles*, Chicago: Forbes and Co.

  1909, *Ethnographic Notes from the Congo Free State: an African Miscellany*, Proceedings of the Davenport Academy of Sciences (Davenport, Iowa) 12: 96–222.

  1912, *Congo Natives. An Ethnographic Album*, Chicago: Printed for the author by The Lakeside Press.

Steiner, Christopher 1986, "Of Drums and Dancers," *The Harvard Review* 1(1): 104–29.

  1994, *African Art in Transit*, Cambridge: Cambridge University Press.

Stengers, Jean, and Jan Vansina 1985, "King Leopold's Congo, 1886–1908," in John D. Fage and Roland Oliver, (eds.), *The Cambridge History of Africa*, VI Cambridge: Cambridge University Press: 315–59.

Stepan, Nancy 1982, *The Idea of Race in Science: Great Britain, 1800–1960*, Hamden: Archon Books.

Stewart, Susan 1984, *On Longing: Narratives of the Miniature, the Gigantic, the Souvenir, the Collection*, Baltimore: Johns Hopkins University Press.

Stocking, George W., Jr. (ed.) 1985, *Objects and Others: Essays on Museums and Material Culture*, Madison, Wisconsin: The University of Wisconsin Press.

  1987, *Victorian Anthropology*, New York: The Free Press.

Sunday Star Helig, Sterling 1913, "Unique Gift for the Smithsonian," (Washington, D.C.), March 16: 2–3.

Szalay, Miklós (ed.) 1990, *Der Sinn des Schönen. Aesthetik, Soziologie und Geschichte der afrikanischen Kunst*, Munich: Trickster.

Theye, Thomas (ed.) 1985a, *Wir und die Wilden: Einblicke in eine kannibalistische Beziehung*, Reinbeck bei Hamburg: Rowohlt.

  1985b, "Optische Trophäen," in Thomas Theye (ed.), *Wir und die Wilden. Einblicke in eine kannibalistische Beziehung*, Reinbeck bei Hamburg: Rowohlt: 18–95.

Thomas, H. B. 1960, "Richard Buchta and Early Photography in Uganda," *Uganda Journal* 24: 144–19.

Thomas, Nicholas 1991, *Entangled Objects. Exchange, Material Culture, and Colonialism in the Pacific*, New Haven: Harvard University Press.

Thompson, Robert F. 1974, *African Art in Motion: Icon and Act in the Collection of Katherine Coryton White*, Berkeley: University of California Press.

  1993, *Face of the Gods, Art and Altars of Africa and the African Americas*. New York: The Museum for African Art.

Thornton, John K. 1983, *The Kingdom of Kongo. Civil War and Transition, 1641–1718*, Madison, University of Wisconsin Press.

Thornton, Lynne 1990, *Les Africanistes: Peintres Voyageurs, 1860–1960*, Courbevoie (Paris): ACR Edition Internationale.

Torday, Emil 1905–08: vol. I, 591. Department of Ethnology, Museum of Mankind, London.

1908, Letter to T. A. Joyce, December 17, II, Department of Ethnology, Museum of Mankind, London.

1909, Letter to T. A. Joyce dated January 20, II, Department of Ethnology, Museum of Mankind, London.

1910a, "Les migrations des Peuples au Kasai," *Bulletin de la Société Belge d'Etudes Coloniales* 17(12): 857–69.

1910b, "Land and Peoples of the Kasai Basin," *Geographical Journal*, 34: 26–57.

1911, "Bushongo Mythology," *Folklore* 22: 41–47.

1913a, *Camp and Tramp in African Wilds. A Record of Adventures, Impressions, and Experiences during Many Years Spent among the Savage Tribes round Lake Tanganyika and Central Africa, with a Description of Native Life, Character, and Customs*, London: Seeley, Service & Co.

1913b, "Comment on a Paper by Sir H. H. Johnston, 'A Survey of the Ethnography of Africa,'" *Journal of the Royal Anthropological Institute* 43: 415–16.

1925, *On the Trail of the Bushongo. An Account of a Remarkable & Hitherto Unknown African People, Their Origin, Art, High Social & Political Organization & Culture, Derived from the Author's Personal Experience Amongst Them*, London: Seely, Service & Co.

1928, "The Influence of the Kingdom of Kongo on Central Africa," *Africa* 1: 157–69.

and Thomas Athol Joyce 1911, *Notes ethnographiques sur les peuples communément appelés Bakuba, ainsi que sur les peuplades apparentées: Les Bushongo*, Brussels: Musée Royal de l'Afrique Centrale (Tervuren).

1922, *Notes ethnographiques sur des populations habitant les bassins du Kasai et du Kwango oriental*, Tervuren: Musée Royal de l'Afrique Centrale.

Twain, Mark 1905, *King Leopold's Soliloquy: A Defense of his Congo Rule*, Boston: P. R. Warren.

Tylor, Edward B. 1871, *Primitive Culture*, 2 vols., London: John and Murray.

Van Overbergh, Cyrille and Eduard De Jonghe 1909, *Les Mangbetu*, Brussels: Institut international de bibliographie, Albert de Wit.

Vansina, Jan 1962, "Trade and Markets Among the Kuba," in Paul Bohannan and George Dalton (eds.), *Markets in Africa*, Evanston: Northwestern University: 190–210.

1964, *Le Royaume Kuba*, Musée Royal de l'Afrique Centrale, Anthropology and Ethnography, No. 49, Tervuren.

1966, *Kingdoms of the Savanna*, Madison: University of Wisconsin Press.

1972, "Ndop: Royal Statues among the Kuba," in Douglas Fraser and Herbert M. Cole (eds.), *African Art & Leadership*, Madison, Wisconsin: University of Wisconsin Press: 41–55.

1978, *The Children of Woot. A History of the Kuba Peoples*, Madison, Wisconsin: University of Wisconsin Press.

1984, *Art History in Africa: An Introduction to Method*, London: Longman.

1987, "The Ethnographic Account as a Genre in Central Africa," *Paiduma* 33: 433–44.

1990, *Paths in the Rainforest. Toward a History of Political Tradition in Equatorial Africa*, Madison: University of Wisconsin Press.

Vellut, Jean-Luc 1983, "Mining in the Belgian Congo," in D. Birmingham and P. Martin, II, 126–62.

Verner, Samuel Phillips 1903, *Pioneering In Central Africa*, Richmond, Virginia: Presbyterian Committee of Publication.

Vinson, Thomas C. 1921, *William McCutchan Morrison. Twenty Years in Central Africa*, Richmond: Presbyterian Committee of Publication.

Vogel, Susan 1980, "Beauty in the Eyes of the Baule: Aesthetics and Cultural Values," in Philip L. Ravenhill (ed.), *Baule Statuary Art: Meaning and Modernization*, Philadelphia: Institute for the Study of Human Issues.

(ed.) 1991, *Africa Explores: 20th Century African Art*, New York: The Center for African Art.

Ward, Herbert 1890, *Five Years with the Congo Cannibals*, London: Chatto and Windus, Piccadilly.

1910, *A Voice from the Congo*, New York: Charles Scribner's Sons.

Ward, Sarita 1927, *A Valiant Gentleman*, London: Chapman and Hall, Ltd.

Washington Herald 1913, "Dark Continent Trophies Given to Smithsonian: Herbert Ward, Famous Sculptor, will Send Valuable Collection to Capital" (Washington, D.C.), March 15.

Wees, William C. 1972, *Vorticism and the English Avant-Garde*, Toronto: University of Toronto Press.

Wharton, Conway 1927, *The Leopard Hunts Alone*. New York: Fleming N. Revell Company.

Willett, Frank 1976, "True or false? The False Dichotomy," *African Arts* 9(3): 8–14.

Wissmann, Hermann 1889, *Unter deutscher Flagge quer durch Afrika von West nach Ost. Von 1880 bis 1883 ausgeführt von Paul Pogge und Hermann Wissmann*. Berlin: Walther and Apolant. (Fourth printing)

Wolff, Janet 1981, *The Social Production of Art*, Cambridge: Cambridge University Press.

Women's Foreign Missionary Society, M. E. Church, South 1895, "How Sheppard Made his Way into Lukenga's Kingdom," published leaflet, February, American Presbyterian Congo Mission Papers, Department of History, Montreat–Anderson College, Montreat, North Carolina.

Zeidler, Jeanne and Mary Lou Hultgren 1988, "Things African Prove to be the Favorite Theme: The African Collection at Hampton University," in Danto, A. (ed.), *Art/Artifact*: 97–111.

Archives

Emile Christiaens, Dossier Emile Christiaens, Papiers Emmanuel Muller, Archives Historiques, Musée Royal de l'Afrique Centrale, Tervuren, Belgium.

American Presbyterian Congo Mission Papers, Department of History, Montreat–Anderson College, Montreat, North Carolina.

Records of the Anthropology Department, National Anthropological Archives, Smithsonian Institution.

Gordon Gibson Papers, National Anthropological Archives, Smithsonian Institution.

Walter Hough Papers, National Anthropological Archives, Smithsonian Institution.

Herbert Krieger Papers. National Anthropological Archives, Smithsonian Institution.

Herbert Lang, Field Notes, Department of Anthropology, American Museum of Natural History.

Herbert Lang Papers, Archives, Library of the American Museum of Natural History.

Muller, Emmanuel n.d., Papiers Muller, Dossier Emmanuel Muller, Archives Historiques, Section Historique, Musée Royal de l'Afrique Centrale, Tervuren, Belgium.

(MRAC), Musée Royal de l'Afrique Centrale, Tervuren, Belgium. Accession Archives of the Ethnology Department.

Frederick Starr, African Diaries, Frederick Starr Papers, Regenstern Library, University of Chicago, Chicago, Illinois.

Emil Torday Papers, Department of Ethnology, Museum of Mankind, London.